ID0745810

In Defense of Music

Musica as personified in
Gregor Reisch, *Margarita philosophica,* 2d ed.
(Strasbourg, 1504), folio O

DON HARRÁN

IN DEFENSE OF MUSIC

*The Case for Music
as Argued by a Singer and Scholar
of the Late Fifteenth Century*

UNIVERSITY OF NEBRASKA PRESS

LINCOLN & LONDON

The paper in this book meets the minimum requirements
of American National Standard for
Information Sciences – Permanence of Paper for Printed
Library Materials, ANSI Z39.48-1984.

Set in Linotron Bembo by Keystone Typesetting, Inc.
Printed on 55lb. Glatfelter paper by Thomson-Shore.
Designed by Richard Eckersley.

Library of Congress Cataloging-in-Publication Data
Harrán, Don.
In defense of music: the case for music
as argued by a singer and scholar of the late
fifteenth century / by Don Harrán.
p.   cm.
Bibliography: p.
Includes index.
ISBN 0-8032-2347-1 (alk. paper)
1. Church music – Catholic Church – 15th century.
2. Church music – France – 15th century.
3. Le Munerat, Jean, 15th cent.
4. Music and language.
I. Title.
ML3027.H37   1989   783'.02'6244 – dc19
88-27792   CIP   MN

TO ROY
*For whom music needs
no defense*

. . . let this mark
the beginning of a discussion,
wherein we submit
to the experience, reasoning,
and judgment of
the listeners and arbitrators.

Jean Le Munerat,
1493

(see page 106)

Contents

Illustrations

Preface

When I started this project in the later 1970s, Jean Le Munerat was for me little more than a name: I had run across Le Munerat, in connection with a treatise of his authorship, in various short references, especially the one in Hans-Heinrich Unger's book on *Die Beziehungen zwischen Musik und Rhetorik im 16.–18. Jahrhundert*.[1] The title of the treatise was intriguing: "On the Regulation and Concordance of Grammar and Music." Behind the title stand a number of questions relative to the definition of music and "grammar," i.e., language, and to their affiliation in composition, in performance. I myself had treated the topic of word-tone relations in two studies that sounded humanism as the main theme of development.[2] But Le Munerat's writings—I say "writings," for his one music treatise actually turns into two—did not conveniently fall into the patterns of thought I outlined there. Where I had been preoccupied for some time with the humanist side of early music, often to the exclusion of other sides, I now found a concrete example of a countertendency.

Le Munerat pointedly assumed a position against the humanists. If we regard humanism in music as, broadly speaking, an adaptation of music, after ancient precept, to the structure and content of speech, Le Munerat went the opposite way by describing and justifying situations where speech was to submit to the authority of music. Le Munerat sets the whole question of humanism as a movement within Renaissance music into sharper profile: though, in time, it came to dominate musical thought of the sixteenth century, humanism did not unfold unilaterally, but rather in conjunction, and often in conflict, with other developments. Le Munerat's treatises reveal the play of different tendencies, the tug of war, in music of the French church and, more generally, in music of the Renaissance, between reformists and traditionalists, between advocates of speech and advocates of music. The author places the contest within a living practice: the music performed in the chapel of the College of Navarre, where he resided as singer and scholar. What lent edge to his descriptions was the special role the college is known to have played as a springboard for humanism in France.[3]

Le Munerat's writings on music record the tensions that prevailed in the college and, by implication, in the University of Paris. The author refers to disputes in the French church over the rights of music versus language. He entered into a controversy which, at root, concerned the nature and purpose of music and language as separate *artes*. His second treatise is, to all appearances, a transcript of the words he pronounced in a live debate held in 1493. Both there and in the first treatise, Le Munerat thought it his duty to defend music against the arguments of his opponents by deploying his skills in scholastic disputation. In the battle of wits that followed, Le Munerat attempted to define and delimit the functions of music and speech in the celebration of the Mass and Offices. He believed that the two could be smoothly coordinated if each kept to what it was supposed to do and did not infringe upon the privileges of the other. By adopting a policy of "to each its own," Le Munerat pressed for a practical settlement of their differences: since language made its demands on music, and music, in the author's opinion, could not always comply with these demands, a way had to be found to connect and combine the two. Thus a treatise "on the regulation and concordance of grammar and music." The problem to which Le Munerat addressed himself—namely, how to coordinate music and language in composition and in performance—has been and, no doubt, will ever remain the foremost problem of vocal music. Le Munerat's comments are assured of wider significance, then, in discussions of word-tone relations in the theory and practice of music at large.

I could not have written this book without the help of many persons, many institutions. Early conversations with Michel Huglo and Ruth Steiner enabled me to form a clearer picture of Le Munerat's contribution to the history of chant. Mary Berry graciously allowed me to obtain a film, from the Cambridge University Library, of her dissertation on the performance of plainchant in the fifteenth and sixteenth centuries; the dissertation, of which I first learned from her entry on Le Munerat in *The New Grove,* contains the only reasoned discussion, in the modern literature, of Le Munerat's treatises in relation to plainchant practices.[4] I am grateful to the French Ministry of Culture for a research grant permitting me to work on Le Munerat at the Bibliothèque Nationale in Paris for a short period during the summer of 1982. A word of thanks goes to my colleagues and my students, who, known or unbeknown to them, provided me with a soundboard for testing my ideas: in the process, I gained many more from them in return.

Preface

For special favors, or counsel, I am indebted to Inge Dupont (Pierpont Morgan Library), Terence Ford (Répertoire International d'Iconographie Musicale), Pierre Gasnault (Bibliothèque Mazarine), Paula Higgins (Duke University), Andrew Hughes (University of Toronto), Emily Lihani (University of Kentucky Libraries), James W. McKinnon (State University of New York at Buffalo), Gilbert Ouy (Centre National de la Recherche Scientifique), Nicolas Petit (Bibliothèque Sainte-Geneviève), H. Colin Slim (University of California at Irvine), Ernest Trumble (University of Kentucky), and Jeremy Yudkin (Boston University). For permission to reproduce the various illustrations in this volume, I acknowledge the courtesy of the Bibliothèque Nationale, Paris (figures 1–6), and the Music Library of the University of California at Berkeley (frontispiece). Howard Mayer Brown (University of Chicago) reviewed the manuscript from cover to cover, and Thomas W. Mathiesen (Indiana University) checked, and commented on, my Latin translations:[5] I could not have asked for two more perceptive readers.

The manuscript is dedicated to my son Roy, the musician in the family; much of it was written to the sound of Bach's cello suites in the background. A sublime accompaniment to Le Munerat's praises of music.

The bibliography could have been expanded in a number of directions: the history and performance of chant, with particular reference to Bourges, Sens, and Paris; French medieval and Renaissance universities, especially the University of Paris; the growth of French humanism; the concept of battle in the theory and practice of music;[6] and more. I have limited it, and the general treatment, to those items that, in relation to the main theme, an early "defense of music," seemed to me indispensable to setting the life and works of Jean Le Munerat into initial focus.

Hec pauca a me . . . preces deposcente
exarata que ab eruditioribus poterunt
amplius dilatari.[7]

PART ONE

Jean Le Munerat
Singer and Scholar at the
College of Navarre

CHAPTER I

The Man

The name Jean Le Munerat will be new to most readers of music history. With one notable exception,[1] Le Munerat has been excluded from the standard reference works. Or most of them at least: he may be found in two rather outdated lexicons, François Fétis's *Biographie universelle* and Robert Eitner's *Quellen-Lexikon*. Yet both of them cover his life and works in a mere six lines.[2] Of Le Munerat's two treatises on music, the larger one is listed in the basic inventory of theoretical works to 1800 known as "Printed Writings on Music."[3] The treatise, as we shall see, has far-reaching implications for the knowledge of Renaissance music. For all its importance, though, it has been almost entirely neglected in the literature.[4] In this and later chapters, we will provide some of the material necessary for a clearer assessment of Le Munerat's achievement.

Le Munerat's biography, as fragmentary as it is, may be reconstructed from earlier authors, particularly Jean de Launoy and Jean LeBeuf. In their brief reports they refer to Le Munerat's connections with the College of Navarre and, along with other writings, to one of his music treatises. Further information can be gleaned from the treatises themselves, as well as from other works that Le Munerat either edited or supervised.[5]

Jean de Launoy (1603–78)[6] wrote extensively on theology and on the history of schools from the time of Charlemagne to the seventeenth century; among other subjects, he traced the vicissitudes of Aristotelian doctrine at the University of Paris.[7] After his death, his writings were collected and published in a ten-volume edition.[8] They evidence his scholarship, for which he appears to have been widely respected. His contemporary César Boulay, for example, described him, in his monumental study on the University of Paris, as "a most renowned teacher and a most learned man, if ever there was, in the early history of churches and colleges."[9] Launoy composed a thumbnail sketch of Le Munerat for his two-volume history of the College of Navarre, of which the author himself was an alumnus. The history first appeared in 1677 under the title *Regii Navarrae gymnasii parisiensis historia;* it was reprinted, in 1682, now under the title *Academia parisiensis illustrata.*[10] In part III, Launoy reviews the life and works of 134 writers associated with the college.[11] Proceeding chronologically, he eventually comes to Le Munerat, of whom he says the following:[12]

> Jean Le Munerat, who refers to himself as a scholastic theologian of the Parisian College [of Navarre], had two distinguished headmasters for his studies. One of them was Jean Raulin, who, after serving as grand master at Navarre, became a monk of the Cluniac order. The other was Louis Pinelle, who, after serving as grand master at the same school, became a chancellor of the University of Paris; then after serving as chancellor, he became a bishop of the church of Meaux. Whether Le Munerat occupied diverse theological posts cannot be determined. The little that can be determined, however, is that he received neither the master's degree nor the degree of licentiate in theology. He was prevented from doing so by other occupations or, perhaps, by the office of *concentor,* so called, that he held in the church of the College of Navarre. He edited Usuard's Martyrology in 1490 and elucidated its individual birthdays, in fact, with numerous statements of the holy fathers. Yet he took no account of older copies, whereby he might have noted the additions made after Usuard's time. He capped the martyrology with two supplementary tracts. One is about the way to celebrate the Divine Office according to the decrees of the Council of Basel; the other is about the regulation and concordance of grammar and music in church services. In 1494 he made public a treatise, in quarto, on the consecration of the Parisian [church of] Notre Dame; it was abridged [for publication] in 1516.

Jean Lebeuf (1687–1760), a second source of information, wrote prolifically on a wide number of subjects, from archeology to church history. His fifteen-volume history of Paris and its ecclesiastical districts ranks as one of his more substantial works.[13] In the field of music, Lebeuf composed a thoroughly original monograph on the history and practice of plainchant (1741). There, under a discussion of "the poor pronunciation which still can be heard in various churches when Psalms are sung," he refers to Le Munerat, quoting from his first treatise to strengthen his arguments.[14] Lebeuf intersperses certain bio-

4

bibliographical data among his remarks. He notes that in matters of accentuation Le Munerat was respected as an authority, and that his music treatise on this topic occurred at the end of Usuard's Martyrology, edited by Le Munerat in 1490 and reprinted "in 1535" [*recte* 1536]. We are told that Le Munerat belonged to the University of Paris and that he supervised the publication of most of the liturgical works commissioned for the Parisian church. Among these works Lebeuf singles out a "beautiful Gothic edition, in folio, of the Parisian breviary (1492),"[15] referring to one copy in the library of Notre Dame and another in the Barnabite convent.[16] Though scanty on details, the discussion erects a framework for the evaluation of Le Munerat's music treatise: by assigning it to the "history and practice of plainchant," and by recognizing its author as an expert, Lebeuf classifies the treatise, for later generations, in its subject matter and the reliability of its presentation.

Le Munerat seems to have begun his career in Bourges. Whether he was born in Bourges or he came to reside there at a later period cannot be determined. His connections with Bourges were strong enough, however, to lead Boulay in his history to report his name as "Ioannes le Munerat Bituricens[is]."[17] Though most of the copies of his edition of Usuard's Martyrology were dedicated to the bishop of Paris, at least one of them carries a dedication to Pierre Cadouet, archbishop of Bourges from around 1485 to his death in 1492.[18] In addressing Cadouet, Le Munerat identifies himself as a canon of Beata Maria de Salis, that is, Notre Dame de Sales, one of seven collegiate churches that functioned in Bourges prior to the Revolution.[19] He turned to him, no doubt, out of camaraderie, for Cadouet himself was canon and prior of Notre Dame de Sales from 1462 until his accession to the archbishopric in the mid-eighties.[20] Nor did this later post make Cadouet any less accessible, for the archbishop's residence adjoined the church. Le Munerat and Cadouet might have known each other from the 1460s on, during which period Le Munerat is likely, for a certain time, to have officiated as canon at Notre Dame. Though Le Munerat can be traced to Paris in the 1450s and, perhaps on a more permanent basis, after 1465,[21] he might have returned periodically to Bourges in one or another capacity. A close association with Bourges may be assumed, moreover, from his having written a commentary on a sequence (*prosa*) from the Biturgian Ordinary[22] and from his references in his larger music treatise to variant readings in the Biturgian chant books, with which he seems to have been well acquainted.[23]

We are on firmer ground in plotting Le Munerat's connections with the Parisian College of Navarre. He appears to have enrolled as a student in the arts faculty of the college in the 1450s: in a list of students admitted to the faculties of grammar, the arts, and theology from 1400 to 1500, Launoy names a Ioannes Munerati under the *artistae* who matriculated in 1456.[24] In addition to grammar and rhetoric, he would have studied philosophy: the arts faculty emphasized dialectic, taught mainly according to Aristotelian method. Course work in the arts, leading to a master's degree, usually lasted six years or thereabouts. It is unknown how long Le Munerat studied in the arts faculty. He probably received a bachelor's degree along the way;[25] he might have even completed work toward a *license,* which was preliminary to earning a master's.[26] In medieval universities it was customary for students to receive a degree in the arts prior to undertaking studies in theology, law, or medicine.[27] Le Munerat, at any rate, is recorded among those admitted to the theology faculty in 1465.[28] He appears to have studied intermittently over a number of years, for two of the teachers to whom he is said to have been assigned, Jean Raulin and Louis Pinelle, became *magistri* at the college much later than the sixties. Raulin enrolled in theology in 1474 and is listed as a teacher in the faculty of theology from 1479; Pinelle enrolled in theology in 1483 and is listed as a teacher in the same faculty from 1491.[29] It is not clear whether Le Munerat studied directly under the two or merely consulted them as "advisors." Launoy's words, it will be remembered, were that "Le Munerat had two distinguished *moderatores* for his studies." Raulin served as *moderator* at the college during the years 1480–90, while Pinelle did so during the years 1490–1509.[30] A *moderator* may be identified with a *magnus magister,* signifying a grand master or headmaster.[31] Each of the three faculties of the college was directed by its own *magister,* and the *magister* of the theologians acted as *magnus magister* of the college as a whole. The *magnus magister* was concerned largely with administrative questions, yet he received an extra allowance for teaching.[32] Whatever his relationship with his tutors, Le Munerat figures as late as 1497 among the *scholares,* or body of students and teachers, associated with the faculty of theology.[33]

Le Munerat described himself on at least two occasions as a "scholastic theologian" at the College of Navarre.[34] Just what his "scholastic" credentials were cannot be ascertained. The designation *scholasticus theologus,* however imposing, means little more than Le Munerat's having engaged in theological studies. From Launoy we know that Le Munerat did not earn a licentiate in theology, hence he was barred from teaching at the college. But Launoy reported no more than what he purposed. He did not mention, for example, that Le Munerat, in the course of his studies, acquired a bachelor's degree in the arts and perhaps in theology, as we are left to assume from the inscription "Jean Le Munerat of Bourges, bachelor's from [the College of] Navarre" that appears in a document relating to the University of Paris.[35] Nor did Launoy mention that Le Munerat was held in such high regard as a scholar by the Parisian church that, at its behest, he undertook many more projects beyond the two to which Launoy specifically referred (the edition of Usuard's Martyrology, the treatise on the consecration of Notre Dame). On this latter point, we might recall Lebeuf's description of Le Munerat as one who enjoyed the respect of his contemporaries and who "supervised [the publication of] most of the liturgical works of the Parisian church."

Launoy remarks that Le Munerat seems to have been too busy to go on for a higher degree or to become a teacher. According to the original statutes drafted for the University of Paris in 1215, a scholar was permitted to lecture in theology after the age of thirty-five and after a course of studies extending for at least eight years, of which the last five were spent in attending lectures in theology.[36] Le Munerat probably met the requirements but for various reasons did not obtain the degrees. Launoy offered two explanations: one is that "other things" preoccupied Le Munerat—by "other things" he means, apparently, his various scholarly undertakings; another is that a good portion of Le Munerat's time was spent in fulfilling his duties as *concentor* in the chapel choir at the college.

The term *concentor* is as unfamiliar to us today as it appears to have been to Launoy in the seventeenth century. Launoy drew the term from the dedication to Le Munerat's edition of Usuard's Martyrology. There Le Munerat described himself as a "*concentor* in the royal chapel of that French school in Paris commonly known as [the College of] Navarre."[37] In the handwritten inscription on the back page of the copy of the martyrology deposited in the library of the college, Le Munerat is named again as a chapel *concentor*. As far as can be determined, no other references to *concentor* occur in the musical literature. Yet the term has several cognates: *discantor, precentor, succentor,* all of them from the root *cantor;* they do, in fact, have precedents in the literature.[38] If a *succentor* is subordinate to the main *cantor,* as implied by the prefix *sub* (here *suc-*), then a *concentor,* literally construed, is a person who sings in conjunction with the main *cantor,* hence con-*centor.* One wonders, though, whether the term is not to be understood in the more general sense of "chorister."[39] It would seem not, for Le Munerat refers to his duties as if out of the ordinary. Nor would the role of mere chorister have absorbed so much of Le Munerat's time as Launoy would have us believe. What Le Munerat did as *concentor* was, in short, to join the *cantor,* or *precentor,* in singing the soloistic portions of the chant.

Le Munerat may not have been a teacher, but he does appear to have occupied an administrative post at the University of Paris. And a very responsible post at that, as rector of the university for the year 1497. His name figures on a list of "rectors . . . who ruled the university in this [i.e., the fifteenth] century" under the designation "Ioannes le Munerat Bituricens[is] Baccal[aris] Navar[rae] 24 Iunij 1497."[40] Le Munerat was therefore appointed rector on June 24, 1497, following Pierre Mesnart, whose tenure commenced on December 15, 1496. Five months after entering upon his duties, on October 10, 1497, Le Munerat was himself succeeded by Ioan[nes] Andreas de Bohemia, coming from the diocese of Prague. The reason for Le Munerat's short tenure cannot be determined: he might have resigned of his own will or he might have been released from his post. Another possibility is that illness or death terminated his office.

A poem of Le Munerat's was published in 1499,[41] the last date we have for him; it is not clear, though, whether Le Munerat wrote it in the same year or at an earlier date. From the evidence at hand, he appears to have been active, in his various editorial and supervisory occupations, until the mid-nineties. His death may have occurred before the turn of the century, at which point his name drops out of the literature.

CHAPTER 2

The Works

Turning from biography to bibliography, we shall be concerned, in the following paragraphs, with establishing the canon of Le Munerat's works. Twelve titles may be determined, representing at least three different categories: nos. 1–5, editions of liturgical books; 6–10, various Christian writings (commentary, dialectical prose, spiritual verses, liturgical rubrics); 11–12, music theory. Of the twelve titles, Jean de Launoy already referred to four and Jean Lebeuf to three;[1] the others, seven in number, figure here for the first time. We list them, within each category, in order of publication.

EDITIONS OF LITURGICAL BOOKS

Le Munerat's editorial activity covers two kinds of works: those that Le Munerat himself prepared, and those that others prepared under his supervision. In the first kind, he is called an *ordinator;* in the second, a *director.* As *ordinator,* Le Munerat was responsible for two Parisian breviaries (1488, 1492), a missal for the diocese of Châlons-sur-Marne (1489) and an edition of Usuard's Martyrology (1490, reprint 1536). As *director,* he was responsible for a Parisian missal (1489).

In four of the editions, Le Munerat inserts the formula "Pray for Master Jean Le Munerat . . . May he rest in peace. Amen."[2] One would expect the formula to be reserved for books issued or donated after the death of whoever happens to be named, and so it usually is. Limiting ourselves to items once belonging to the College of Navarre, we find the words "orate pro eo" inscribed, for example, in a volume that Pierre d'Ailly (d. 1420) left to the theology faculty, his commentary on Peter Lombard's *Sentences;* and we find the words "requiescat in pace" inscribed in a copy of the Bible owned by a certain Guillaume Leduc, formerly a student of the college, and left by him to the library in 1391.[3] But since Le Munerat was still alive at the time his editions were published, why did he ask to be allowed to rest in peace? Le Munerat may have been thinking ahead to the years after his decease when his works for the church continued to be used, though their editor was no longer there to reap the laurels of his efforts. By having future readers say a prayer for him, he hoped, perhaps, to be remembered and assured of permanent rest in the afterlife.

A similar example of providing for oneself after death comes to mind from the musical sphere: Dufay's four-voice motet "Ave regina caelorum," which the composer, in his will, designated to be performed at his own obsequies.[4] But it does not easily compare with the instances in Le Munerat's works: where Dufay referred to himself as "ailing" (the liturgical text carries the insertion "Have mercy on your ailing Dufay"), Le Munerat referred to himself by implication as dead and buried, or so at least one would assume from "May he rest in peace."

1. *Breviarium parisiense.* Paris: printed by Pierre Le Rouge for Vincent Commin, 1488.

Fol. 279^v (= ō 3^v), col. 2, carries the following inscription: "Orate pro Magistro iohanne le munerat huius ordinarii[5] ordinatore. Requiescat in pace. Amen."

The explicit on fol. 280^v (= ō 4^v) reads thus: "Ce present breviayre fut imprime a paris La(n) Mil. cccc. iiiixx. et viii au moys de septe(m)bre pour Vince(n)t co(m)min marchant et libraire demoura(n)t a paris a la rose en la rue neufve [de] nostre dame par pierre le rouge libraire et imprimeur du roy nostre sire."

For the bookseller Vincent Commin, see Philippe Renouard, *Répertoire des imprimeurs parisiens,* 91; also Anatole Claudin, *Histoire de l'imprimerie en France au XVe et au XVIe siècle* II: 508–9. It seems that the archbishop of Sens was opposed to Commin's engaging in commerce within the Senonic diocese. Yet the French parliament overruled his opposition; it issued an edict, on January 8, 1486, authorizing Commin to sell breviaries and missals in the bishopric of Sens and elsewhere. Commin not only printed works but also entrusted commissions to second printers, among them Pierre Le Rouge. On Le Rouge, who, after working in Chablis, established a printing shop in Paris[6] where he was active from 1478 until his death in 1493, see Renouard, *Répertoire,* 270–71, and Claudin, *Histoire* I: 455ff.

The *Breviarium parisiense* is listed as no. 2906 in Marie Pellechet, *Catalogue général des incunables des bibliothèques publiques de France* II: 217. Shelf number for copy in Paris, Bibliothèque Nationale: B 27802.[7]

2. *Missale parisiense.* Paris: Guillaume Le Caron, Jean Belin, and Jean Dupré, 1489.

After an initial calendar, the missal opens with the words "Incipit missale s(e)c(un)d(u)m usum ecclesie parisien(sis)," etc.

Explicit (fol. 268): "Ad instantia(m) et impegnis magistri Joha(n)nis belin Guillermi lecaron et Johannis de prato librarorium iuratorum universitatis parisien(sis). hoc prese(n)s opus impressum extitit . . . Johannis le Munerat opus secu(n)du(m) directione. Requiescat in pace. Amen."

For the printer Jean Dupré (elsewhere Du Pré, de Pratis, a Prato, Pratensis), see Renouard, *Répertoire,* 130–31, and Claudin, *Histoire* I: 209ff., also II: 554f. Dupré was active between the years 1481–1504.

The *Missale parisiense* is listed in Ludwig Hain, *Repertorium bibliographicum . . . usque ad annum MD* II: 434 (no. 11342); in Paul Marais, *Catalogue des incunables de la Bibliothèque Mazarine,* 289–90 (no. 560); and in Louis Polain, *Catalogue des livres imprimés au quinzième siècle des bibliothèques de Belgique* III: 582.[8]

3. *Missale ad usum ecclesie cathalaunensis.* Paris: Jean Dupré, 1489.

This missal prepared for Châlons numbers 411 pages. Le Munerat's name appears on page 268 (right-hand column) thus: "Orate pro magistro iohanne le Munerat hui(us) missalis ordinatore. Requiescat in pace. Amen." The inscription is followed by various musical staves, three of them with three different versions of "Ite missa est," one with a single reading of "Benedicamus Domino" and another empty one with "Benedicamus Domino" written underneath. After the last of the staves, the words "Requiescant in pace" (now in plural) were reprinted.

Explicit (p. 411): "Impressore q(ui)de(m) Joha(n)ne de prato. Anno d(omi)ni. M. cccc. iiii^{xx} ix. in vigilia s(an)ctor(um) symonis et iude." For Jean Dupré, see above, no. 2.

The missal is listed in Polain, *Catalogue* III: 582. Shelf mark for copy in Paris, Bibliothèque Nationale: Rés. Vélins, 157; B 215.

4. [Usuard], *Martirologium.* Paris: Guy Marchant, 1490.

Le Munerat dedicates the edition to Louis, Bishop of Paris, in the following incipit: "Revere(n)do in xr(ist)o patri ac d(omi)no D(omi)no ludovico. divina miseratio(n)e parisiensi ep(iscop)o Suus iohannes:[9] cappelle regie schole francie

nare infirmitatem.lauare feditate.
illuminare cecitatem.ditare pauper
tatem.uestire unditatem.ut te pane
angelorum:regem regum:z dominu
dominantium.tanta reuerentia z ti
more suscipere tanta contritione et
amore ualeam:tantaq3 fide et puri
tate:tali proposito z humilitate sicut
expedit saluti aie mee. Da michi q3
so illius dominici corporis z sangui
nis non solum suscipere sacramen
tum: sed etiam uirtutem sacramen
ti.O mitissime deus da michi susci
pere corpus unigeniti filii tui domi
ni mei quod traxit de uirgine:ut cor
pori suo mistico merear incorporari
z inter eius membra connumerari.
O pater amantissime : concede mi
chi dilectum filium tuu3 quem nuc
quidem uelatum accipere propono:
reuelata tandem facie contemplari
Qui uiuis z regnas deus.Amen.
Post celebrationem misse.

Gratias ago tibi dulcissime dne
iesu criste.lux uera.salus crede
tium. solatium tristium , gaudium
angelorum.speq3 cunctorum: q3 me
miserum z magnum peccatorem fa
mulum tuu3 hodie sacratissimo cor
pore z sanguine tuo pascere digna
tus es.Ideo ego miserrimus z innu
merabilibus criminibus ifectus.la
crimosis precibus imploro benignis
simam misericordiam tuam: z sum
mam clementia3 ut hec dulcissima
refetio summa et incomprehensibi
lis communio nota sit michi in iu
diciu3 aie me:sed prosit michi i

remedium ad euacuandas omnes i
sidias et nequicias dyabolice. frau
dis:ita ut nulla eius dominetur ini
quitas in corde:corpore:anima: z sen
sibus meis.sed tua clementia me p
ducat ad superna conuiuia angelo
rum:ubi tu es uera beatitudo:clara
lux:z sempiterna leticia.Amen

Orate pro magistro iohanne le
muncrat hui9 missalis ordinatore

Requiescat in pace. Amen.

Ite missa est

Ite missa est

Ite missa est

Benedicamus domino

Benedicamus domino

Requiescant in pace

Missale ad usum ecclesiae cathalaunensis
(Paris, 1489), page 268

vulgo navarre parisii concentor. ac gi[m]nasii parisiensis scholasticus theologus. honore(m) ac famulatu(m)." Bishop Louis may be identified as Louis I of Beaumont de la Forêt (born in 1446). His term as bishop of Paris lasted from 1472 until his death in 1492.[10] It was Louis who commissioned the edition of the martyrology, as he did various adaptations of other liturgical works for the Parisian church. We learn as much from Le Munerat's dedication, which continues as follows (fol. a iv):

Desiderasti prestantissime pater. pastoralis dignitatis officiu(m) rite exequens: commissiq(ue) tibi gregis no(n) immemor: sed p(er)vigil assiduus. ipsius profectus ac co(m)moda procura(n)s: ut post rep(ar)atu(m) seu adaptatu(m) tue ecclesie tam misse q(uam) horaru(m) quas canonicas dicu(n)t ordinariu(m): atq(ue) arte seu industria nostris ob id felicissimis diebus adinventa multiplicatu(m):[11] qua codicillos quib(us) quid deo psallere aut legere quisq(ue) debeat (c)o(n)tinetur: quo ipsi plasmatori facilius co(m)modiusq(ue) debitis lectio(n)ibus atq(ue) or(ati)onibus incu(m)bitur ipso largie(n)te facile obtineat: si q(ui)d in ecclesiasticis officiis necessariu(m) aut opportunu(m): exemplandu(m) videretur. consimili industria co(m)poneretur. adaptaretur ac multiplicaretur: ad dei laude(m) et ecclesie seu ecclesiasticor(um) ampliore(m) instructione(m) atq(ue) profectu(m). Cui sancto desiderio pro posse satisfacere satagens: occurrit ear(um) que ad horam diei qua(m) prima(m) vocat ecclesia: quotidie in ip(s)a proferu(n)tur lectionu(m): quarum prima aliquid discipline ecclesiastice

Most eminent father, duly performing the functions of your pastoral office, and not unmindful of the flock entrusted to you, but rather watchful and attentive, looking after its improvement and its welfare! You [first] wished to have the ritual of both the Mass and the so-called canonical hours of your church repaired or revised, and to have it reproduced with the arts or skills devised in our therefore highly auspicious times, so that anyone might easily procure from a distributor the writings containing whatever he is supposed to chant or read to God; from appropriate readings and prayers he thus becomes more easily and securely drawn to his Maker. After that, [it was your wish that] if anything necessary or advantageous to the ecclesiastical services appeared to need copying, it too might with similar skills be arranged, adapted, and reproduced, to the praise of God and for the greater instruction and improvement of His church or churchmen. I endeavored, to the best of my ability, to satisfy this holy wish, turning to those readings that are daily recited in the church at the hour of day known there as Prime. The first part of them contains something for churchly instruction; the second part enumerates the deeds of the

13

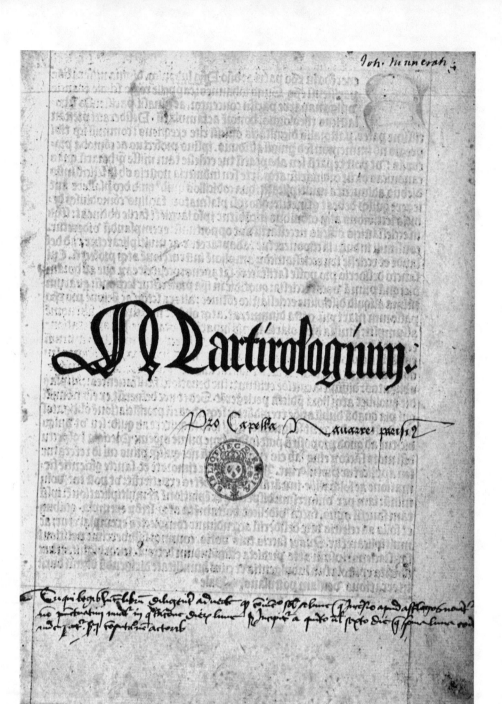

Martirologium (Paris, 1490), title page

co(n)tinet: altera s(an)ctor(um) ac
p(rae)cipue pro xr(ist)o passorum
martyru(m) gesta dinumerat. atq(ue)
ob hoc martirologii. sibi nome(n)
assumpsit: p(rae)missa diei solaris
necno(n) lunaris quotatione seu
annotatione textus co(m)poneretur:
ac p(rae)missis qui in diversis eccle-
siar(um) codicibus inveniu(n)tur debitis prologis. arte sepedicta multiplicaretur: quo q(ui) devotiores seu
observa(n)tiores inter sacerdotes tuos:
ac alias divinor(um) officior(um) lectionibus obligatos: divina largitio(n)e
existunt: sue devotioni satisfacientes:
easipsas die quolibet atq(ue) hora
p(rae)dicta perlegere(n)t. Sed et nec
defueru(n)t ex eis no(n)nulli qui pia
quada(m) dubitatio(n)e trepida(n)-
tes: seq(ue) ad earu(m) pronu(n)cia-
tione(m) obligatos arbitra(n)tes:
adieceru(n)t se ignorare atq(ue) ideo
inquirere ad quid: se [recte si] ut
vulgo dicitur ad quod propositu(m)
post ipsius hore prime or(ati)o(n)em
(Preciosa i(n) (c)o(n)spectu d(omi)ni
mors sa(n)ctor(um) eius) ab eis
enu(n)cietur: cu(m) nec quicq(uam)
prius cui id referatur seu applicetur
protulerint.[12] Ideoq(ue) pro sue ti-
morate et sancte (c)o(n)scientie firma-
tione ac solidatio(n)e. insta(n)tissime
require(n)tes expetieru(n)t: ut post
tot voluminu(m): iam per universum
dispersor(um) exe(m)platione(m) ac
multiplicatione(m): ipsu(m) tam
sanctu(m) opus. sacra videlicet hor-
tame(n)ta atq(ue) s(an)ctor(um) ex-

*saints and especially the martyrs who
suffered on behalf of Christ, whence the
name martyrology. [As to the latter], it
seemed right to arrange the text with an
introductory mention or indication of the
solar as well as lunar day and, using the
arts to which we already referred, to
have it reproduced together with the fitting introductory prefaces to be found in
various church manuscripts. By so doing,
those of your priests who are more de-
vout or observant and, moreover, are responsible for the Divine Office readings
(of which there is a divine abundance)
might satisfy their devotion by reciting
the same on any day and at the appointed hour. But some of them hesitated
on account of a certain pious uncertainty.
Holding themselves responsible for the
delivery of these readings, they added
that since they do not know, they need to
search for evidence whether, as is commonly said in this regard, they may recite it [the martyrology] after the prayer
of the same first hour ([the verse] "Pretiosa in conspectu Domini" [and its re-
sponse] "Mors Sanctorum eius"). Yet
they could produce no earlier evidence to
refer or apply to this. Perceiving an
urgent need, and wishing therefore to
harden and strengthen their reverent and
holy conscience, they strove, after so
many volumes had been copied and reproduced, then distributed all over, to
have the present work reproduced: so
holy [in character], it contains, to be
sure, sacred encouragements and the
saints' examples, from which alone we*

empla. quibus et solis ad celestis vite
desideriu(m) accendimur complec-
te(n)s exemplaretur: ac multiplicaretur. Quare sacris tuis votis.
eorumq(ue) saluberrime petitioni
satisfaciens: ipsum arte predicta
effigiandum decrevi. tueq(ue) dig-
nitati hac adiecta epistola sub indul-
gentia et cum humilitate dirigen-
du(m) dignu(m) duxi: in erratibus
veniam postulans. Vale[.]

*are inflamed with the desire for heavenly
life. Satisfying thereby your sacred
wishes and their [your priests'] most salutary demands, I decided that the same
[work] ought to be prepared with the
aforementioned arts, and with this added
letter I gently and humbly judged it
worthy to commend it to your office, requesting pardon for my mistakes.
Farewell!*

Usuard's Martyrology represents a historical martyrology: it differs from
mere lists of martyrs, of which examples may be cited from the fourth century
on, in appending information on the lives and sufferings of those who sacrificed
themselves for the church. Historical martyrologies composed before the one
by Usuard include those from the eighth and ninth centuries by Bede, Rhabanus
Maurus, Florus of Lyons, and Ado of Vienna. Along with others, they paved
the way for the compendium prepared by Usuard, a Benedictine monk at the
Abbey of Saint Germain-des-Prés, in the later ninth century.[13] Usuard's chief
source, however, seems to have been Ado of Vienna's Martyrology, which, in
its adaptation by the Benedictine monk, laid the foundation for the present
Roman Martyrology.[14] But Usuard's Martyrology outlived all previous ones to
become, in the later Middle Ages, the most famous and widespread document
of its kind. Some fifty-six manuscript copies of the work may be found in the
Bibliothèque Nationale in Paris alone.[15]

The first printed edition (known as the *Maxima Lubecana,* having been issued
in Lübeck) dates from 1475.[16] It was followed by two others of Italian provenance (1486, Florence; 1487, Rome), and by one, predating Le Munerat's
edition, from Paris in 1489.[17] In 1490 alone, three editions of Usuard's Martyrology left the press, one from Paris (Le Munerat's), another from Colonia
Agrippina, i.e., Cologne,[18] and a third from Lübeck (probably a reprint of the
Maxima Lubecana).[19] Why Le Munerat undertook another edition when others
were already available or being prepared is unclear. Le Munerat implied, in his
dedication to Louis, that the martyrology needed to be revised in line with
changes in the Parisian ritual. The relation of the various printed editions of
Usuard's Martyrology both to one another and to manuscript sources must be
clarified if we are to understand Le Munerat's motives. Launoy, it will be

remembered, cast some light aspersions on Le Munerat's scholarly procedure, saying that Le Munerat had taken no account of "older copies" with their particular addenda.[20]

The Bibliothèque Nationale owns five different copies of Le Munerat's edition from 1490: they bear the shelf marks Rés. H 277, H 362, H 996, H 1005, and B 186. All but one of them are dedicated to Louis I of Beaumont de la Forêt. The one in question is H 996, which basically is identical with the other copies, except for having its first two lines revised to read as a dedication to Pierre Cadouet, the archbishop of Bourges.[21] Le Munerat obviously had his reasons for making the change (which typographically involved a stop-press substitution procedure). One can only speculate on them: Did Le Munerat fall out with Louis? Did he hope for monetary gain from Cadouet? Was there a birthday, or other festive occasion, for which a presentation copy to Cadouet might have been warranted? The result of the change is a dedication that anomalously attributes to Cadouet the same achievements as were hailed in the one to Louis.

Of the various copies extant, three or more may be traced to the library of the College of Navarre. B 186 seems to have been Le Munerat's own personal copy that he himself presented to the college: the title page bears the handwritten inscription "Pro Capella Navarre parisi(orum)." The Bibliothèque Mazarine owns two other copies once belonging to the college.[22] Copies of the martyrology no doubt reached the college immediately after publication on July 30, for the printer, Guy Marchant, worked nearby in a building that was college property. The explicit, with Marchant's inscription, reads as follows: "Parisii per guidonem mercatoris: p(ro)pe regia(m) scola(m) fra(n)cie vulgata(m) navarre. ac domo possessio(n)is eiusde(m) scole. arte i(m)pressionis multiplicata. Anno d(omi)ni millesimo. CCCC nonagesimo Mensis iulii die ultimo" (fol. o vi^v).

Guy Marchant (d. 1505) began printing in 1483 in the Champ-Gaillard, where he had a shop directly behind the College of Navarre. His first publications carry the signature "In magno domo Campi Gaillardi retro collegium Navarrae . . . Apud amoenissimam domum vulgatam du Champ gaillard de possessione dictae scholae." He was active until the early 1500s (his later publications give different addresses). For biographical information, see Renouard, *Répertoire*, 293; Claudin, *Histoire* I: 335ff.; also Arthur Christian, *Débuts de l'imprimerie en France*, 16–17. Marchant's publications include moral and philosophical works by Thomas Aquinas, Bonaventura, Jean Gerson, Raymond Lull; allegorical works for spiritual edification, e.g., Denis le Chartreux (Dionysius the Carthusian, 1402–71), *Speculum aureum animae peccatricis* (see below);[23] a letter by Christopher Columbus on his geographical discoveries (*Epistola de insulis repertis de novo*); a practical manual on epistolography; the *Calendrier des bergers,* a lexicon of agricultural, hygienic, meteorological, and ethical knowledge for all strata of society; and so on.[24]

Le Munerat's 1490 reading of Usuard's Martyrology is listed in Hain, *Repertorium bibliographicum* IV: 498–99 (no. 16112); W. A. Copinger, *Supplement to Hain's "Repertorium bibliographicum"* III (viz., pt. II, vol. II): 134 (no. 5915); Polain, *Catalogue des livres imprimés* III: 141–42 (no. 2631); British Library, *Catalogue of Books Printed in the Fifteenth Century* VIII: 58 (shelf mark: IB. 39611).

A second edition of the martyrology appeared in Paris in 1536. The colophon, replacing that at the end of the earlier print by Guy Marchant, reads as follows: "Imprimebat desiderius Maheu / bibliopole parisij i(m)pensis honesti viri Ambrosij Girault. anno a nato christo. M. D. xxxvj. Mense Januarij." (Shelf mark for copy in Bibliothèque Nationale: Rés. H 1000.) The volume bears the same letter of dedication to Pierre Cadouet that appeared in at least one copy of the first edition (see above). As a reprint, the 1536 edition keeps more or less to the original page layout. It differs from it in its composition of lines and in its variant punctuation and abbreviations.

Usuard's Martyrology, as read by Le Munerat, runs to fol. n iii[v] in the earlier and later prints. For other items that the editor included along with it in the same volume, see nos. 9, 11, and 12 below.

5. *Breviarium magnum ad usum parisiensem.* Paris: Jean Dupré, 1492.

Marais lists a copy of this work among the incunabula of the Bibliothèque Mazarine (*Catalogue des incunables,* 345), no. 663 (636). Whether the *Breviarium magnum* is a reprint of the *Breviarium parisiense* published in 1488 (see item no. 1) or a separate edition remains to be determined. The explicit, as it appears in Marais's catalogue, reads thus: "Actum parisii per Joh(ann)em de prato. Anno d(omi)ni MCCCC. IIII. XX. et Xij. Junii IX. Pontificat(ur) reverendi in xr(ist)o patris d(omi)ni Ludovici divina miseratione parisien(sis). ep(iscop)i. Anno XX. Orate p(er) magistro Joha(nne) le munerat hui(us) ordinarii ordi(n)atore. Requiescat in pace. Amen."

The formula "Pray for Jean Le Munerat . . . May he rest in peace. Amen" is familiar from the earlier breviary. What is new in the present explicit is the indication that Bishop Louis was in his twentieth year of office when the edition went to press.

Hain designates the breviary as no. 3869 in his *Repertorium bibliographicum* I: 536.

VARIOUS CHRISTIAN WRITINGS

a. *Commentary*

6. Commentary on a sequence (*prosa*) belonging to the liturgy for Bourges.

The Bibliothèque de l'Arsenal owns a manuscript listed by Henri Martin as a "Commentaire sur la prose du Saint-Esprit extraite de l'Ordinaire de Bourges" (no. 848 [581 K. T. L.] in his *Catalogue des manuscrits de la Bibliothèque de l'Arsenal* II: 130–31; also VII: 333a). Dating from the fifteenth century, the manuscript numbers seventy folios, divided into four sections. The second section consists of a "well-known poem or song, a prose on the Holy Ghost, drawn from the Ordinary of the Biturgian [i.e., of Bourges] church" ("Carmen seu canticum vulgatum, prosa de Spiritu sancto, excepta ex ordinario ecclesie Bituricensis," fol. 55): its first words are "Veni, summe consolator." In the third section, Le Munerat traces the contents of the poem to Scriptures and to various biographical accounts of the saints (the section begins with the words "In prescripto carmine, prosa seu cantico multa Spiritui sancto attribuuntur, quorum quedam ex sacra Scriptura, quedam ex historiis fide dignis sic demonstrantur," fol. 56ᵛ).[25] He signs the section with the remark that "these few comments were set down by me, Jean Le Munerat, requesting your prayers [in return]; they could be more amply expanded by others of greater learning" (for Latin, see above, end of preface). Various Latin prayers follow for the last section (from fol. 59 on).

b. *Dialectical prose*

7. *De dedicatione ecclesie parisiensis*. Paris: Guy Marchant, 1496. 8 fols.

The treatise carries a dedication by Le Munerat to Jean Simon, who, in 1494, succeeded Louis I of Beaumont de la Forêt as bishop of Paris.[26] Le Munerat begins by describing himself as currently a "theological scholar" at the College of Navarre and a *concentor* in its chapel choir, yet formerly a schoolmate of Simon's, presumedly at the college: "De dedicatione ecclesie Parisiensis. Reverendo in xr(ist)o patri / d(omi)no Joa(n)ni / divina miseratione parisie(n)si ep(iscop)o Suus ioa(n)nes le munerat quo(n)da(m) scholastic(us) soci(us) / et ia(m) feliciter in xr(ist)o fili(o) capelle regie schole fra(n)cie vulgo navarre co(n)-ce(n)tor modicus ac scholasticus theologus Honorem: et vestre benedictionis consecutionem" (fol. a i). Shelf mark for copy in the Bibliothèque Nationale: Rés. B 2496.

We are told, in the continuation, that Louis I was much preoccupied with the question of whether the Church of Notre Dame had been properly dedicated. Louis believed that it had not been, and seems to have contemplated an official consecration ceremony. Death terminated his plans, and the matter was eventually transferred to the jurisdiction of Jean Simon. At Simon's behest, perhaps, Le Munerat debated the issue *more dialectico* in writing. For various reasons, he advised against dedicating or, as the case may be, rededicating the church.

The explicit (fol. a viii[v]) reads as follows: "De dedicatione ecclesie et precipue Parisiensis questio nova feliciter explicit. Advisata seu excogitata atq(ue) ordinata sacra arte multiplicari in regia schola fra(n)cie vulgo navarre parisii pro co(m)muni utilitate. Multiplicata vero p(er) Guidonem mercatorem apud amenissima(m) domu(m) vulgatam du champ gaillard de possessione dicte schole. Anno domini. M. cccc. iiiixx. xvi mense amenissimo Mayo."

Launoy wrote that the treatise was abridged and reprinted in 1516.[27] We have not located this edition, which might have been the model for the later one, with slight omissions, published in Paris by Pierre Targa in 1633. The latter numbers twenty-seven pages (shelf mark for copy in Bibliothèque Nationale: 8° LK[7] 6949; a handwritten annotation indicates that it once belonged to the Church of Notre Dame). Its omissions are interesting precisely from a musical standpoint: expunged are the names of certain chants performed during dedication ceremonies, namely, "Jerusalem et Syon filie cetus,"[28] "Rex Salomon fecit templum,"[29] and "Quam dilecta tabernacula domini virtutum et atria"[30] (mentioned on fols. a vii[v]–viii[r] of first edition). The explicit has likewise been shortened, though retaining the original date: "De Dedicatione Ecclesiae et praecipuè Parisiensis quaestio nova foeliciter explicit. Anno Domino millesimo cccc. iiij xx. xvj. Maio."

c. *Spiritual verses*

8. A set of verses, twenty lines long, under the title *Sancta et salubris cogitatio* ("A Pious and Salutary Reflexion"), printed at the end of Denis le Chartreux, *Speculum* (or *Opusculum*) *aureum anime peccatricis* (Paris: Guy Marchant, 1499), fol. c iv (= 36[r]).

The verses begin as follows: "O q(uam) qui astra numerat: / Et terram palmo ponderat: / Est colendus et tremendus" ("Oh how we should worship and dread / Him who counts the stars / And weighs the earth in His palm!"). Le Munerat reveals his identity in the last distich: "Hasq(ue) dotans uberius / Donis beatis Munerat" ("Le Munerat abundantly provides these [thoughts] / As gifts for the blessed").

The explicit follows: "Speculu(m) aureu(m) anime peccatricis finit feliciter. Impressum Parisij in Bellovisu a magistro Guidone mercatore. Anno d(omi)ni 1499. Die 24. Septembris." Chartreux's volume is listed as no. 14910 in Hain,

Repertorium bibliographicum II: 341, and as no. 4325 in Pellechet, *Catalogue général des incunables* III: 184. Shelf mark for copy in the Bibliothèque Nationale: D 13121 (5).

According to Pellechet, the verses were later printed in Jean Raulin's *Collatio de perfecta religionis plantatione, incremento, et instauratione* (Paris: Guy Marchant, 1499), fols. 19ᵛ–20 (the *Collatio* is listed as no. 3308 in Polain, *Catalogue des livres imprimés* III: 581–82).

d. *Liturgical rubrics*

9. *Ex sacro basiliensi concilio Canonica regula* ("The Canonical Rule according to the Holy Council of Basel"); fols. n iv–o iiᵛ of the volume containing Le Munerat's edition of Usuard's Martyrology (Paris: Guy Marchant, 1490; see item no. 4).

The Canonical Rule was established by the Council of Basel during its twenty-first session (terminated on June 9, 1435). Of the rule's twelve articles, seven (nos. 1–4, 6–7, 9) offer instructions for the proper celebration of Mass and the Divine Office. They have been reproduced in appendix 1 (see there for details).

The five remaining articles deal with collateral issues, hence their omission from appendix 1. They carry the following headings (all numerals are additions to the source):

V. De pignorantibus cultum divinum ("On those offering securities to release them from divine worship")

VIII. De tenentibus capitula tempore misse ("On those holding meetings during Mass")

X. De concubinariis ("On those who cohabit with women")

XI. De exco(m)municatis non vitandis in casu ("On excommunicates not to be shunned in an emergency")

XII. De interdictis indifferenter non ponendis ("On prohibitions that should not be set indiscriminately")

For modern editions of the texts relating to the council and its deliberations, see Jean Hardouin, *Conciliorum collectio regia maxima* (1714–15) VIII: 1103–1910 (session XXI, cols. 1196–99), and Gian Domenico Mansi, *Sacrorum conciliorum nova, et amplissima collectio* (1759–98) XXIX: 1–1280 (session XXI, cols. 104–08). They refer to Le Munerat as a source along with such later writers as Johann Albert Fabricius (*Bibliotheca latina mediae et infimae aetatis* [1734–46] and later editions) and Pierre Le Brun (*Explication literale, historique et dogmatique des prieres et des ceremonies de la messe, suivant les anciens auteurs, et les monumens de la plupart des eglises* [1716–26] and later editions).

On the Council of Basel and its liturgical provisions, as they relate to the musical practice described by Le Munerat, see the discussion in chapter 4.

10. *Compendium divinorum officiorum sive Tabula sine quo esse nolo.* Paris: Jean Dupré, 1496 (October 22). 28 fols.

The *Compendium* is listed as no. 3541 in Copinger's *Supplement to Hain's "Repertorium bibliographicum"* II (i.e., pt. II, vol. I): 357, and as no. 7120 in Pellechet's *Catalogue général des incunables* IX: 7063. A copy is held by the Bibliothèque Sainte-Geneviève (shelf mark: OE XV 824, pièce 2, Rés.). Incipit: "Compendium divinorum officiorum quod est repertorium contentorum in rationali divinorum officiorum." Explicit: "Explicit repertorium seu tabella libri rationalis divinorum officiorum quod alio nomine vocatur compendium divinorum officiorum sine qua esse nolo." The *Compendium* amounts to an index, in alphabetical order, to the contents of the well-known *Rationale divinorum officiorum* by Guillaume Durand, Bishop of Mende (d. 1296). In this work, Durand reviews and symbolically interprets the various items relevant to the Christian liturgy (its sacraments, utensils, garments, ornaments, etc.).

MUSIC THEORY

11. *De moderatione et concordia grammatice et musice* ("On the Regulation and Concordance of Grammar and Music"). It covers fols. o iv–vi^v (*recte* o iii–v^v) of the volume containing Le Munerat's edition of Usuard's Martyrology (Paris: Guy Marchant, 1490; see above, item no. 4).

The treatise ends with the printer's colophon for the whole volume: "Parisii per guidonem mercatoris: p(ro)pe regia(m) scola(m) fra(n)cie vulgata(m) navarre ac domo possessio(n)is eiusde(m) scole. arte i(m)pressionis multiplicata. Anno d(omi)ni millesimo. CCCC nonagesimo Mensis iulii die ultimo" (fol. o vi^v [*recte* o v^v]).

Le Munerat considers the respective roles of music and grammar in determining the accentuation of words in plainchant. The College of Navarre appears to have been the theater for a lively debate on the subject, with Le Munerat speaking for music and his opponents for grammar. Le Munerat reviews, then refutes the arguments for a grammatical approach, hoping thereby to put an end to the controversy. For the original and its translation, see part II; for a discussion of contents, chapter 5.

A d inuestigandam veritatem· et sedandam discordiã. que frequenter in ecclesiis super obseruatõne mẽsure seu quantitatis sillabarũ oritur; volunt enim qdam qp quecũqp sillaba longa vel breuis est secundũ precepta gram matice prosodie vel prosodice: tam i simplici littera qp in littera notis seu notulis modulata: longa vel breuis suo modo pronũ cietur: quod qui vellet obseruare oporteret omia gradalia et an tiphonarios destruere: et noua seu nouos condere: cum i ipsis passim super syllabas breues multe note ; super longas vero vnica tantũ adiiciatur) Sciendũ est qp in ecclesiastico officio qtũ ad pronunciationẽ: duo sunt regulatiua; Cantus: et accentus· Cantu regulãtur quecũqp nota seu notis modulãtur: vt sunt antiphone. respõsoria. hymni. introitus. offertoria: et cetera quecũqp in gradali. antiphonario: libro processionũ et similib9 libris inscribũtur. Accentu regulantur quecũqp simplici littera hoc est sine nota describuntur· vt sunt lectiones in matutinis· epistole: et euangelia. collecte seu oratiões. et similia. Que opor tet etiam per virgulas. puncta. et comata: distingui· Et sicut accentus est sine cantu seu preter cantũ. vt nomen sonat: sic et cantus sine accentu. sunt enim sciente disparate: cum tamẽ in vnius tertii: scz officii diuini tendant obsequiũ seu famulatum Vnde sicut in conflictu seu bello corporali: non semper z in omi loco quilibet magistratus belli sua arte vel industria vtitur:cũ ad vnũ finem scz victoriã regis contendant. sed tantũ p vices Nam si congrediente hostes magistro militũ: magister machi narũ sua arte vel industria hostes concuteret: propriũ exercitũ cum aduerso dispderet: sic valde timendũ est ne nisi loca sua et vices agnoscant cantus et accentus: magnã in ecclesiastico offi cio qfusione pariat eoz indiscretus conflictus· Iam cui non est qui audeat Magnificat secũdi et octaui toni: vti notatũ est a pa trib9 inchoare: ob hoc qdem qz eius penultima syllaba scz fi.du plici nota scz vt. fa. moderatur vel modulatur: z vt longa per sonatur seu personari videtur. Similiter hymnũ Sanctorum meritis inclyta gaudia. secũdi toni. trium scilicet z ir. lettionũ more psio: vbi sup sillabã di. de gaudia duplex nota. s. sol fa mo dulatur: nõ audẽt qdam sicut notatũ est decantare: sed sup gau·

O·IIII

De moderatione et concordia
grammatice et musice (1490), from volume
containing *Martirologium*, folio o iv

As listed in *Écrits imprimés* I: 495, the treatise is extant in three copies: one in Paris, Bibliothèque Nationale; another in Brussels, in the Jesuit convent of Saint Michael's; and a third in the British Library. Yet as many additional copies may be located as remain for Le Munerat's edition of Usuard's Martyrology in its earlier and later printings (for the five copies in the Bibliothèque Nationale, see under item no. 4).

12. A second treatise with the incipit *Qui precedenti tractatu nullam adesse rationem vel demo(n)strativam* [Paris: Guy Marchant, 1493].

Occupying one folio, the treatise may have been printed, at Le Munerat's expense, as a broadside to be distributed among the *scolares* of the College of Navarre. It forms a sequel to the previous treatise, which, instead of terminating the controversy over the rights of music and grammar in the liturgy, appears to have stimulated further argument. A debate was held in the college in 1493, and, to all intents, what we read in *Qui precedenti* may constitute a transcript of Le Munerat's remarks. The author had a copy of the one-leaf tract bound, as the last folio, to his own personal copy of Usuard's Martyrology, which he later presented to the chapel library (it is now in Paris, Bibliothèque Nationale, Rés. B 186). It appears to preserve the only known copy of the tract.

The origins of *Qui precedenti,* as described above, may be reconstructed from the handwritten annotation on the back flyleaf of the presentation copy. There someone in charge of recording acquisitions wrote, in garbled Latin, as follows:

Ex dono eiusd(em) Ioh(ann)is le munerat hui(us) cappelle conce(n)toris ipsi cappelle[.] Et est hic ultim(us) tractat(us) i(n)vectiva co(n)tra quosda(m) ecc(lesi)asticos vocali i(n)terdum secu(m) disceptatio(n)e oppositu(m) sustinentes[.] Anno d(o)m(ini) mille(sim)o. cccc. iiii xx. xiii. festo sanctj ludovicj. Stallo[31] sinist(ro). Requiescat i(n) pace Ame(n)[.] Et a(n)i(m)e o(mn)i(um) fideliu(m) r(equies)c(ant in pace).

From a gift of the same Jean Le Munerat, a singer in the chapel, to the said chapel. This last treatise is an invective against certain churchmen who continue to sustain an opposite viewpoint in the live debate [they held] with him in the year of our Lord 1493 on the Feast of Saint Louis in the left [choir] stall. May he [the donor] rest in peace, Amen! And may the [departed] souls of all faithful rest in peace!

The debate to which the writer refers took place on August 25, the feast day of Louis, the patron saint of the chapel.[32] It was one in a number of debates, in Louis's honor, that date back to the early years of the college (see chapter 3).

Qui precedenti tractatu [1493],
added to one copy of the *Martirologium*,
folio o vii

Handwritten inscription on back flyleaf
of volume containing
Qui precedenti tractatu

The volume containing the treatise seems to have been deposited in the college chapel, at Le Munerat's behest, shortly after his death. Its connection with the chapel is emphasized not only in the inscription just quoted, but also in three other handwritten annotations: "Pro Capella Navarre parisi(orum)" on the title page of the martyrology; "De libris Cappelle collegii Navarre" and "De libris sacelli collegii navare" on the back flyleaf. The volume belonged, then, to the books originally housed in the small chapel library, to be distinguished from the general library of the college.

No colophon is given. The treatise differs from item no. 11 above in being set in a separate type font (bastard) and in using virgules (instead of periods) for commas. Guy Marchant may perhaps be assumed to have undertaken the printing, if only because he prepared item no. 11, but we cannot be sure of this.

For the original Latin and its translation, see part II; for a discussion of contents in relation to item no. 11, see chapter 5.

CHAPTER 3

The College of
Navarre

The College of Navarre, where Le Munerat was active as scholar and singer, has a history dating back to the fourteenth century.[1] It was founded in 1304 by Jeanne, queen of Navarre and wife of the French king Philip IV ("The Fair"). Jeanne, who died in 1305, endowed the college with an annuity deriving from the liquidation of part of her property. In her will she specified that the college be installed in her palace, the Hôtel de Navarre, at Bussy.[2] Yet the executors of the will preferred to sell the *hôtel* and, with the monies received, to purchase a tract of land for erecting the college on Mount Saint Genevieve, on the Left Bank in Paris. Construction began in 1309; with the completion of the original core of buildings in 1315, the college provided separate lodgings for each of the three faculties (grammar; the *artes,* i.e., principally logic; and theology) and a common chapel, where students and teachers met for prayer on Sundays and feast days.[3]

The College of Navarre belonged to the network of colleges, including the Sorbonne, that formed the University of Paris (the university was granted its royal charter in 1200).[4] From their beginnings in the thirteenth century, the colleges were largely charitable institutions, offering room and board to needy scholars. According to its terms of foundation, the College of Navarre admitted seventy such scholars to its faculties (twenty to grammar, thirty to the *artes,* and twenty to theology). Each of the faculties was directed by its own *magister,* and the *magister* of the theologians acted as the *magnus magister* of the college as a whole. Students and teachers, as customary in other colleges, were grouped into *nationes,* according to regional provenance. Yet where some colleges restricted admission to one or another "nation," as, for example, the College of

29

Harcourt whose *scolares* were drawn from the province of Normandy, the College of Navarre accepted all Frenchmen regardless of cultural or political affiliation. In 1458 a commission was charged with reconstituting the college for an increase in revenues. It enacted various changes, among them the admission of students paying tuition, which comes as no surprise, for most of those required to pay belonged to families of the high nobility. By the later fifteenth century some eighteen colleges were in full operation, enlarging their facilities and expanding their activities as part of the university. Yet the College of Navarre seems to have won a special reputation for its distinguished teachers and alumni. Many celebrated figures of early and later times were educated there, including Henri III, Henri IV, Bossuet, Cardinal Richelieu, Cardinal Fleury, and Prince Eugene of Savoy. François Mézeray (d. 1683) described the college in his *Histoire de France* as "the cradle of French nobility and the honor of the University of Paris."[5]

But a college cannot exist on its *scolares* alone; it needs books. Jeanne of Navarre had the foresight to recognize the importance of a library:[6] in her will she specified that whatever sums of money were received as an increment to the yearly allowance be set aside "for buying books of grammar, logic, philosophy, and theology, to be put to the common profit of the poor schoolboys in their studies."[7] Jeanne's words were incorporated in Latin into a special act (*Statutum speciale fundationis navarricae*). The *magni magistri* were entrusted with the responsibility of developing the library. And so they did: Pierre d'Ailly, Jean Raulin, Louis Pinelle, and other *magni magistri* were instrumental during their terms of office in increasing its holdings. The library was enlarged, moreover, by the deposition of books once belonging to various teachers and alumni. Sometimes whole libraries were bequeathed, as was the precious collection of manuscripts owned by Pierre d'Ailly (d. 1420). Other times two or more volumes reached the college upon the decease of their proprietors.[8] It appears to have been the custom for those affiliated with the college to deposit one copy of their own works in the library. Many volumes have annotations that preserve the memory of their donors. One of the oldest may be traced to Nicolas Laginius (or Laginiis), who studied at the college in 1352. Still another is the copy of Usuard's Martyrology that Le Munerat designated for use in the chapel library.[9]

The library grew quickly, acquiring a collection that, at an early stage, rivaled that of the Abbey of Saint Victor or of the College of the Sorbonne.[10] It was during Louis Pinelle's term as *magnus magister* that the construction of a new and elegant set of quarters for housing the library was completed.[11] One eyewitness from the later sixteenth century reported of the library that "by comparison it hardly falls short of that of Saint Victor, whether it be in the number of its books or in the beauty and singularity of the volumes by authors [writing] on all sciences and in all languages."[12] He may have overestimated its size. Only in the seventeenth century, with the absorption of certain private collections, does the library seem to have made significant increases in its holdings. Even so, its capacity, by present standards, is small. In 1706, for example, it numbered about eight thousand volumes.[13] They were arranged in two large cupboards more or less according to their sizes: the smaller volumes were set on the upper shelves and the heavier larger ones on the lower shelves.

Various inventories were taken of the library from the first part of the eighteenth century. They appear in the handwriting of the particular librarian who was in charge of the collection at the time. Étienne Milanges prepared a catalogue of theological titles in 1708, appending a list of "books preserved in cabinets either because they are duplicates or because they ought to be exchanged."[14] A new, ten-volume catalogue of the library's complete holdings was undertaken by Pierre Davolé (or Duvollé) in 1721.[15] The first three volumes cover theology, the next three individually law, history, and the *humaniores litterae* (i.e., grammar, literature, philosophy), and the last four various indices. A third catalogue, largely of manuscript items, was completed by Gabriel Masson in 1741: it consists of a single volume, numbering 268 folios.[16] To these three catalogues should be added the recent list by Émile Châtelain of addenda and emendanda to the one by Masson.[17]

The catalogues prove useful for tracing the items mentioned by Le Munerat in his music treatises. To start with, Le Munerat's edition of Usuard's Martyrology, to which the treatises were attached, figures in two different copies in the college library.[18] Other liturgical works, for the period prior to 1500, include a selection of missals and breviaries. The lives of the saints are represented by various manuscripts, among them a *Summa de vitis sanctorum* (with the incipit "Cum plurimi sacerdotes") and a volume *De vitis sanctorum* (with the incipit "Ab inventione sanctorum Abraham, Isaac et Jacob").[19] Le Munerat could have consulted a number of volumes for writings of the church fathers: for example, an anthology entitled *Variorum patrum opera* (with the incipit "Liber Ambrosii de bono mortis") from the eleventh century, or another one entitled *Sanctorum patrum excerpta* (with the incipit "Incipit liber in libro Confessionum S. Augustini") from the twelfth century.[20] Works by Saint Gregory were collected in a book *S. Gregorii Papae dialogi* from the fifteenth century.[21] There is a manuscript, again from the fifteenth century, comprising various decrees of the Council of Basel;[22] Le Munerat might have used it in preparing his tract *Ex sacro basiliensi concilio Canonica regula.*[23] Few works relate to music—one can only wonder about the contents of the volume *De musica* that was described as a "codex vetus," or of the manuscript said to "begin with the words 'Benedictus Dominus' and be provided with musical notation."[24] The grammarians, on the other hand, were represented by a large number of items. Priscian, whom Le Munerat names in his second music treatise, could be read in a manuscript titled *Priscianus grammaticus de latinitate sermonis,* or in two Venetian prints from 1488 and 1492 titled *Priscianus grammaticus de octo partibus orationis.*[25] The collector of historical curiosities Valerius Maximus, also mentioned by Le Munerat in the same treatise, could be read in a volume titled *Valerii Maximi dictorum factorumque mirabilium exempla.*[26]

None of these or the remaining volumes in the college library carries a particular label. Their connection with the library can be ascertained in the majority of cases from annotations on the flyleaves. On the basis of these annotations, usually in the hand of the librarian, it is possible to identify part of the collection of books from among those in the various libraries to which the collection was dispersed after the college was definitively closed in the early years of the nineteenth century. The Bibliothèque Nationale acquired 124 volumes, including at least one of the copies of Le Munerat's edition of Usuard's Martyrology held by the college library.[27] The Bibliothèque de l'Arsenal acquired 102 volumes, of which only forty-nine carry an inscription.[28] More than 130 volumes now belong to the Bibliothèque Mazarine.[29] Additional volumes no doubt found their way into these and other libraries, though they have yet to be identified.

Not all the books were originally deposited in the general library of the college. Some appear to have been held in a smaller collection in the chapel. One of them, as we know, is Le Munerat's edition of Usuard's Martyrology (Bibliothèque Nationale, B 186).

The chapel[30] was the center of Le Munerat's activity as *concentor.* It also played an important role in the lives of the teachers and students. According to the original college statutes, "all scholars were, at the strike of the bell, to assemble, in an orderly fashion, in the chapel on solemn feasts and on Sundays to recite Matins, the Mass, and other canonical hours."[31] Le Munerat was probably obliged to participate in the services of the chapel on a daily basis. Otherwise it is hard to understand why his duties there absorbed so much of his time as to prevent him, according to Launoy, from pursuing his studies toward a degree in theology.[32] In the course of a day Le Munerat might often have betaken himself to the chapel for the celebration of Mass and various offices; he might have used its library in the time that remained for working on his editions.

The cornerstone of the chapel was laid in 1309, four years after the founding of the college. A tablet appears to have been set at the entrance to the chapel, reporting that "in the year of our Lord 1309, on Saturday, the twelfth of April, namely, the Saturday following Quasimodo Sunday,[33] the reverend father, his lord Simon Festu, by the grace of God the bishop of Meaux and the executor of the [estate of our] most excellent lady Jeanne, Queen of France and of Navarre, laid and placed the first stone at the entrance to the church or chapel of the congregation of scholars of [the College of] Navarre."[34] The official dedication of the chapel took place in 1373. Another tablet, to the right of the entrance, appears to have been inscribed with the words "In the year of our Lord 1373, on Sunday, the sixteenth of October, in accord with Declaration No. 11, this chapel was dedicated by the reverend servant of Christ the lord Pierre de Villars, at the time bishop of Nevers, in honor of the Holy Trinity, the Most Victorious Cross of Christ, the Most Glorious Virgin Mary, the Blessed King of France Louis, the Blessed Virgin Catherine, and the whole assembly of celestial citizens."[35]

The chapel possessed a collection of sacred relics, mentioned as early as the dedication ceremonies.[36] References to the chapel treasures can further be found in subsequent documents, as in one from 1487 that regulated the handling of *iocalia* and "ecclesiastical ornaments and other valuables."[37] *Iocale* is a medieval Latin word, invented after the French *joyau;* it is used in the singular for a "theca reliquiarum," i.e., a box of relics, while in the plural (*iocalia*) it designates jewels or precious gems.[38] In this connection, Le Munerat's remark, in his first treatise, about ancient French manuscripts of chant that are "preserved and displayed as a precious collection of relics" ("pro iocali precioso conservantur et ostenduntur") has a special ring.[39] Like the relics of the chapel, old books are the pride of their possessors; they deserve special handling.

An organ was installed in the chapel upon the initiative of the French nation in 1487: "The teachers, superintendents, chaplain, and bursars of the College of Navarre acknowledge by contract that the organ placed in the chapel of the said college belongs to the teachers of the French nation, at whose expense it was constructed."[40] In 1552, the organ was replaced by an instrument ordered from the "master builder of organs and other musical instruments" Josse Lebel. He received 230 pounds minted in Tours for "the construction of the organ built by him and delivered to the church of the College of Navarre, for the said nation of France."[41] Perhaps the earlier organ proved inadequate, hence was sold and supplanted by a new, improved instrument. We know of the organ, for exam-

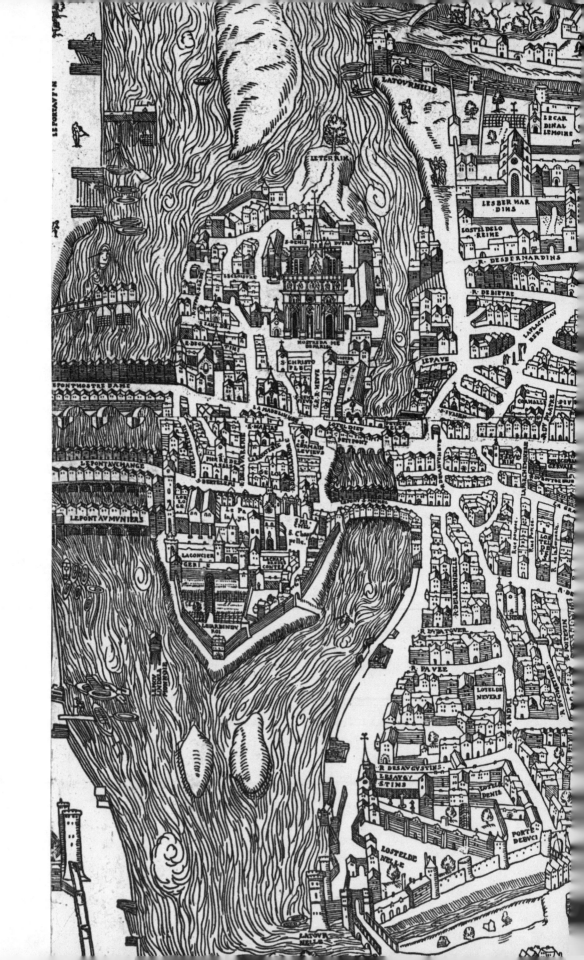

The College of Navarre as depicted in a map of Paris from 1552 (fragment; see chapter 3, note 3). To the left, the Île-de-France, dominated by the cathedral of Notre Dame; to the right, the Left Bank, with its numerous colleges.

ple, in the Sainte-Chapelle du Palais, originally installed in 1299, that it "was sold because it was neither good nor satisfactory for such a church."[42] Whether the organ in the college chapel was used to accompany the chant or for instrumental preludes or postludes cannot be determined.

The patron saint of the chapel was Louis. He appears to have been associated with the chapel from its inception: "In 1309, on Saturday, the second of April, Master Simon Festu, Bishop of Meaux, was, of those [named to execute Queen Jeanne's will], the one who cast the first stone for the foundation of the chapel, dedicated thereafter to Saint Louis."[43] Louis IX, who reigned as king of France from 1226 to his death in 1270, was canonized in 1297. Various reasons may be given for his being chosen as patron saint. He was remembered for his religious ardor: as the last of the crusaders, he led two expeditions against the infidels, the first in 1248–49, the second, during which he died, in 1270. Under his patronage the Sainte-Chapelle was constructed and Robert of Sorbonne founded the College of the Sorbonne, which became the main seat of the theological faculty of the University of Paris. Louis was officially recognized as patron saint of the college chapel during its dedication in 1373.[44]

Louis's feast day fell on August 25, and it seems to have been marked annually by a public sermon or debate in the chapel. The custom of "holding a public address or sacred sermon on the feast day of Saint Louis, in whose honor the shrine or chapel was dedicated"[45] dates from the early years of the college. Master Simon pleaded for its inauguration as a regular yearly activity in 1364 ("we read in the Regulations of the English nation, which is now called the German [nation], that 'on the last day of July, in the year 1364, Master Simon, a doctor of theology, petitioned the university to allow holding an annual address [meeting? discussion?] on the aforementioned feast day of Saint Louis' "). His request was granted.[46]

Music was not absent from the debates at the college. In 1444 Fernando of Cordova, a brilliant youth, is reported to have held forth on the subject against more than fifty adversaries, with an audience of three thousand in attendance. Nothing remains of his remarks or of the others' retorts, except for a general description by one of the disputants:[47]

With us in the school of Navarre he engaged in disputation, although we numbered more than fifty of the most perfect masters. I omit three thousand others and more who attended the bout . . . He argued four doctors of the church out of countenance; no one seemed comparable to him in wisdom; he was taken for antichrist.

In 1493, another debate on music took place: facing one or more grammarians, Jean Le Munerat argued for the rights of music as opposed to those of grammar in determining the pronunciation of Latin in church services. Here we are fortunate to have what seems to be a fairly accurate transcript of Le Munerat's comments. They form the short treatise that their author appended to his first music treatise in the copy presented to the chapel library.[48] From the handwritten annotation on the back flyleaf we learn that the debate occurred "on the Feast of Saint Louis in the left stall [of the chapel]." Like Fernando of Cordova before him, Le Munerat seems to have stood alone against his opponents; he pleaded his cause, as a single musician perhaps, against a band of grammarians and grammatically schooled theologians[49] for whom not notes but words regulated the performance of the liturgy. Music does not seem to have been much favored at the college. "The elders of the choir," Le Munerat wrote in his first music treatise, "are for the most part adequately schooled in grammar and many other sciences, but only scantily acquainted with music. Therefore they underrate music, as may be expected, for everyone cultivates what he knows but scorns and spurns what he knows not. In all places and for all needs, they propose grammar or its laws and would have them rule [any other considerations]. They do not believe that music is fit for the schools or that it has any power in the ecclesiastical office to withstand, in particular, the laws or rules of grammar, being rather in all matters subordinate to them."[50]

One can only speculate on the circumstances of the debate. It must have been surrounded with the aura of solemnity that marked the annual convocation on Saint Louis's feast day. The students and teachers of the college probably turned out in full numbers; they may have even participated in the proceedings with words of encouragement or of disapproval. The outcome of the debate is unknown. Yet the lines seem to have been so clearly drawn from the beginning that little room was left for compromise; the grammarians no doubt remained as firmly entrenched in their opinions as Le Munerat did in his. The dispute turned on the rights of words versus those of music. Le Munerat was pleading a lost cause against the grammarians, who represented a literary point of view at a time when words were in the ascendency. It is no wonder that the grammarians eventually carried the day.[51]

The College of Navarre seems to have reorganized its program of studies sometime in the mid-fifteenth century to conform to the new emphasis placed on the *studia humanitatis*. Changes of curriculum date from an even earlier period: Jean Gerson, who taught at the college toward the end of the fourteenth century, initiated the changes. After his example, the teaching of the humanities played an increasingly prominent role in determining the course offerings at the college.[52] Where and how music fit into the curriculum, if at all, is not clear. The place of music in the College of Navarre must be considered along with the broader question of its place in the University of Paris as a whole.[53] It is generally thought that music, as a science and an art, was widely cultivated at the university.[54] But the various references to music occurring in the statutes and records of the university are too fragmentary to permit a consistent account of its uses.

The practice of music was one kind of activity at the university. Music was performed in the college chapels in the celebration of the Mass and the Offices. It was heard on the feast days of saints or on special occasions marked on the university calendar.

The teaching of music was another kind of activity. Knowledge of music as a *scientia* was imparted in the lecture hall. Yet as an *ars* music was taught in the chapel: there the singers received whatever training was necessary to enable them to read the chant books. Not all teachers administered their instruction in the classroom; some of them may have given lessons in their private quarters. It should not be forgotten that music was also taught at the choir schools or *maîtrises* that were connected with the churches or cathedrals.

The music treatises were used as textbooks. They may serve as a gauge to the study of music, both in content and in character. Basically two kinds of textbooks may be signaled: those dealing with music as a mathematical or speculative discipline; and those dealing with it as a practical art. Music, from early times, was grouped with the mathematical sciences of the quadrivium, which, along with the trivium, formed the backbone of university studies throughout the Middle Ages.[55] It may be assumed that the mathematical and speculative textbooks were the ones employed in classroom teaching at the university. Writings of the ancients were still favored, among them Cassiodorus's compendium *De quatuor mathematicis disciplinis*,[56] the *Introduction to Harmonics* (Εἰσαγώ-γη ἁρμονική) by Cleonides (printed in 1497),[57] Boethius's treatise *De institutione musica*,[58] and Martianus Capella's *De nuptiis Philologiae et Mercurii* (in which the author assigned music to the curriculum of studies forming the *artes liberales*).[59] These textbooks were supplemented by writings of more recent authors. Jean de Muris composed a *Musica speculativa* based, in large part, on Boethius's work; it became so popular that it seems to have superseded the latter as a basic textbook in the universities.[60] Another book directed to a university audience was the *Musica libris demonstrata quatuor,* written in the 1490s by Jacques Lefèvre d'Étaples, a *magister artium* at the university and teacher at the College of

Cardinal Lemoine. It too emphasizes the numerical aspects of music—in fact, it forms a digest of Boethian arithmetic.[61] One important treatise by a former student of the university is Jacques de Liège's *Speculum musicae* (early fourteenth century). It brings together a welter of practical and theoretical information on music.[62]

Other works seem to have been intended for use in the college chapels or in the cathedral schools. Such a one is Nicolaus Wollick's *Opus aureum musices* (1501), later expanded and published under the title *Enchiridion musices* (1509) when Wollick taught at the University of Paris. An introductory work, it sets the fundaments of *cantus planus* and *cantus figuratus*.[63] A half century later, the theologian and composer Maximilian Guilliaud, a graduate of the College of Navarre, published a work entitled *Rudiments de musique practique*.[64] Whether anything in it reflects previous training at the college is hard to say (Guilliaud matriculated there in 1552). It might be mentioned that, except for casual mention of polyphony,[65] Jean Le Munerat seems to have regarded plainchant as the predominant form of music practiced in the chapel in his time. Its precepts are summarized in the first part of Guilliaud's treatise. But in the first half of the sixteenth century polyphonic music must also have been heard in the chapel. Guilliaud discusses polyphony, at any rate, in part II of his *Rudiments*.

Another series of treatises, by authors who either were graduates of universities or did occasional teaching there, discourse on a variety of musical topics, such as notation, counterpoint, modal rhythms, etc. Jerome de Moravia's *Tractatus de musica* was designated "for the use of students" (it contained four treatises, among them works by the "academics" Johannes de Garlandia and Franco of Cologne). To what extent the treatise was employed as a textbook for university or private instruction cannot be determined. Similar uncertainty surrounds the uses of Anonymous IV's treatise on modal rhythm or Johannes de Grocheo's *Ars musica* (Anonymous studied at the university, Grocheo seems to have taught at the Sorbonne).[66]

Not all singers participating in the chapel choir were in need of musical training. Some had received instruction in the rudiments of music while in the cathedral schools; when their youthful voices changed, they were generally encouraged to go on to studies at the university. In 1475, for example, two Notre Dame choristers were granted scholarships to study at the College of Navarre.[67] Thus the colleges could count on a nucleus of musically literate singers to staff their chapel choirs.

Beyond the plainchant renditions in chapel services at the College of Navarre, music may have been performed as part of the theatrical productions known to have been put on at the college from the fourteenth century on.[68] The *scolares* in the faculties of grammar and the *artes* were authorized, on certain conditions, to present works of their own composition before their teachers and fellow students. Their plays tended to treat moral subjects (evidence remains for short *moralités* presented in the years 1426–27). Yet a farce may be dated to the end of the fifteenth century (*La Farce du Cousturier et d'Esopet*), and Latin tragedies and comedies were enacted in the sixteenth century. It is likely that music enjoyed the same privileges in these productions as were accorded to it in the French theater at large:[69] the subject needs to be investigated along with the whole complex of matters that relate to the uses and functions of music in the French schools.

What happened to the College of Navarre in later times? The college had its subventions cut off at the beginning of the Revolution. It was closed in 1792, only to reopen in 1800, when an attempt was made to revive its program of studies. A promotional leaflet was put out,[70] describing the college as "the ancient, celebrated House of Navarre . . . whose graduates number so many great figures of the [French] Church and State." The curriculum consisted of mathematics, logic, ethics, rhetoric, and languages. Anyone was qualified to enter the college "provided he knew how to read and write." Tuition was required of all except those who were lodged in the student hostel (*pensionnat*). An insignia was prepared, with the device "when His winds blow, the waters flow" ("Flabit spiritus ejus et fluent aquae").[71]

But the "winds" and "waters" soon subsided. The attempt to breathe new life into the college was short-lived: a few years later it closed down and its library became public domain. The history of the college formally ended when, in November, 1805, the École Polytechnique (founded in 1794) was established in its buildings.

Writer's postscript. In September, 1982, on the last morning of a ten-day stay in Paris, where I researched Le Munerat in the libraries, I paid a visit to the erstwhile College of Navarre. Walking the narrow, winding streets of the Mount Saint Genevieve, I eventually came to the college grounds on rue Descartes.[72] Little remained of the old buildings except for the one that contained the library. The École Polytechnique had made physical changes in the building: it divided the ground floor, once the Salle des Actes, into two stories, installing rooms for fencing on the lower level and its own library on the upper one. Above that, what was originally the second story, holding the library of the college, was converted into a room for draftsmanship. Yet in the meantime even these arrangements had changed. The École Polytechnique no longer occupied the college; in 1967, it moved to the rue de Saclay, in Palaiseau, on the outskirts of Paris. Ten years later, the Auguste Comte Institute was formally settled in its buildings. The French government had pinned great hopes on the institute, an advanced center of technological studies dedicated, according to the official decree of its inauguration, "to administering a complementary education focusing on the economic and international consequences of the evolution of [industrial] science and technology, as well as on the human problems connected with the development of the forms of production," etc.[73] But the institute did not live up to the hopes of its founders. It eventually closed down, and in its place the government established the offices of the Ministry for Research and Industry.

On the morning of my visit, bulldozers were clearing the area, workmen were busy deconstructing, reconstructing. I looked for remnants of the college. A sign pointed to the office of the Friends of the École Polytechnique. The woman in charge of the office spoke wistfully of the former days of the *école,* complaining about the wasted efforts poured into the Comte Institute. I asked if she had any pamphlets, maps, or designs relating to the *école* and, perhaps, to the College of Navarre. Stacks of papers lined the floors; the office, she explained, was being reorganized. She pulled out a booklet on the institute and a couple of newsletters of the Friends. Why don't I drop by another day, she said, once the files had been put in place... I left with mixed feelings: it was clear that the College of Navarre had passed into history.

CHAPTER 4

Three Traditions of Chant, One Mode of Performance

Jean Le Munerat's writings on music may be studied from various points of view. In the present chapter we shall consider the chant traditions with which Le Munerat was acquainted and the regulations that he seems to have acknowledged as binding for an orderly practice of the liturgy; in the following chapter we shall consider the arguments he formed in defense of music against the attacks of the grammarians. Other topics relevant to evaluating the position of Le Munerat's writings in Renaissance musical thought will be deferred to the epilogue.

Le Munerat includes no written musical examples, yet his discussion is rich in references to chants. In the first treatise, twenty-eight titles are mentioned, covering a number of types: hymns, antiphons, Psalms, responsories, introits, alleluias, sequences, and so on. The author knew the chants from firsthand contact and presumed a similar familiarity with them from his readers. Though the greater part of the chants may be identified and reconstructed,[1] we cannot today pretend to any more than an imperfect knowledge of them as they functioned within the liturgy. By citing a single name, Le Munerat awakened in his readers a range of associations which for us, at a distance of nearly four centuries, is considerably dimmed.

Much remains to be done to clarify the history and practice of chant in the French church of the fifteenth century.[2] Yet the chants themselves, or at least the ones designated by Le Munerat, command attention at first encounter for belonging to more than one tradition. One might suppose that, as a member of the University of Paris, Le Munerat would have chosen his examples from the Parisian tradition. Not so: three usages are represented, the Parisian, the Biturgian (i.e., of Bourges), and the Senonic (i.e., of Sens). Le Munerat admits to having examined a large number of chant manuscripts, from both regular and secular churches.[3] He is familiar with variant readings of single chants. Thus he freely recalls the melody of "Ait Petrus" according to the Parisian and Biturgian rites, comparing it with its version in the Senonic books.[4] He demonstrates how individual churches added ornaments to the chants or altered the placement of syllables as they saw fit. His acquaintance with two or more traditions was taken for granted in the French church, with its active interchange between members of separate dioceses. The Parisian church[5] was subject to the jurisdiction of the archbishop of Sens, in the same way as, say, the different churches of the Roman Catholic rite, since the sixteenth century, look to the pope in Rome for their leadership. Bishops, canons, deacons, and others from outlying districts were invited to deliver sermons in Parisian churches, to dedicate their chapels, to sanctify their altars. The Biturgian church possessed its own chapel in Paris, as did the Senonic church. Thus Paris became the seat of diverse traditions, practiced by their local representatives.

It is not surprising, then, to have Jean Lebeuf refer, in his treatise on plainchant, to a particular ending in the Dorian mode preserved "in the old and new [chant] books of Sens, Paris, Rouen, Langres, Tours, Auxerre, Lisieux, la Rochelle."[6] Lebeuf's book was written nearly a century and a half after Le Munerat's treatises. In the interim, the process of unifying the church in its ritual and its music had gradually eliminated the plurality of traditions so characteristic of its early development; or if not eliminated them, at least reduced the differences among them to variants of questionable significance. The only situation comparable today to the erstwhile diversity, then increasing uniformity, of music in the French church may be found in non-European musical traditions that, under the socio-cultural pressures of Westernization, change in form and function.

Le Munerat's connections with the Parisian church stem from his activities at the University of Paris. As a *scholasticus theologus*, Le Munerat seems to have made a sufficient name for himself to be entrusted with preparing various editions for the church. He received his commissions directly from the bishop of Paris, first from Louis I of Beaumont de la Forêt, then from Jean Simon. Yet Le Munerat was also tied by personal and professional bonds to Bourges. He seems to have spent his early years there, numbering among his friends the future archbishop of Bourges Pierre Cadouet.[7] The friendship dates from the period when the two officiated at the collegiate church of Beata Maria de Salis. Cadouet worked his way up the ranks from canon and prior of Beata Maria in the 1460s to become the Biturgian archbishop in the mid-1480s; all we know of Le Munerat is that at some point he was named canon of Beata Maria. Le Munerat seems to have received certain favors from Cadouet, for he chose to dedicate to him one or more copies of his edition of Usuard's Martyrology, printed in 1490 (the dedication, as we know, reappears in the second edition from 1536).[8]

The Biturgians were known in ancient times as a Gallic tribe occupying a strip of land between the Atlantic and the left bank of the Garonne. They are mentioned by, among others, Caesar, Livy, Strabo, Pliny, and Ptolemy.[9] At an early date the tribe seems to have divided into two large families settled in separate portions of the territory named Aquitania: the *Bituriges vivisci* whose capital was Bordeaux, and the *Bituriges cubi* whose capital was Bourges. The Church of Bourges was founded after A.D. 250; it laid claim to primacy in Aquitania. Though Aquitania disappeared from political geography from the thirteenth century on, even today the archbishop of Bourges retains the title of primate of Aquitania. Bourges played an active role in the history of the Gallic church. It was the seat of many councils, among them the renowned convocation in 1438 that, in promulgating the Pragmatic Sanction, enforced the decrees of the Council of Basel. The Cathedral Saint-Étienne was built in the thirteenth century; it is of importance, from an artistic standpoint, for being one of the purest examples of Gothic architecture.[10]

It is difficult to establish which chant books belonged specifically to the Church of Bourges. The Bibliothèque Municipale of Bourges holds a missal in manuscript dating from the fifteenth century.[11] Some nine printed missals connected with Bourges may be traced from the end of the fifteenth to the mid-eighteenth century.[12] The Bibliothèque Mazarine, in Paris, owns an antiphonary in manuscript (dated 1543) that has, among the items for the Proper of the Saints, a service on January 17 for Sulpice the Good-Natured ("Le Débonnaire"), bishop of Bourges in the early seventh century.[13] Other books are less easily identified.

Sens was the capital of the Senons, who in Roman times occupied one of the seven provinces of Gaul, namely, the province known as Senonia or Lugdunensis quarta (it comprised seven cities: Sens, Chartres, Auxerre, Troyes, Orléans, Paris, and Meaux). During the Frankish Empire the vast territory was divided into five districts, or *pagi,* of which the *pagus senonicus* roughly corresponds to the area covered today by Sens and its outlying districts. It was then that the diocese of Sens made rapid strides in its consolidation as an ecclesiastical unit.[14] From the eleventh century on Sens was attached to the royal domains, thus strengthening the relationship between the Senonic and Parisian dioceses.

In 1306, the archbishop of Sens (Étienne Bécard) was authorized by his chapter to purchase a domicile for residence in Paris. From the proceeds of its sale in 1365 a new set of lodgings was constructed, eventually to become the Hôtel de Sens.[15]

Until the seventeenth century, Paris as a bishopric was subservient to the metropolitan church in Sens. The superior position of Sens dates as far back as the fourth century, when the various districts of the Senonic territory were placed under the jurisdiction of the archbishop. Thus Paris, Chartres, Orléans, and other dioceses were subject to the authority of the Senonic church. In the eighth century, the popes in Rome conferred on the Senonic archbishop the title "Primate of the Gauls and of Germany." The result was that throughout the early history of the French church, Senonic prelates played a major role in governing its affairs. In the twelfth century, for example, the See of Sens rose to such eminence that Pope Alexander III, expelled from Rome, took up residence in Sens (1163–65), from which he governed the whole of Christendom. The Senonic archbishops, by virtue of their status as metropolitans of Paris, were involved in court affairs as well. Many of them, in fact, were named to governmental posts as chancellors or were entrusted with political missions. The authority enjoyed by the Senonic church lasted until 1622: with the transformation of the bishopric of Paris into an archbishopric, the Parisian church was effectively removed from the control of Sens to become an independent entity. But to return to the period with which we are concerned, the later fifteenth century, the Parisian church was to all intents responsible to the Senonic archbishop. Three archbishops officiated from 1422 to 1519: Jean II of Nanton (1422–32), Louis I of Melun (1433–76), and Étienne Tristan de Salazar (1476–1519).[16] The last of them confirmed the appointment of the two bishops of Paris with whom Le Munerat was connected, Louis I of Beaumont de la Forêt and Jean Simon.

The archbishop's see at Sens was renowned, among the churches of France, for its cultivation of plainchant. In the thirteenth century, "li chanteor de Sens" earned praise for their art,[17] as practiced, particularly, in the Cathedral Saint-Étienne de Sens (completed in 1168). Until such time as a systematic inventory of Senonic musical sources is taken, it is hard to say how much of the chant tradition has been preserved. Yet certain sources may be connected with a fair degree of certainty with the diocese. The Bibliothèque Nationale owns a twelfth-century antiphonary written in French notation on staves.[18] Two graduals date from the mid-thirteenth century (both in square notation).[19] A number of manuscript missals belong to the thirteenth to fifteenth centuries, among them three presently in the Bibliothèque Nationale.[20] Five missals were printed during the sixteenth century, along with an *Antiphonarius ad ritum et consuetudinem . . . senon(icae) ecclesiae* from 1554.[21]

The performance practice that Le Munerat tacitly acknowledged as relevant to the various chant traditions appears to be the one prescribed by the Council of Basel (1431–49). Originally convened by Pope Martin V, the council was concerned mainly with defining, or as it turned out delimiting, the powers of the pope versus those of the national churches. It recommended that papal reservations and expectancies be abolished; that appeals to Rome be restricted to *causae majores;* that the French church be subject to the authority of the king, not of the pope.[22] It is clear why the council, which was pro-French and anti-papal, won the favor of the French king Charles VII (1422–61). Its early decrees were ratified in 1438 at the Council of Bourges. In the Pragmatic Sanction, the latter council asserted the superiority of the church council to the pope; it confirmed the autonomy of the French church as a national entity affiliated with, though not governed by, Rome. True, Louis XI revoked the Pragmatic Sanction (in 1461), seeking rapprochement with the papacy; but his decision did not impair the sovereignty of the national church, now firmly under the crown.

The conciliar movement might have found itself a natural habitat at the College of Navarre. Two of its early ideologists were the college associates Pierre d'Ailly and Jean Gerson, active at the Councils of Pisa (1409) and Constance (1414–17), both of which were convened to end the Great Schism. The Council of Basel must have awakened similar enthusiasm at the college, as it did in the larger framework of the University of Paris, prone to endorse policies of self-rule.

In its deliberations, the Council of Basel dealt with liturgical ceremonial in the twenty-first session (June 9, 1435). It issued a Canonical Rule, including a number of instructions for the celebration of the Mass and the Offices.[23] Le Munerat appended the rule to his edition of Usuard's Martyrology.[24] Those of its regulations pertaining specifically to the performance of the liturgy have been extracted and printed, in order of appearance, in the first appendix. We refer to them according to their numbering there.

The Canonical Rule was to be enforced "in all cathedrals and collegiate churches" (app. 1, no. 1). It did not eliminate local or individual practices; rather it was concerned with their proper realization. Le Munerat seems to have subscribed to the rule as the basis for the performance of chant, regardless of the tradition to which the chant belonged. In a parenthetical comment to one of its provisions, he wrote that they were specified not only to be remembered, but

47

also to serve as a stimulus to "other churches both secular and regular, [so that] if any possibly do not observe [them], they may be aroused to a similar observance."[25] Thus the provisions were for all churches and, like the Church itself, for all times.[26] They represent the culmination of a long tradition of ecclesiastical writings on the propriety of liturgical observance. The tradition began with the church fathers, who emphasized the need for full participation in rendering the psalms, the need for the singers to coordinate in pitch, in speed, in dynamics. It was strengthened by the provisions of various rules, most notably the Rule of Saint Benedict (c. 540),[27] and by the decisions of earlier councils, among them the Councils of Toledo (589), of Cavaillon (650), of Tours (813).[28] In the *Instituta patrum* from the early thirteenth century, one finds a number of regulations concerning the propriety of song[29] which are repeated thereafter in writings by the music theorists: Conrad of Zabern, Rutgerus Sycamber, Biagio Rossetti, and others treating the performance of chant in the liturgy.[30]

The instructions of the Council of Basel fall into two kinds, separable in content yet related in spirit. In content, the first kind stresses the importance of striking a suitable tone of devotion in the celebration of the Mass and Offices; the second kind concerns the maintenance of discipline among the celebrants. In spirit, the key word for both is reverence: the words must be reverently recited, reverently chanted (app. 1, nos. 1, 6). Only when they are so delivered can one hope for them to be "accepted by God" (app. 1, no. 6).

Turning to the first kind of instructions, we are told that the words should be pronounced clearly, which means that they should be measured in their utterance. They should therefore not be rushed ("a pronunciation [that is] not hasty, but distinct": app. 1, no. 1); nor should they be formed "in the throat, or filtered through the teeth, or swallowed or stammered" (app. 1, no. 6). In order for the words to be understood, they ought also to be correctly articulated. The singer must therefore insert pauses, paying particular attention to the division of the psalm verse at its *mediatio* ("with seemly pauses, especially in the middle of any psalm verse": app. 1, no. 1). He must read or sing the words in a voice that is loud enough to be heard by those present at the service: he should not mumble or sing in an undertone ("reading the Mass in so low a voice that it cannot be heard by the bystanders": app. 1, no. 9). Much depends on the choice of a suitable tempo: "the divine praises . . . should be pronounced not hastily or quickly, but slowly" (app. 1, no. 1). Yet slowness does not rule out *alacritas*: the singers are enjoined to intone the psalms, hymns, and canticles with joy, with gladness (app. 1, no. 3).

The occasion determines the mode of performance: "A proper differentiation should be made between a solemn and ferial office" (app. 1, no. 1). The celebrant is not instructed how to do so, but it is likely that the provision refers to variations in the speed of delivery. A faster tempo would seem plausible for regular weekday Masses and Offices, whereas a slower one befits an occasion of greater solemnity, including Sundays and major feast days.

Turning to the second kind of instructions, those regarding the conduct of the officiants, we find that the latter are advised to pray to God in the same way they would address a ruler of state ("exhibit an honest appearance, seemly gestures": app. 1, no. 1). It is essential "to maintain the gravity that the place and office require" (app. 1, no. 2). The singers should not prattle with their fellows, "nor should they read letters or other writings." The first order of the day is obedience; he who presides should see to its maintenance ("the deacon or whoever discharges his duties ought, hereafter, to keep diligently on the alert, watching out lest anything be done irregularly": app. 1, no. 4). As an expedient for assuring order, the council urges the celebrants to consult the chart that hangs in the choir: it lists the various portions to be read and sung during the week or over larger periods of time (app. 1, no. 8).

The members of the choir are to appear promptly for the celebration of Mass and the Offices (app. 1, no. 5). Nobody may absent himself from the choir except by special permission requested and granted in advance. By the same token, nobody may presume to fulfill his obligations by reading Mass in private: attendance in chapel service is mandatory (app. 1, no. 9). The reason for communal recitation of the Mass and Offices must be sought in the ancient ordinance that prescribed group prayer as a means toward religious cohesion— Saint Basil (d. 378) wrote, for example, that when men raise their voices to chant the psalms, they are united by the bond of harmony.[31]

Not only must all be present, but they must take an active part in the performance. No one should stand idly by with his mouth closed (app. 1, no. 3). Rather he should perform eagerly, taking care never to skip a portion of the chant or omit an item altogether (app. 1, no. 9). It may be that these skippings and omissions occurred with such frequency as to induce the council to take a firm stand against them. Another practice that needed to be eradicated was that of interspersing secular tunes among the plainchants, which the singers seem to have done for fun or out of boredom. They are reprimanded by the council for their unseemly conduct.

It was not enough for the singers to perform their parts in an orderly manner. A suitable ambiance had to be created for them to discharge their duties honorably. When the choir sang, all private readings or devotions were to cease, so that the singers may not be distracted (app. 1, no. 4). No one should wander around the church, impeding the celebration of the services (app. 1, no. 7). Games, theatrical stunts, banqueting, trafficking in goods, these and other secular pursuits are to be excluded from the church premises (app. 1, no. 10). The council denounces the antics practiced under the name of the Feast of Fools. Further condemnation of the feast may be found in a letter, dated March 12, 1445, in which the faculty of theology of the University of Paris asked the prelates of the churches to exercise a "greater and keener repression" of this "pestiferous" rite.[32] In its colorful description, the letter reads as a more detailed complement to the tenth provision of the council. It refers to

> those priests and clerics whom they [the prelates] see at the time of the Divine Office masked, with monstrous faces, or in the clothing of women or panders, or leading choruses of actors, singing shameful songs in the choir, eating rich morsels at the altar rail near the celebrant of the Mass, shaking dice there, censing with foul smoke from the leather of old shoes and parading through the whole church, dancing, not blushing at their shame, and then going through the town and public places in chariots and base vehicles to infamous spectacles, making shameful gesticulations with their bodies to excite the laughter of the bystanders and those accompanying them, and uttering most immodest and scurrilous words.[33]

As mentioned, the prescriptions of the Council of Basel may be traced to the church fathers. In their writings, the fathers laid the groundwork for a tradition of song meant to befit the hallowed character of the liturgy. Devotion, reverence, order, decorum: these are the earmarks of a performance that does justice to the sacred words. The same point of view was expressed in various church statutes and ordinances, from the Rule of Saint Benedict to that, in the twelfth century, of the Cistercian order. It passed over into other writings that, in the fifteenth and sixteenth centuries, served in the church as a basis for its ritual. One of them was the short *Compendium musices* that appeared as an independent tract or, more often, as an introduction to the *Cantorinus* or the *Rituale*.[34] It seems to have become a standard "textbook" for music among the clergy. Its instructions for performing the chant read as follows:

> The singing of the clerics should not be languid, nor should it be broken or disconnected. Rather it should be respectable, grave, uniform, and, in all parts, unaffected. Psalmody should more reflect sweetness of mind and humility or devotion than any ostentation. The reason is that the mind is

not free from sin when the note pleases the singer more than the matter being sung. It is thoroughly abominable to God when a voice is raised more for the benefit of the listeners than for that of God.[35]

The *Compendium* refers to two ways of delivering the chant. One of them is a performance governed by the word as an expression of faith. Its characteristics are gravity, humility, devotion, or more specifically, accuracy, smoothness, uniformity. The other, of which it did not approve, is a performance guided by non-verbal considerations, such as a preference for the sonic qualities of the music over the meanings of its words or a desire to display vocal skills. Though the Council of Basel did not outwardly say so, this second kind of performance was, by implication, excluded from its prescriptions; the council maintained that only when the words were devoutly performed were they agreeable to God.

The battle between a textual versus musical or, at times, theatrical approach to singing was fought as early as the church fathers. They insisted that the performance accord with the sanctity of the place in which the singers assembled and with the significance of the words they intoned. Singers were warned against ostentation, against secularization, against adopting the tragic gestures of the actor.[36] John of Salisbury (d. 1180) lashed out against "the excesses of a wanton voice, its seeming extravagance, its womanly ways of dividing notes and words."[37] Ailred (d. 1167) scoffed at the singer

whose voice is now constrained, now broken, now stumbling, now prolonged in an extended sound. Sometimes, I am ashamed to say, it is forced into horselike neighs; sometimes, putting aside its manly strength, it is sharpened into the slenderness of a female voice, or then again twisted and retwisted through a certain artful winding. You may see, at times, a man, with his mouth open, not sing, but expire as if his breath had been stifled, and with a certain ridiculous interception of his voice almost threaten silence; now [you may see him] imitate the sufferings of the dying or the rejoicings of the suffering. Meanwhile, with certain histrionic gestures, his whole body is shaken, his lips are twisted, his shoulders roll and spin, his fingers bend in correspondence to the separate notes. And this ridiculous dissoluteness is called religion.[38]

The word-music battle continues in the writings of Jean Le Munerat. He seems to accept the prescriptions of the Council of Basel, as they appear in its *Canonica regula* or are reflected in other writings directed to the clergy, among them the *Compendium musices,* as a valid mode of performance for church song. Yet he modifies the stand of the ecclesiastics somewhat by noting that where the content of the words directs the expression, that is, the character of the performance, the content of the music makes its demands upon syntax and accentuation. Le Munerat recognizes a musical logic, then, that stands apart from a grammatical logic.[39] He goes so far as to outline a system of melodic analysis based on principles of motivic articulation.[40] He does not, as the humanists were wont, dismiss the melogenic approach of the *cantores* for whom musical considerations outweighed textual ones, nor does he make light of the logogenic approach of the ecclesiastics for whom music was subject to words. In the arguments he puts forth in defense of music, to be outlined below, he takes a middle road between the extremists; he differs from almost all other writers of the time in asking that not only the words, but the music be duly considered in performing the chants. After all, his first treatise was entitled the "regulation and concordance" of music and grammar. To achieve a seemly performance of the liturgy, Le Munerat does not force the text on the music or the music on the text. Rather he divides up the ecclesiastical domain so that the text rules in readings (*accentus*) and the music rules in song (*cantus*). His is a pragmatic solution, intended to avert conflict; in the political sphere it has a long history, dating back to Roman times ("divide et impera"). It is less well known in the musical sphere, where its history, as far as can be determined, begins with Le Munerat.

CHAPTER 5

In Defense of
Music

The question of accentuation aroused controversy in the churches. Two schools of thought may be recognized: a musical one and a grammatical one. Their adherents quarreled over the rights and privileges of music versus those of grammar in the liturgy. In this chapter we shall review Jean Le Munerat's arguments against the proponents of a grammatical approach to accentuation. His writings form another chapter in the story of the age-old contest between music and language for superiority in musical composition and performance. The dispute over their prerogatives intensified in the Renaissance with the emergence of humanism, placing new emphasis on language and its proprieties. It was abetted by the recalcitrance of its participants, refusing to consider any arguments beyond their own. Human nature is such, we are told, that one "cultivates what he knows but scorns and spurns what he knows not."[1]

As an example of contradictory procedure, Le Munerat mentions the intonation of "Magnificat."[2] Where the musicians did not think twice about singing two notes to the short syllable "fi," the grammarians were aghast at singing anything that would extend or emphasize the syllable beyond its inherent brevity. As much may be said for the syllable "di" of "gaudia" (in the hymn "Sanctorum meritis inclyta gaudia"):[3] Le Munerat tells us that to prevent the placement of two notes on "di," the grammarians simply reassigned the first note to the previous syllable "gau." What bothered Le Munerat was that the grammarians felt no scruples about tampering with the tradition established in the old chant books.

Le Munerat set out to put an end to the controversy. In his first treatise, he reveals his intention at the outset: "My purpose is to investigate the truth and

53

settle the dispute, of frequent occurrence in the churches, over the observance of the measure or quantity of syllables."[4] The question up for debate was how to accentuate and articulate the words of the chant. Should one proceed from a grammatical point of view or from a musical one? Le Munerat proposed to weigh the value of both in order to clarify the roles of grammar and music in the church service. His aim was not to accept one and reject the other, but rather to conciliate them: his first treatise concerns "the regulation and *concordance* of grammar and music,"[5] while his second treatise pursues the same theme with new arguments. The varying approaches to accentuation had produced confusion, which Le Munerat hoped to dispel by the force of his reasoning ("after noticing so much discord in the church and wishing to produce concord").[6]

Le Munerat's discussion stands as the first of its kind. No ancient or medieval author had compared grammatical and musical practices in setting words to music. Le Munerat himself admitted to being unacquainted with previous treatises on "the regulation of melody and accent."[7] Nor could the "ecclesiastics," to whom he turned for assistance, refer him to any. With no earlier writings to fall back on, Le Munerat was obliged, for better or worse, to break fresh ground. He developed his ideas in conformity to his purpose: to reconcile differences. In short, whatever its merits, Le Munerat's discussion was original. The author did not make light of the difficulties attendant upon striking out on a new path in the literature.[8] Demurring at his innovation, he asked at the end of his second treatise that his arguments be taken as the groundwork for a serious debate in which logic and objectivity prevail in forming judgments (see the epigraph to this book).

The grammarians, as depicted by Le Munerat, stood for a humanist approach to setting Latin to music. They were concerned with preserving the quantities and stresses of syllables,[9] with clarifying the syntax of words and the linear construction of verses.[10] They insisted that the short "di" of "gaudia" be set to no more than one note, lest it be misconstrued as a long. They paused at the end of verses in hymns, such as "Sanctorum meritis" and "Sacris solemniis," to mark the cadence. To free the setting from verbal improprieties, they were not averse to reworking the chants, assigning syllables to other notes for the sake of an improved accentuation or articulation. Nor were their alterations limited to the collegiate chapel of Navarre. Le Munerat describes them as common practice in the French churches.[11]

Two principles seem, then, to have guided the grammarians. The first is that the durations of language (longs, shorts) and its acute or grave accents should be correspondingly set to more or fewer notes of music or, when only single notes were available, to notes prolonged or contracted in performance. The second is that the division of words into their syntactical components and of verses into separate lines should be maintained in the division of the chant into its phrases and smaller motives. Said otherwise, the language should be reflected accentually and syntactically in the music. By "language" Le Munerat means both prose and verse—he uses the word *prosodia,*[12] which applies as much to the poetry of hymns as it does to the prose of introits, responsories, antiphons, and so on. In poetry the accentuation was quantitative; it followed the metrical scheme that underlay the scansion. In prose the accentuation was qualitative; it followed the natural stresses of Latin speech, with its differentiation into acute and grave accents.

Why is it that the grammarians felt no qualms about altering the music to have it accord with the words? The answer provided by Le Munerat is that the grammarians held music in little regard.[13] Le Munerat identifies these same grammarians as the elders of the choir. He was therefore surrounded by a number of senior choristers who had their own adamant opinions about how the music should be performed; he seems to have been in the minority. The elders are described as having received a broad scholastic education, yet as not having been trained in music; they did not think that music was worthy of the schools or that it had any rights in the church service. All in all, they were intolerant of music and its demands.

For Le Munerat, the matter of preserving the accentuation of speech or of heeding its syntactical divisions held no water. By promoting musical considerations over others, the theorist openly defies the grammarians in his views on the pronunciation of Latin. From his treatises we are led to conjecture the course of events regarding chant practices at the chapel of the college, and in French churches at large, as proceeding in two directions. One of them was a humanist direction: music should conform to the grammatical and syntactical dictates of the text. The other was a non-humanist direction, whereby textual demands ceded to musical ones or, more correctly, to the demands of musical tradition. The field divided into the humanists versus the traditionalists, or, keeping to the terms of reference established by Le Munerat, into the grammarians versus the musicians. Le Munerat resorted to a military analogy at the beginning of his first treatise to describe the tug of war between adverse forces fighting for supremacy in the field of battle, in this case the celebration of the liturgy.[14] The term "grammarians," as used today, often connotes persons of an exacting, if not pedantic disposition. Le Munerat, however, equated "grammar" with "language," hence "grammarians" with persons concerned with the proprieties of language. As used by him, the term "grammarians" indicates the new humanist tendency under way in the French schools, one which seems to have been particularly marked at the College of Navarre.[15] Le Munerat tried to stem the tide of change, to keep the humanist movement at bay. Yet his actions were ineffective in preventing the forces of humanism from capturing the minds of musicians and music theorists in increasing numbers from the later fifteenth century on.[16]

Le Munerat addresses the grammarians in the sonorities of a forensic orator. He charges them with a lack of respect for the accomplishments of the church fathers (Jerome, Ambrose, Gregory).[17] Not only are they ignorant of the laws and properties of music, he declares, but they have no feeling for musical tradition, for the practices codified in the old chant books. Le Munerat refers to the original chant as "healthy grain" which the new generation of grammarians, with their feeble teeth and sunken jaws, can no longer chew or swallow.[18] Thus the grammarians mince it into bits and pieces, resorting to devious changes to preserve the durations or stresses of syllables; they debilitate the once sturdy chant by forcing on it humanist principles of accentuation.[19] The tone turns sardonic: "But I ask of these same gentlemen, who have such pious and tender ears that they are not at all capable," etc.[20] Le Munerat is battling an adversary.

Turning from invective to reason, Le Munerat points up holes in the grammarians' argumentation. Despite their insistence on proper accentuation, both quantitative and qualitative, they lengthen the first short syllable of a Latin dissyllable, such as the short "bi" of "bibet," to adjust it to its stress;[21] or, in a hymn, they extend the final note of verses by rhythmic prolongation, even though the note falls on a short syllable.[22] What do they have to say for that? he asks.

Le Munerat reports an imaginary conversation between music and grammar in which music is said to inform its sister art that if it does not submit to its musical laws, the two had best go their separate ways.[23] Music can dispense with grammar, or so it boasts, for its procedures are ordered whereas those of grammar are not.[24] The implication is that grammar is severely in need of music, for without it it lacks coherence.[25]

Lest he be accused of speaking out of malice, at the end of his second treatise Le Munerat strikes the motif of "gratefulness to one's first teachers" to show that he is basically of a mild and reasonable disposition.[26] He acknowledges his

debt to grammar, "which supported [him] as well as others from childhood."
He saves his one last rhetorical trump for the conclusion: despite his unflinching
loyalty to grammar, honesty impels him, he says, to reveal the truth about the
roles of grammar and music in the liturgy.[27] Not his truth, however, but that
truth that God commanded him, in keeping with catholic doctrine, to reveal.
Thus Le Munerat appeals to God as supreme authority for the arguments he
devises in favor of music. Would the grammarians dare question the will of
God?

So much for rhetoric. Let us review the various allegations on which Le
Munerat builds his case in the first treatise for a musical approach to chant. What
appears in the first treatise is often reinforced in the second, hence our references
in footnote to the latter as well. Le Munerat emphasizes four points:

1. *Grammar and music belong to separate traditions.*[28]

The grammatical tradition rests on the authority of the early grammarians and
rhetoricians, among them Priscian and Cicero, and on spoken and written
practices.[29] The musical tradition rests on the authority of the church fathers
and on the usages preserved in the old chant books.[30]

Musical considerations directed the compilers of the chant books (graduals,
antiphonaries).[31] The compilers were not restricted, then, by the demands of
proper quantitative or qualitative accentuation. As a result, they had few mis-
givings about letting several notes appear on short syllables or a single note on a
long one.[32] They observed proper accentuation where they could, but did not
let it take precedence over matters of intervallic construction, the contour of
lines, the conventions for opening a phrase, for reciting on certain pitches, for
coming to cadences.[33] Any attempt to force grammatical accentuation upon the
chant books would mark a total break with tradition. The grammarians who so
proceed would have to revamp all the books in order to make them practicable
for their purposes ("yet for anyone to observe this [procedure], all graduals and
antiphonaries would have to be destroyed and new ones compiled").[34]

Le Munerat would have the grammarians acknowledge the viability of the
musical principles that govern the chant. In a passage to which we already
directed attention, he claims that their lack of knowledge awakens their hos-
tility.[35] The elders of the choir obdurately uphold grammar "in all places and for
all needs" without regard for the demands of music. Le Munerat implies that the
problem could be solved were music given proper coverage in the school
curriculum.

2. Grammar and music control different parts of the liturgy.
Le Munerat refers to grammar as "accent" (*accentus*) and to music as "melody" (*cantus*).[36]

Grammar, alias accent, governs recitations, that is, the lessons, Epistles, Gospels, collects, orations, and so on.[37] The role of grammar here is to see to it that these items are properly accentuated and sensibly articulated. Yet Le Munerat seems to recognize two kinds of recitation, one without music, the other with music added to it ("accent occurs without melody or, as its name implies, with melody adjoined to it [*ad-cantus*]").[38]

Music, alias melody, governs the purely musical portions of the Mass and Offices, that is, "antiphons, responsories, hymns, introits, offertories, and any other portions inscribed in the gradual, the antiphonary, the processional, and similar books."[39] In these items music imposes its own restrictions on the setting of the texts.[40] How the text is accentuated or articulated takes second place to how its music is designed ("necessity begets the law . . . whereby speech is required to suffer a distortion in the quantity of its syllables").[41] Like grammar, so vocal music appears to consist of two varieties: one sung to words, another sung to pitches alone ("melody [may] occur without accent").[42]

The psalm tone, according to Le Munerat, represents a special case: it is directed by grammar, in conjunction with music, in its medial and terminal portions, yet by music alone at its opening.[43] Thus the psalm tone offers an example of how grammar and music have learned, at least in this one category, to adjust to each other in their operations. Each knows and keeps to its role.

3. Grammar is subject to music in all portions that heed musical principles of construction. This point follows as a corollary to the preceding one. Le Munerat contends, as a basic premise, that in the song portions of the liturgy, music binds grammar "to her laws and fits it to her rhythms and measures."[44] Yet he finds it hard to sustain this premise by rational argument.[45] He invokes the authority of Archytas and Aristoxenos, who, as reported by Quintilian, maintained that grammar was subject to music.[46] Beyond that, he adduces three pieces of circumstantial evidence:

First, it is difficult, in practice, to accommodate music to grammar.[47] Composers of polyphonic music will attest to this, he asserts, from their everyday labors in constructing vocal works.[48] Music cannot be forced into the mould of speech, for "its numbers and measures are, for the most part, different from the measures of its words."[49] Music, moreover, has its own syntactical logic, often at odds with the logic of grammatical syntax.[50]

Second, it is unreasonable to expect two arts exerting contrary demands to reach an understanding. Grammar and music tear in opposite directions, as "two untamed horses" that pull a carriage now to one side, now to another.[51] The only way to have them move in a single direction, according to Le Munerat, is for music to subordinate grammar to its requirements.[52] For want of any better evidence to justify such a form of tyranny, Le Munerat recalls the decision of the "two philosophers" (Archytas, Aristoxenos).[53]

Third, it is foolhardy to overlook the demands of "tradition": music has developed along the lines of a certain tradition which itself may be adduced as an "authority." (We alluded to the question of musical tradition under point no. 1 above.) "Our lords the jurists . . . say that usage or habit is a certain law."[54] The musical customs of one or another church cannot be neglected; neither can the usages that are codified, for one or another rite, in the ancient manuscripts.[55] From a study of these customs and usages, Le Munerat was led to conclude that correct grammatical accentuation was of no consequence in the formation of *cantus,* the musical portions of the liturgy.[56] As an example, he mentions the word "Dominus" that, in so many chants, has its second short syllable lengthened.[57]

Just as Le Munerat cited the "two philosophers" to justify his counsel that music dominate grammar, so now he refers to the authority of the church fathers to sustain his approbation of "tradition."[58] Various popes, bishops, and doctors (Jerome, Damasus, Celestinus, Gelasius, Ambrose, Gregory) are mentioned as having inaugurated the musical practices of the church: they assembled the repertory of chants, ordering them into the scheme to be followed by the antiphonary ("they not only devised the textual sequence of the Divine Office, but also established its melodies").[59] Gregory is singled out for special praise: building on and completing his predecessors' work, Gregory compiled the first antiphonary ("he established the melodies for the services").[60] All later chant books written in France were derived, according to Le Munerat, from his primordial compilation for the Schola Cantorum in Rome. Le Munerat thus perceives the overall development of Gregorian chant from an early Roman practice to a later Frankish one, a development confirmed in its broad outlines by current historical research.[61] The oldest French manuscripts, traceable to the original Roman chant, constitute a body of evidence in support of a musical approach to chant: Le Munerat looks upon them with veneration ("[they] are preserved and displayed as a precious collection of relics").[62]

Realizing that he advocated an extreme position in this point no. 3, Le Munerat moderated it, in various statements, by striking a more conciliatory attitude. As the main theme of his treatise, he thus suggested that, for their benefit,

4. *Grammar and music must learn to live with each other.*

The practitioners of the two arts are called to recognize and respect their particular duties in the Mass and Offices.[63] Music controls the melodic portions, grammar the declamatory ones. By no means should they impose their requirements on items not falling within their jurisdiction. If grammar and music do not reach some form of accommodation, one can only expect confusion in the celebration of the liturgy[64]—the officiants will be constantly bickering over their rights and privileges.[65] Grammar and music "form separate sciences," though obliged to "submit and conform to [the dictates of] a third [science], namely, the Divine Office [and the Mass]."[66]

Psalmody has already been mentioned as an example of how music and grammar can, in fact, collaborate as partners in the church service.[67] The grammarian adds the preestablished psalm tone in its medial and terminal portions to his recitation, adapting the needs of speech to the conventions of melody ("here grammar and music well agree in their paces").[68] As other examples of how the two *artes* meet on common ground, Le Munerat names the preface, the Pater noster, the lessons of the boys for the Tenebrae services of Holy Week, the Passions, the Book of the Generations, and so on.[69]

The main conclusion to which Le Munerat was drawn in his first treatise is that one should leave the chant books untouched.[70] The author admonishes the grammarians not to tamper with the notation, for as inadequate as they may find it, it is supported by a long tradition. Were anyone to alter the tradition, he does so in violation of the regulations fixed by the ancient fathers. For Le Munerat, these regulations apply to two dimensions of the music. The first is music as it is written: one should not modify the note groupings for the sake of an improved accentuation (removing melismas from short syllables, reassigning them to long ones).[71] The second is music as it is performed: in portions subject to music ("melody"), all notes should be equally performed regardless of their association with long or short syllables.[72] (We already know, from an earlier passage, that "no matter whether the first, second, or third syllable is short or long, or whether the word is monosyllabic or polysyllabic, Latin or foreign, it is uniformly chanted.")[73] It makes no difference whether the notes appear at the opening, middle, or end of the phrase—Le Munerat firmly warns against the practice of protracting the long penultimate (or antepenultimate) syllable of words, word groups, or sentences.[74]

As a corollary to his first conclusion concerning accents, Le Munerat states a second one concerning syntax.[75] To his mind, no attention need be paid to syntax in those portions governed by *cantus:* rests are inserted, not according to the punctuation of the text, but rather according to musical divisions. Nor does it matter whether the rest falls between inseparable members of a sentence, as between "Regina" and "caeli" or between "Ruga carens et" and ["macula"].[76] The only time the grouping of words (or their accentuation) determines the performance of the music is in reading lessons, Epistles, and all other portions governed by *accentus.*[77] Thus the singer should be trained to recognize whatever pertains separately to music and to grammar. Only then will confusion be averted.

Le Munerat no doubt came under attack for the feeble arguments he presented in defense of music in his first treatise. The principal point he failed to demonstrate was that grammar must submit to music in the *cantus* portions of the liturgy. He anticipated the objections of his critics, bound to charge him with "making assertions, yet offering little proof."[78] Not only was he unable to refer to written documents, excluding a second-hand report of ideas imputed to Archytas and Aristoxenos,[79] for the authority of his remarks. But he was unable to sustain his ruling that music govern speech, and he even doubted whether it could be sustained: "In truth, I do not know how to explain the logic behind my observations, nor do I believe that it can be explained."[80]

Le Munerat had time following the publication of his treatise to reconsider his evidence. He eventually felt the need to make a second, more effective plea in defense of music. The opportunity seems to have presented itself in the form of a public debate held on the feast day of Saint Louis in the chapel of the College of Navarre.[81] There Le Munerat shaped his ideas into a scholastic argument consisting of two premises and a conclusion. The first, or major, premise is that any conjunction of two entities, of which one is regular and the other irregular, should be effected through the regular one.[82] The second, or minor, premise is that music is regular and grammar irregular.[83] It follows as a conclusion that for music and grammar to be connected, grammar must submit to music as its leader.[84] Le Munerat thus constructs a classic syllogism used to reinforce two points made in the first treatise: one should hearken to the authority of the philosophers (Archytas, Aristoxenos), who maintained that grammar is subject to music;[85] one should hearken to the authority of musical tradition, which, in song portions, carries more weight than grammar.[86]

As a deductive argument, Le Munerat's new set of statements makes sense: A (major premise) and B (minor premise) lead inevitably to C (conclusion). Yet the question is whether A and B can be confirmed by supporting evidence. How does Le Munerat justify the proposition, for example, that regular and irregular entities are combined through the regular one, a proposition for which he claims the backing of right and reason ("de omni iure et secundum omnem intellectum")?[87] He does so by appealing to the logicians' assertion that "such things are subjects as are allowed by their predicates."[88] What Le Munerat seems to be saying, then, is that in the proposition "speech is sung," "speech" is the subject and "is sung" is the predicate: since the predicate allows for speech to be sung, it follows that speech is "subject" to song. Le Munerat later admits that his assumption that (irregular) grammar is ruled by (regular) music holds only if one concedes that speech is sung and not that song is spoken.[89] (Were song spoken, it would follow, according to the same logicians' argument, that song is subject to speech.)

The failure to consider the possibility that song may in fact be spoken constitutes an appreciable weakness in Le Munerat's reasoning. Had he considered it, he would have been forced to acknowledge the predominance of speech in the *accentus* portions of the liturgy, as he already did in his first treatise;[90] he would have returned, then, to the basic premise, in the same treatise, that music and speech are two separate though equal disciplines, each superior in its own sections of the liturgy. Yet Le Munerat probably did not want to get embroiled in the difficulties attendant upon providing a logical explanation for his basic premise; he would most certainly have had to grapple with these difficulties in any demonstration, such as that in his second treatise, pretending to dialectical contingency. He decided to make one final plea for the superiority of music, strengthening it by concentrating on *cantus* alone. His omission of *accentus* suggests a subtle yet significant change of emphasis: where in the first treatise Le Munerat appears to recognize the superiority of music and grammar in their own domains, in the second one he appears to divest grammar of all privileges. By excluding grammar from his discussion, he leaves us to assume that for him only music, at all times and in all circumstances, determines the notation and performance of the chants. He has the musicians say that "as far as [they] are concerned, [they] have no need of speech."[91]

Another argument that Le Munerat advances in support of his first, major premise is that music is governed by a logical ordering of numerical quantities, whereas speech lacks consistency in its succession of longs and shorts.[92] It follows, then, that music must impose its intrinsic numerical order on speech in order for speech to be regulated, or so at least Le Munerat concluded:[93] "As it is the case that you [as grammarians] do not observe meter or measure, then it remains for you to observe us [as musicians]."[94] Yet, again, no convincing evidence is proffered to corroborate the assumption that the numbers of music are inherently logical whereas those of speech are arbitrary.

To sustain his second, minor premise, Le Munerat had to explain in what way and to what extent grammar is unregulated and music regulated. The ancient authorities, he reports, maintain that grammar is regulated in its principles and their unfolding toward their conclusions.[95] Le Munerat is inclined to accept their opinion, though he interjects the epistemological question whether, in fact, grammar can be said to have principles. He suggests that whatever logic it displays may reside in "mere usage," by which he means speech habits or the conventions of written discourse. Thus Le Munerat implicates himself in a contradiction: he employs the same argument to uphold the logic of grammar that served him, in his first treatise, to uphold the logic of music, namely, the weight of tradition, with its attending constraints. Yet where in the first treatise the author implies that the argument as it relates to music cannot be disputed ("usage proves [my assertions]"),[96] in the second treatise he implies that as it relates to grammar it rests more on faith than on fact.[97]

As to the "operations" of grammar, Le Munerat believes them to be totally unregulated.[98] Grammar, according to him, observes no meter or measure; it is inconsistent in its order of durations. As an example, Le Munerat cites the words "Gaudeamus omnes in Domino," remarking that in their sequence "there is no [regular] quantitative proportion with which melody might be able to proceed or advance."[99]

Music, on the other hand, is regulated in its every dimension.[100] It has definite principles directing it toward its natural consequences. So far it resembles "other disciplines," among them, we might add, even grammar (if, to return to Le Munerat's parenthetical query, grammar can be said to have principles). But beyond its teleological processes, music is regulated in its "operations," that is, in its formation as sounds. Le Munerat argues that its sounds are, in essence, numbers; music, for him, constitutes a form of arithmetic inasmuch as its intervals and rhythms are both measured and measurable.[101] The regularity of music, he maintains, may be demonstrated in its performance: music can be "reproduced" in its every detail with utter precision. Whatever is performable with such exactitude, Le Munerat concludes, may be mathematically reckoned, hence music is based on fixed numbers. Fixed numbers are, for the author, logical numbers: music is governed by a calculable ordering of numerical quantities, whereas speech lacks sense or purpose in its succession of longs and shorts. It follows, then, that music must impose its own numerical schemes on speech in order for speech to be systematized.[102] Yet Le Munerat neglects to explain why music, with its fixed quantities, is more rational than speech. He might have referred to Euclid's ideas on "rational" versus "irrational" proportions: the former consist of two quantities that have a common denominator or stand in a superparticular relation; the latter, of two quantities that are mutually incommensurable.[103]

What "music" is Le Munerat talking about? The answer, of course, is plainchant. Yet Le Munerat, to lend additional weight to his arguments, broadens his conception of *cantus* or melody to comprehend the various forms of vocal and instrumental music. He defines music as "the melody produced by the mouth of a living creature or by the aforementioned instruments" (organ, lira, drum, etc.).[104] Polyphonic music is not excluded, as we already know from the first treatise: there the author writes that the composers of polyphony will back him up in his contention that music has laws of measurement at variance with those of speech, hence it cannot be determined in its composition by the words.[105] This enlarged conception of music helps Le Munerat provide a final, clinching argument for his assertion that music has a logic of its own, different from whatever logic may be discerned in words. By conferring on instrumental music the same qualities of exactitude, regularity, and measurability as are apparent in vocal music, Le Munerat implies that music depends for its rationale on its ordering of sounds into pitches and durations, independent of the structure and substance of words. Since instrumental music dispenses with words, yet is no less regulated in its composition, it follows that music in general has no need of words for the construction of its own language as sounds with definite melodic and rhythmic content.

Le Munerat speaks as a non-humanist, as an advocate of the quadrivial sciences, as a reactionary in an era when words gradually assumed leadership over music. Yet by praising music as an autonomous art, the author links with developments preceding him in the Middle Ages and following him in the eighteenth to twentieth centuries. The recognition of music for its inherent rules and reasons is a theme that repeats itself in a multitude of variations throughout music history. Music and words were ever at war, and their defendants assumed diverse positions, ranging from intransigence to conciliation. Though Le Munerat adamantly pleaded for music against the grammarians, he was pliable enough, even in his markedly pro-musical second treatise, not to disclaim grammar—"I should like to speak and express myself more amiably on behalf of grammar, which supported me as well as others from childhood," etc.[106] All in all, he tended to compromise, acknowledging grammar and music for their separate functions. He warned against mixing categories. When dealing with language, one should proceed from a grammatical point of view, but when dealing with music, from a musical point of view. Music, in short, has its own language, not to be confused with the forms and figures of speech: with this crucial argument Le Munerat rests his defense.

The Battle of Music
and Words
in the Renaissance

Vult unum grammatica,
vult aliud et musica.[1]

Why "battle"? Le Munerat invented the bellicose imagery—he likened the confrontation of music and words to the bodily combat of two armies fighting for supremacy in the field.[2] We shall pursue the implications of this imagery for music in the Renaissance.

The battle took place, in Le Munerat's writings, on the level of *cantus* and *accentus*. *Cantus* is a blanket term for song. But what is *accentus*? Accent, for the ancients, meant the tonic inflection of words, the highs or lows that accompanied stressed or unstressed syllables.[3] It was called *prosodia,* after the conjunction of *pros* and *odé,* or as it was translated into Latin, *adcantus* or *accentus.*[4] In early theory, music (*cantus*) was generally expected to reflect the verbal accentuation in its rhythms and intervals. Enfolded, as it were, within grammar, music was therefore subject to the grammatical laws that governed accentuation, both quantitative and qualitative. From a literary point of view, this was a convenient situation, because it assured the superiority of one set of criteria (linguistic) over another (musical), and, moreover, it created a hierarchy of values whereby verbal considerations outweighed all others in the theory and practice of music.

Dissenting voices must have been heard among the musicians. Not always did they follow the longs and shorts of syllables, not always did they curve their melodies according to verbal inflections.[5] By seeming to arrogate certain freedoms to themselves, the musicians posed as a threat to the grammarians. Thus

Plato, in his famous injunction that speech ought to dominate song,[6] wished to curb the powers of music, lest it infringe upon the authority invested by the grammarians in speech. Yet by framing his injunction as he did, he implied a conflict in principle between literary and musical approaches to vocal music. His solution was to impose the hegemony of words on music. Later theorists returned to Plato, repeating his recommendations as basic tenets of neoclassical renewal, be it in the humanism of the Renaissance or in operatic reforms. But music did not complacently submit to the rule of grammar—the practical sources show how often the composers violated accentual and syntactical proprieties. To follow the history of medieval and Renaissance music as it is preserved in the manuscripts and early prints is to follow the vicissitudes of grammar and music clamoring for authority in vocal music. Music theory, with its tendency to reiterate ancient dicta, among them Platonic instructions for a speech–dominated music, reveals one kind of solution to problems of composition; music practice reveals other kinds variously closer to literary or musical ideals.

It was the great innovation of Le Munerat to bring the struggles of music and grammar, which music theory had often thwarted by its unilateral propositions, clearly into the open. But before entering the fray of battle, as described in Le Munerat's and others' writings, let us return to *accentus* for its treatment in later sources.

Of the various theorists dealing with *accentus,* Johann Spangenberg (d. 1550) might serve as example—his works enjoyed considerable popularity in the northern schools.[7] Spangenberg defines *prosodia* as "the art that teaches the kind of accent to be used in pronouncing each syllable of a word."[8] In his treatise so named, the theorist discusses, among other topics, the durations of syllables, the varieties of feet, of meters; and he caps the volume with a musical supplement, four works for four voices, illustrating different meters (Phalaecian, Asclepiadean, Sapphic, and Elegiac). Thus through music the student learns the rudiments of Latin quantitative accentuation as they pertain to the construction of poetic meters.[9]

How does *accentus* relate to *prosodia?* Spangenberg defines *accentus* as, specifically, a "law for raising or lowering a syllable."[10] In quantitative verse, the accents are metrical longs or shorts, or the same combined with stresses. Spangenberg discerns two species, one extended, another shortened: "An extended [accent] occurs when, by nature, a syllable is raised, as in 'fortúna' or 'natúra.' A shortened one occurs when, by nature, a syllable is lowered, as in 'dòminus' or 'tàbula.' "[11] Thus Spangenberg connects an extended accent with acuity, and a shortened one with gravity, or to cite his own examples, the long syllable "tu" of "fortuna" or "natura" receives an acute accent, while the short syllable "do" of "dominus" or "ta" of "tabula" receives a grave accent. What Spangenberg is describing, then, is a form of quantitative verse, built from preestablished patterns of long and short, in which all longs correspond to acute accents and all shorts to grave ones.

Different considerations apply to the accent as it functions in qualitative verse or in prose. In both, the length or brevity of syllables is of no consequence; the construction depends on the stress properties of syllables as parts of words. Thus Spangenberg defines *accentus* slightly differently now as "a law for raising or lowering the syllable of any speech particle [i.e., word]." Three accents may be distinguished, acute, grave, and circumflex. "Acute is when a syllable of a word is raised or lifted, as in 'sum,' 'es,' or 'est.' Grave is when a syllable is lowered or pressed downward. Circumflex is when a syllable winds in a circle and stops in the middle."[12]

Till now we have discussed *prosodia,* or accents as they function in speech (verse, prose). But accent theory plays a significant role in the recitations of the church as well. There it was codified in a series of regulations for textual declamation: they appear in treatises by Guerson, Wollick, and Ornithoparcus,[13] and, again, in those by Spangenberg. The theorists concentrate in their discussion on two aspects of the relation between music and words, the word accent and the syntax structure. About the first of them, Spangenberg writes that *accentus,* by which he means an accentual recitation, "is a melody which systematically presents the syllables of words according to the requirements of their natural accentuation."[14] Two kinds of accents are described, acute and grave, for which he gives six different rules. As an example, we quote the first of them, concerning the pronunciation of monosyllables and foreign words. "Monosyllabic words, along with any foreign, Greek, and Hebrew ones not having a Latin inflection, are given an acute accent, as in 'me,' 'te,' 'se,' 'nos,' 'vos,' 'sum,' and 'est,' or in 'Ascaroth' [= 'Ashtaroth'?], 'Senaherib' [= 'Sennacherib'], 'Babylon,' and 'Abraham.' Exceptions are the enclitic conjunctions 'que,' 'ne,' and 've,' which have a grave accent."[15]

For the rules that govern the relation between verbal syntax and musical articulation, we refer to another theorist, Lampadius. He says that the "ecclesiastical accent" may be recognized by "a point set in the text," that is, by a punctuation mark (virgule, comma, colon, period, question mark). Different melodic formulae correspond to different kinds of punctuation. Thus "if a distinction [i.e., a break, or caesura] occurs in a text between several words, it

69

shows that they are to be delivered on a single pitch. Yet if a comma, that is, [a sign of] two points [:] occurs, then the last syllable is lowered a third, with the exception of a monosyllable and a Hebrew word, which are raised to the neighboring second. When, however, a colon, that is, a point [.] before a capital letter is found, it indicates that the last syllable ought to be lowered a fifth, though not in a Hebrew word and a monosyllable, which must be raised to the place of their descent according to the quantity of the syllables,"[16] and so on. The theorists recognized various weights of "distinction" according to function: the *plena distinctio* marks the end of a sentence; the *media distinctio* divides the sentence into two halves; and the *subdistinctio* coincides with smaller divisions of the sentence. It was their opinion that the proper placement of the musical distinction, that is, the cadence, helps to uncover the sense of the text.[17]

But accented singing admitted exceptions to grammatical exactitude. Le Munerat scoffed at the grammarians, who insisted on proper accentuation yet were unconcerned about lengthening the first short syllable of a two-syllable word: "But I ask of these same gentlemen, who have such pious and tender ears that they are not at all capable of hearing a short syllable prolonged or protracted (or the contrary) [viz., a long syllable curtailed or contracted], whether it is necessary according to the rules of their grammar for the first syllable, however short, of any word forming a Latin dissyllable to be made long in conformity to its accent?"[18] The inconsistency seems to have been built into the system. Returning to Spangenberg, we read that a "dissyllabic word receives an accent on its first syllable, whether it be long or short."[19] The theorist gives a musical example, with three dissyllables:

Here the first syllable of "fugit" and "velut" is short while the first of "ombra" is long. Were the example written out with the rhythmic changes that Spangenberg implies in its rendition, it would read as follows:

The situation we have been describing is one in which speech and song were ruled by grammar. No problems arose, for grammar unconditionally set the laws of accentuation and articulation. Grammar thus acted as a regulating force for the elements of speech or song. Yet the order it maintained was disrupted when certain tensions within the two *artes* could no longer be repressed. Eventually they broke into the open, leading to conflicts over the rank and relation of elements. The conflicts developed first within grammar, i.e., speech, then within music.

Within grammar, what started as a difference between the rules that govern the subject and predicate portions of the sentence ended in open hostilities between nouns and verbs. Andreas Guarna was first to record the events in his "Grammatical War between the Kings Noun and Verb, Contending with Each Other for the Leadership of Speech."[20] The tract made a tremendous impact, for its *editio princeps* from 1511 was succeeded by no less than seventy-five editions during the sixteenth century and twenty-six editions during the seventeenth century, not to speak of translations into Italian, English, French (one appeared as late as 1811), German, and Swedish.[21] Even Spangenberg reworked the tract for a German edition published in Wittenberg in 1534,[22] whence its diffusion over Germanic territory. Guarna's *Bellum* so captured the imagination of the public that it formed the source of theatrical adaptations produced in England, Germany, and France in the 1590s and in 1759.

Guarna set out to define the functions of the various parts of speech. He describes an erstwhile Golden Era in which two kings ruled placidly over the domain of Grammar. Verbum, alias Amo, governed verbs (*verba*), while Nomen, alias Poeta, governed nouns (*nomina*). Eventually they began to quarrel over their rights and privileges as assured by the law of seniority. The question up for debate was who preceded whom. Nomen claimed priority on the basis of the word God (*Deus*), a noun. Yet Verbum countered with the Biblical quotation "In the beginning was the *Verbum,* and the *Verbum* was with God, and God was a *Verbum.*"[23] The next day the kings took to the battlefield. Verbum's supporters were adverbs; Nomen's were pronouns and prepositions. Both sides suffered great losses, whereupon it was decided to undertake peace negotiations. Upon the recommendation of the ancient grammarians Priscian, Servius, and Donatus, three Italian humanists were chosen to arbitrate the dispute, namely, Raffaelo Brandolino, Tommaso Inghirami (called Phaedrus), and Pietro Marso.[24] In their decision, they struck a compromise between the conflicting demands of Nomen and Verbum, delegating authority to the one or the other under specific conditions. Nomen, they asserted, may rule over Verbum in the *casus rectus,* i.e., in the nominative and vocative cases, whereas Verbum may rule over Nomen in the *casus obliquus,* i.e., in the remaining cases of noun declension (genitive, dative, accusative, and ablative).

Within music, the battle of opposites involved *cantus planus* and *cantus mensuralis* struggling for sovereignty in church music. Following the example of Andreas Guarna, the music theorist Claudio Sebastiani composed a "Musical War between the Kings of Plainchant and Polyphony, Fighting to Obtain Leadership in the Province of Music."[25] Sebastiani explicitly names his model, asserting that what Guarna did for grammar, he did for music: "Although he [Guarna], to be sure, described the war of nouns and verbs in grammar, I, however, considered in addition the controversies surrounding gods, muses, men, beasts, birds, musical instruments along with those known to be their inventors, and, as far as I could remember, any other musical topics."[26] Another source on which he drew for his information was Andreas Ornithoparcus's *Micrologus*. Sebastiani borrowed from it for the content of his chapters on consonances, cadences, the theory of *accentus,* the reading tones for Epistles, Gospels, and prophecies, concluding the exposition with Ornithoparcus's set of ten rules for singing.[27] His debt to Ornithoparcus, whom he regarded as "a man of remarkable erudition,"[28] extends, in fact, to all other practical musical data in the manual.

Sebastiani relates the mounting tensions that led to warfare between Musaeus and Linus. As Apollo's sons, they govern the separate territories of plainchant and mensural music, yet are constantly bickering over their rights. With no peaceful alternative for settling their differences, they go to battle, summoning their respective armies. On the side of plainchant stand popes, monks, nuns, peasants, badly trained singers, and nine angel choirs; on the side of mensural music stand choir directors, organists, trumpeters, Lutherans, Zwinglians, Jews, and Anabaptists. After a number of mishaps, the fighters call a truce, and preparations are made for signing a peace treaty. The assembly counts a line of famous musicians from Tubal and Orpheus to Heinrich Isaac and Ludwig Senfl. Four judges are named to arbitrate the dispute: Pope Gregory, Bishop Ambrose, Jacques Lefèvre d'Étaples,[29] and, as might be expected, Ornithoparcus, whose laws for music are pronounced as those that bind on the parties.

Echoes of battle in musical writings can be heard well into the seventeenth century. Without mentioning sources, Erasmus Sartorius composed a treatise recalling Sebastiani's, though now entitled "Belligerence, or the Story of a War that Began in a Musical Realm." He reports a conflict between Biston[30] and Orpheus, so-called sons of Apollo, who are entrusted with the rule, respectively, of *musica choralis* and *musica figuralis;* they argue over their rights of succession to the once undivided musical domains administered by their father.[31]

In literary circles, Guarna is thought to have been the first to present the dichotomies of grammar as precipitating a war.[32] Yet he was preceded by Le Munerat, for whom the war occurred not in language, but in the interdisciplinary area that stretches between language and music. Le Munerat touched in his writings on the fundamental epistemological questions that concern the origins and development of language, both as an independent art and in relation to music. His priority over Guarna extends, further, to music theory: by dividing the church service into portions governed by grammar and others governed by music, Le Munerat anticipated the writings of Ornithoparcus and Biagio Rossetti. Like Le Munerat, they too recognized the conflict between words and music and sought to mediate their separate claims to authority. Ornithoparcus, for example, mythified the opposition into a story of two brothers, Accent and Concent, fighting for control of the ecclesiastical domain ruled by their father Sound (*Sonus*). The story begins thus (we quote from the translation of John Dowland):[33] "*Accent* hath great affinitie with *Concent,* for they be brothers: because *Sonus,* or *Sound,* (the king of Ecclesiasticall Harmony) is Father to them both, and begat the one upon Grammar; the other upon *Musicke.*" At the death of Sound, the problem of succession was solved by dividing his lands equally between the sons: Accent was appointed to rule over all things read (Gospels, Epistles, lessons, orations, prophecies); Concent was appointed to rule over all things sung (hymns, sequences, antiphons, responsories, introits, tropes). The story illustrates a number of points already signaled by Le Munerat: the origins of the two *artes* grammar and music in "sound"; their parity as brothers (or, in Le Munerat's writings, sisters) with commensurate rights; their equal participation in the church service; the need for their coordination, in celebrating the liturgy, by specifying their duties.

Rossetti pursues the speech–music antinomy one step further by noting two kinds of relation between music and grammar: one in which music is mistress and grammar its servant; another in which the elements are reversed, with grammar now the mistress and music its servant. The first kind occurs in embellished music, that is, music with two, three, or more pitches to each syllable, as in introits, graduals, and responsories.[34] The second kind occurs in simple chants, with one or sometimes two notes to a syllable, as in hymns, sequences, Psalms, and antiphons.[35] Thus Rossetti divides music (or *cantus*) into two categories: embellished (*ornatus*) and plain (*simplex*). All examples may be assigned to one or the other. The only variety of chant Rossetti fails to consider is *accentus,* i.e., accented singing, as employed for the recitation of Epistles, Gospels, lessons, and so on. It would seem to be subsumed, though, under the category of simple chants. Like Le Munerat, Rossetti recognized two types of composition, one speech-dominated, the other music-dominated; like him, he sought to designate the characteristics of each, in order for them to be combined without confusion in the Mass and Offices. Only thus could basic divisions in the realm of sound be mended, the divisions, that is, between pitches and phonemes, between intervals and syllables, between musical phrases and larger speech units. Rossetti strove for the "regulation" and "concordance" of speech and music, as did Le Munerat, by tying them to a higher principle: the sacred service,[36] with its demands for order and propriety.

Not only did grammar and music wage a battle in Le Munerat's treatises for supremacy in the church. But Le Munerat himself waged a battle to keep grammar from infringing upon the rights of music. He pleaded for their complete separation: grammar pertains to speech-dominated portions, music to music-dominated portions of the liturgy. They should of course be connected, but, in his opinion, the prescriptions of the one should not be forced upon the other. Le Munerat resisted the infiltration of speech processes into a territory that, in his view, belonged to music; he resisted the rising humanist tendencies in the French schools, which seem to have been particularly evident in the curriculum and activities of the College of Navarre.[37]

The principles that the humanists sought to enact in music, after enforcing them in speech, were basically two. Proper accentuation, for one: music should follow the meters and stresses of the text—the grammarians, alias humanists, decry barbarisms of faulty accentuation. Proper articulation, for another: music should follow the structure of the text, its division, that is, into sentences, clauses, and smaller word groupings. All other rules are secondary to, or derivative from, these two, which stand at the cornerstone of a humanist composition and performance. The two may be traced in a long line of utterances, from the late fifteenth to the early seventeenth century, on accentual and syntactical propriety.[38] As an example, one might mention their classic formulation in the writings of the arch-humanist Zarlino. With regard to accentuation, he urges that "we take care to adapt the words of the text to the notes of the song in such a way, that is, with such rhythms, as to prevent any of those barbarisms that result, in singing, from making a syllable long though it should have been short of delivery, or, on the contrary, from making one short though it should have been long of delivery."[39] With regard to syntax, he urges that we "observe that which many of the ancients already observed, namely, to place such rests nowhere else but at the end of phrases or on the punctuation marks of the text to which the music was composed and likewise at the end of every sentence. Thus it is necessary for composers to see to it, moreover, that the parts of the text are [properly] divided and the meaning of the words heard and grasped in its entirety."[40]

Le Munerat accepted the rules of verbal accentuation and syntax as valid only when song was spoken, which occurred in the reciting tones for lessons, Gospels, etc. (*accentus*). He rejected them as invalid for music proper (*cantus*), whose melodies unfold according to inherently melic laws of stress and articulation. Le Munerat wished to save music from becoming speechified, to prevent it from succumbing to the forces of verbalization that directed the efforts of musicians from the late fifteenth century on.[41] To be sure, not all musicians surrendered to the lure of humanism. Vincenzo Galilei writes, toward the end of the sixteenth century, that "among the most renowned there has been and still is no lack of those who first compose notes by whimsy, then adapt to them whichever words they see fit, not at all being concerned that between the words and their notes there exists the same or an even greater incompatibility than that which was said[42] to exist between the dithyramb and the Dorian 'harmony' [i.e., melody type]."[43] Though certain composers were less word-conscious than others, as is only natural, still the major trend in Renaissance composition, from the time of Josquin to that of Orlando di Lasso, via the generation of Adrian Willaert, was humanism: the history of music in the fifteenth and sixteenth centuries is, in effect, one of a growing preoccupation with speech as a determinant of musical procedure.[44] Le Munerat protested; he sought, as a countermeasure, to steer music onto an intrinsically musical course of development.

The humanist movement took hold at the College of Navarre and in other French schools along with churches in the fifteenth century. Its supporters pressed for reforms in plainchant. They immediately entered into dispute with those who upheld the integrity of the chant tradition represented by the older manuscripts.[45] We learn as much from Le Munerat, who, at the outset of his discussion, resolved "to settle the dispute, of frequent occurrence in the churches, over the observance of the measure or quantity of syllables." On the one side stood those who "believe that whatever syllable is long or short according to the rules of grammatical accentuation . . . ought to be pronounced after its measurement as long or short."[46] They wished to revise the chant, which would mean rewriting its books, for "if anyone were to observe this [kind of accentuation], all [the old] graduals and antiphonaries would have to be destroyed and new ones compiled."[47] Enter Le Munerat, taking his place on the other side as an adherent of the venerable chant tradition dating back to the church fathers: in his two treatises he attempted to still the voices clamoring for reform. His treatises are the earliest to refer to the gradual tendency in the church to alter the chant in conformity to grammatical demands. He fought the tendency, but his was a losing battle. One generation later, we find, in the churchman Rossetti's treatise, practical advice for removing abuses of accentuation: the author advocates the differentiation of accented and unaccented syllables by commensurate rhythmic changes.[48] And in the final years of the Council of Trent, originally convened in 1542 by Pope Paul III to discuss reforms in the church, various decrees were issued for regulating the liturgy, such as the "Decree on what should be observed and avoided in celebrating the Mass" (1562). Particular emphasis was placed, in the decisions of the council, on the intelligibility of the words in reciting and singing the chants. The decisions were implemented, in different ways, in the years from 1562 to 1614. A revised Roman breviary appeared in 1568, a revised Roman missal in 1570. Pope Gregory XIII, in 1577, commissioned Palestrina and Annibale Zoilo to improve the chant melodies, accommodating them to the emended texts. The work was eventually entrusted to a team of six composers, led by Felice Anerio and Francesco Soriano. It resulted in a revised gradual published by the Medici Press in Rome in 1614–15 (the *Editio Medicea*). Here the humanist propensity for renovation in line with linguistic precepts came to full fruition.

Today we are inclined to look back on the revamped Roman gradual as a historical aberration:[49] we ask how could the church discard hundreds of years of musical tradition, as recorded in countless manuscripts from the later Middle Ages to the Renaissance? How could it alter the chants according to principles alien to the development of the plainchant repertory? The questions were put by Le Munerat at the end of the fifteenth century: he opposed the incursion of speech principles into the chant repertory; he used his pen, he lifted his voice in debate, to avert the tendencies that, in his view, could only spell the downfall of chant as he knew it, as he wished to have it preserved. The tendencies were to culminate, in the later sixteenth and early seventeenth centuries, in a wide-sweeping reform that modified the character of chant for hundreds of years until the counterreform inaugurated by the Benedictine monks of Solesmes in the later nineteenth century. Le Munerat tried to break the process at its inception. Yet the humanist movement, against which he fought, was a more powerful, more resilient opponent; it grew in strength, generating developments in literature and in music over which he had no control.

Le Munerat spoke out of genuine concern for maintaining the integrity of music as a discipline subject to its own logic. His efforts on behalf of music seem futile when judged in relation to the sixteenth century, where humanism carried the day. But viewing his treatises in a larger perspective, we are reminded of other periods in which music did not so easily surrender to the forces of speech: medieval chant, large parts of the repertory from the eleventh to thirteenth centuries, or of that from the seventeenth to nineteenth centuries, and especially music composed in the twentieth century: in all of them music often held its own against speech, asserting its rights as an autonomous art with its own set of grammatical, syntactical, and semantical laws. What Le Munerat did in his treatises was formulate the basic dialectical conflict between music and speech, one that has underlain their growth from antiquity to the present. Music and speech have been fighting greater and lesser battles for domination of vocal music ever since its beginnings. Now the one prevailed, now the other. Le Munerat pleaded the case for music in an era in which music gradually submitted to linguistic principles. He might have lost in his campaign for its independence toward the end of the fifteenth century. Still, the broader ideas he uncovered in his exposition, and the almost passionate arguments he formed "in defense of music" as an art of its own, have been vindicated by music history in earlier and later phases of its development.[50]

PART TWO

The Texts and Their Translation

De moderatione
et concordia grammatice
et musice (1490)[1]

1. [Fol. o iv][2] De moderatio(n)e[3] et c(on)cordia gra(m)matice et musice

2. Ad investigandam veritatem. et sedandam discordiam. que frequenter in ecclesiis super observat(i)one me(n)sure seu quantitatis sillabaru(m)[4] oritur (volunt enim q(ui)dam q(uod) quecunq(ue) sillaba[5] longa vel brevis est secundu(m) precepta grammatice prosodie vel prosodi-[a]ce:[6] tam i(n) simplici littera q(uam) in littera notis seu notulis modulata:[7] longa vel brevis suo modo pronu(n)cietur: quod qui vellet observare oporteret om(n)ia gradalia et antiphonarios destruere: et nova seu novos condere: cum i(n) ipsis passim super syllabas breves multe note: super longas[8] vero unica tantu(m) adiiciatur).[9]

3. Sciendu(m) est q(uod) in ecclesiastico officio q(uan)tu(m) ad pronunciatione(m): duo sunt regulativa: Cantus: et accentus.

1. *On the Regulation and Concordance of Grammar and Music*

2. *My purpose is to investigate the truth and settle the dispute, of frequent occurrence in the churches, over the observance of the measure or quantity of syllables. Some believe that whatever syllable is long or short according to the rules of grammatical accentuation or of prosody, both in plain speech and in speech sung to notes or neumes, ought to be pronounced after its measurement as long or short. Yet for anyone to observe this, all graduals and antiphonaries would have to be destroyed and new ones compiled, for here and there in the former several notes are assigned to short syllables but only one note to long ones.*

3. *It must be known that in the ecclesiastical office there are, as regards pronunciation, two regulators: melody and accent.*

4. Cantu regulantur quecu(m)q(ue) nota seu notis modula(n)tur: ut sunt antiphone. respo(n)soria. hymni. introitus. offertoria: et cetera quecunq(ue) in gradali. antiphonario: libro processionu(m) et similib(us) libris inscribu(n)tur.

5. Accentu regulantur quecu(m)q(ue) simplici littera hoc est sine nota describuntur. ut sunt lectiones in matutinis. epistole: et evangelia. collecte seu oratio(n)es. et similia. Que oportet etiam per virgulas. puncta. et comata: distingui.

6. Et sicut accentus est sine cantu seu preter cantu(m). ut nomen sonat:[10] sic et cantus sine accentu. sunt enim scientie disparate: cum tame(n) in unius tertii: sc(ilicet) officii divini tendant obsequiu(m) seu famulatum[.]

7. Unde sicut in conflictu seu bello corporali: non semper e(t) in om(n)i loco quilibet magistratus belli sua arte vel industria utitur: cu(m) ad unu(m) finem sc(ilicet) victoria(m) regis contendant. sed tantu(m) p(er) vices.

8. Nam si congrediente hostes magistro militu(m): magister machinaru(m) sua arte vel industria hostes concuteret: propriu(m) exercitu(m) cum adverso disp(er)deret: sic valde timendu(m) est ne nisi loca sua et vices agnoscant cantus et accentus: magna(m) in ecclesiastico officio (c)o(n)fusione(m) pariat eor(um) indiscretus conflictus.

4. *Melody regulates whatever portions are sung to a note or notes, as are antiphons, responsories, hymns, introits, offertories, and any other portions inscribed in the gradual, the antiphonary, the processional, and similar books.*

5. *Accent regulates whatever portions are recorded in plain speech, i.e., without notes, as are lessons for Matins, or Epistles, Gospels, collects, orations, and similar portions, which need, moreover, to be punctuated by commas, periods, and colons.*

6. *Just as accent occurs without melody or, as its name implies, with melody adjoined to it, so melody occurs without accent. Indeed, they form separate sciences, though tending to submit and conform to a third, namely, the Divine Office.*

7. *Thus in bodily combat or warfare, an officer does not always use, at every juncture, his warlike skills or stratagems, though directed to one goal, namely, a victory for the king. Rather he uses them in due order of succession.*

8. *For if the officer in charge of munitions were to pummel the enemy with his skills or stratagems at the same time as the commander-in-chief confronted the enemy, he would destroy his own army along with his adversary's. The same holds for melody and accent: it is much to be feared that, unless they know their places and wait their turns, they will produce great confusion in the ecclesiastical office with their undivided combat.*

9. Iam eni(m) non est qui audeat Magnificat secu(n)di et octavi toni: uti notatu(m) est a patrib(us) inchoare: ob hoc q(ui)dem q(uia) eius penultima syllaba sc(ilicet) fi. duplici nota sc(ilicet) ut. fa. moderatur vel modulatur: et ut longa personatur seu personari videtur.

9. *These days no one would dare begin the Magnificat of the second and eighth tone as it was notated by the fathers, for its penultimate syllable, "fi," is shaped or sung to a two-note neume, C-F, whereby it impersonates or seems to impersonate a long [ex. 1]:*

EXAMPLE 1. Magnificat: tones 2, 8 (*LU*, 208, 212)

10. Similiter hymnu(m) Sanctorum meritis inclyta gaudia. secu(n)di toni. trium scilicet et ix lettionu(m) more p(ar)isio:[11] ubi sup(er) sillaba(m) di. de gaudia duplex nota. s(cilicet) sol fa modulatur: no(n) aude(n)t q(ui)dam sicut notatu(m) est decantare:

10. *The same may be said of the hymn "Sanctorum meritis inclyta gaudia" of the second mode, of three or nine lessons in the Parisian custom, where a two-note neume on G-F is sung to the syllable "di" of "gaudia." Few dare to chant it as it was notated [ex. 2]:*

EXAMPLE 2. "Sanctorum meritis": mode 2 (*LU*, 1157)

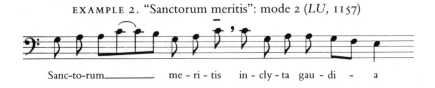

sed sup(er) gau. [o iv^v] prima(m) notam scilicet sol apponu(n)t: a syllaba seque(n)ti quod suu(m) est aufere(n)tes:

Rather they place the first note, G, on "gau," removing it from the following syllable to which it properly belongs [ex. 3]:

EXAMPLE 3. Ibid. (end of line 1)

altered to

atq(ue) in huiusmodi diverticulu(m)
co(n)fugientes.

11. Illos tu(nc) manifeste reddit
(c)o(n)fusos: vocabulu(m) paulopost
sequens: fortia. similiter ultimu(m):
sc(ilicet) optimu(m). quor(um) se-
cunda(m) syllaba(m) ti. s(upra) i(n)
utroq(ue) necessario producu(n)t.

*They take refuge, then, in this kind of
evasion.*

*11. But the word shortly following,
"fortia," clearly makes the singers confused, as does likewise the last one, "optimum." In both of them, to be sure,
they necessarily prolong the second syllable "ti" [ex. 4]:*

EXAMPLE 4. Ibid. (end of lines 2 and 4)

na(m) non adest eis ut prius aptu(m)
diverticulu(m)[.] Alioq(ui)n oporteret totu(m) ca(n)tu(m) illu(m) destruere:[12] qui est multu(m) co(m-
mun)is in ecclesiis francie.

12. Et p(er) decursu(m) hymni in
quolibet versu su(n)t tres vel quatuor
pause morose sup(er) syllabas
breves[13] ut p(atet) canta(n)do.

13. Similiter fieret in hymno
Sacris sole(n)niis in illo ca(n)tu
deca(n)tato[.][14]

*They cannot find a suitable way out as
before without otherwise destroying the
whole melody, as is commonly done in
French churches.*

*12. At the completion of the hymn in
any of its verses, there are three or four
extended pauses on short syllables, as is
apparent in the singing.*

*13. The same thing happens in chanting
the hymn "Sacris solemniis" to its own
melody [ex. 5]:*

EXAMPLE 5. "Sacris solemniis" (end of lines 1, 2 and 4) (Bruno Stäblein, ed., *Die
mittelalterlichen Hymnenmelodien*, 348 [modes 6, 8])

14. Contingit aute(m) iudicio meo
error iste: q(uia) in ecclesiis maiores
de choro: ut plurimu(m) gra(m)ma-

*14. In my opinion, however, these errors
occur because in the churches the elders of
the choir are for the most part adequately*

tica(m) satis: alias etia(m) plurimas sci(enti)as noverunt: musica(m) aute(m) paru(m) didicerunt.

15. Ideoq(ue) musica(m) parvipendentes: sicut vulgatu(m) est. Quod scit quisq(ue) colit. quod nescit spernit et odit: ad omne propositu(m) et in omni loco: gra(m)matica(m) seu ipsius leges proponu(n)t et dominari volunt: non putantes musica(m) esse de gimnasio: nec i(n) officio ecclesiastico habere potestatem aliquam: p(rae)sertim[15] contra leges seu regulas gra(m)matice: sed in omnibus illi subici.

16. Cum econtra quintilianus libro primo i(n)stitutionu(m) oratoriaru(m) cap(itu)lo de laudibus musice: dicat duos philosophos p(rae)dicte utriusq(ue) artis p(rae)ceptores: archita(m) et aristoxenu(m) in hanc devenisse sententia(m): ut dicere(n)t gra(m)matica(m) subiecta(m) musice.[16]

17. Quod firmiter credendu(m) puto. Nam cu(m) littera nuda notis musice moderatur vel modulatur: musica quasi super eam manum apponens: suis eam legibus constringit: modos ei et mensuras suas adiiciens: que tota consistit in numeris.[17] habetque ut plurimum numeros et mensuras a mensuris ipsius littere differentes.

18. Nec esset ei possibile sequi mensura(m) seu q(uan)titate(m) syllabarum littere.

19. Sapiu(n)t hic mecu(m) puto mu-

schooled in grammar and many other sciences, but only scantily acquainted with music.

15. *Therefore they underrate music, as may be expected, for everyone cultivates what he knows but scorns and spurns what he knows not. In all places and for all needs, they propose grammar or its laws and would have them rule. They do not believe that music is fit for the schools or that it has any power in the ecclesiastical office to withstand, in particular, the laws or rules of grammar, being rather in all matters subordinate to them.*

16. *Quintilian, on the other hand, says in his chapter on the praises of music, from book 1 of his* Institutiones oratoriae, *that the two philosophers Archytas and Aristoxenos, teachers of both of the aforesaid arts, reached a decision whereby they declared that grammar is subject to music.*

17. *I feel strongly about their credibility. When bare speech is shaped or sung to notes of music, music, as it were, places her hand over it: she binds it to her laws and fits it to her rhythms and measures. Music consists entirely in numbers, and its numbers and measures are, for the most part, different from the measures of its words.*

18. *Nor is it possible for music to follow the measure or quantity of speech syllables.*

19. *Here, I reckon, the musicians*

sici de minutis vulgariter de rebus factis: qui quotidie nova condu(n)t: q(uam) difficile esset eis illud observare. A quibus accepi inter cetera: q(uod) in suis Magnificat: in dispersit superbos. prima(m) syllabam de: sup(er)bos duplici nota.[18] secunda(m) vero que est longa positione unica minima modulantur.

[= composers], who prepare new works daily, will back me up: they know, ordinarily, from the details of writing part music how difficult it is for them to observe this [i.e., metric quantity]. I learned from them, among other things, that in their Magnificats, on "dispersit superbos," the first syllable of "superbos" is sung to two notes, while the second, which is long by position, is sung to a single minim [ex. 6]:

EXAMPLE 6. Incorrect accentuation of "suPERbos" as "SUperbos" (various quotations from polyphonic settings of the Magnificat, verse 6)

a) Alexander Agricola (d. 1506), "Magnificat secundi toni" (*Opera omnia,* ed. Edward Lerner, III: 90 [4 v.], alto, with identical motives in tenor and bass)

b) Antoine Brumel (d. c. 1515), "Magnificat octavi toni," among works of uncertain authorship (*Opera omnia,* ed. Barton Hudson, VI: 55 [4 v.], tenor, with similar figuration in other three parts)

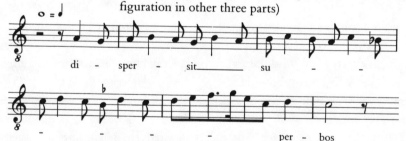

c) Elzéar Genet [Carpentras] (d. 1548), "Magnificat octavi toni," composed between 1513 and 1523 (*Opera omnia,* ed. Albert Seay, IV: 118 [3 v.], alto, with identical motive in bass)

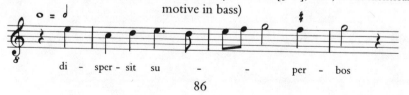

d) Clemens non Papa (d. 1555 or 1556), "Magnificat septimi toni" (*Opera omnia*, ed. K. Ph. Bernet Kempers, IV: 106–07 [3 v.], alto)

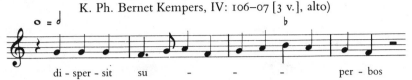

di - sper - sit   su   -   -   -   per - bos

e) Idem, "Magnificat octavi toni" (ibid. IV: 113 [3 v.], soprano, with similar accentuation in other two parts)

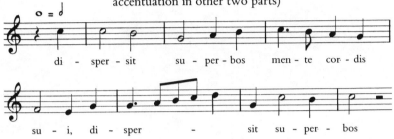

di - sper - sit   su - per - bos   men - te   cor - dis

su - i,   di - sper   -   sit   su - per - bos

f) Claudin de Sermisy (d. 1562), Magnificat section (*Opera omnia*, ed. Gaston Allaire and Isabelle Cazeaux, I: 53 [3 v.], soprano, tenor, the latter identical with motive in alto)

di - sper - sit   su   -   -   per - bos____

di - sper - sit   su   -   per - bos

20. Non igitur video factibile. id-q(ue) tentare. simile videretur: ac si quis duos equos i(n)domitos currui iu(n)gat: quor(um) unus tarde: alius velociter. unus illac. alter istac volet transmeare.

20. *Therefore I do not see how it [i.e., the observance of speech] is feasible, and any attempt to make it so is as if someone were to join two untamed horses to a chariot, with one of them running slowly and the other quickly, or with one of them eager to pull to this side and the other to that.*

21. [o v] Erit igitur oportet cum predictis philosophis musica no(n)

21. *In line with the aforesaid philosophers, music should not then be a horse*

equus seu iumentu(m): sed auriga dirigens currum: litteram. s(upra) nuda(m) et omnes eius syllabas ut dictu(m) est sue dicioni subiiciens.

22. Sed dicet aliquis. Asseris. sed paru(m) probas.

23. Ad veritate(m) nescio ratione(m) demonstrativa(m) eor(um) que dicuntur. nec puto esse.

24. Inquisivi a viris religiosis: si quid scriptu(m) habere(n)t super moderatio(n)e cantus et accentus: sed minime repperi.

25. Quare videns tanta(m) dissonia(m) in ecclesia: ad concordia(m) si possum facienda(m): quod michi de probleumate[19] videtur scribere decrevi.

26. Erit tamen pro assertorum probatione ubi maior pro nu(n)c haberi nequit cum autoritate p(rae)dictoru(m) philosophor(um): q(uod) ea usus probat.

27. Dicunt eni(m) d(omi)ni iuriste: q(uod) usus seu (c)o(n)suetudo est quodda(m) ius.

28. Omnes enim codices antiphonarii: et gradales ecclesiaru(m) tam seculariu(m) q(uam) regulariu(m) quotquot vidimus: et multos vidimus hunc ritu(m) observant: ut sine differentia super syllabas breves et longas et multas et unicam quandoq(ue) tantu(m) notam adiiciant.

29. Patet in hoc nomine dominus. cuius secunda syllaba in inicio[20] prime misse natalis domini trib(us) notulis modulatur.

or a beast of burden. Rather it should be a driver steering the chariot and, as already said, subjecting plain speech and all its syllables to its own discourse.

22. But someone will say: you make assertions, yet offer little proof.

23. In truth, I do not know how to explain the logic behind my observations, nor do I believe that it can be explained.

24. I inquired of ecclesiastics whether they had any writing on the regulation of melody and accent, but I discovered nothing.

25. After noticing so much discord in the church and wishing to produce concord if I can, I resolved to write about what seemed to me the problems.

26. My report may stand, nevertheless, as proof of my assertions when, for now, nothing greater than the authority of the aforesaid philosophers can be had. Usage proves them.

27. Our lords the jurists, in fact, say that usage or habit is a certain law.

28. All codices of the antiphonary and of the gradual (from both the secular and the regular churches), or at least as many as we have seen—and we have seen a good number of them—observe the practice whereby they indiscriminately assign either many notes or sometimes only one note to short and long syllables.

29. It is evident at the beginning of the first Mass for the Nativity of our Lord in the noun "Dominus," the second syllable of which is sung to three notes [ex. 7]:

EXAMPLE 7. Midnight Mass for Christmas: introit, opening (*LU*, 392)

Do - mi - nus di - xit ad me

30. Similiter in Statuit ei dominus. in Gaudeamus omnes in d(omi)no. in Loquetur domin(us) in festo sanctor(um) gervasii et protasii.[21] ubi in omnibus istis: trib(us): quatuor vel sex ut patet in gradali notulis producitur.

30. *Likewise, in "Statuit ei Dominus," in "Gaudeamus omnes in Domino," and in "Loquetur Dominus" (which is for the Feast of the Saints Gervase and Protase), all of these have it prolonged by three, four, or six notes, as is evident in the gradual [ex. 8]:*

EXAMPLE 8

a) Introit "Statuit ei Dominus" (*LU*, 1182)

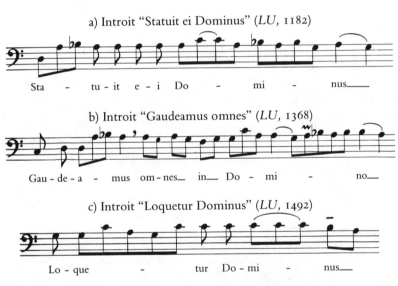

Sta - tu - it e - i Do - mi - nus

b) Introit "Gaudeamus omnes" (*LU*, 1368)

Gau - de - a - mus om - nes in Do - mi - no

c) Introit "Loquetur Dominus" (*LU*, 1492)

Lo - que - tur Do - mi - nus

31. Sic in maiori missa eiusdem natalis d(omi)ni. li. de concilii:[22] quatuor notulis protenditur.

31. *In the major Mass for the above Feast of the Nativity of our Lord, the "li" of "concilii" is extended by four notes [ex. 9]:*

EXAMPLE 9. Major Mass for Christmas Day: from the introit "Puer natus" (*LU*, 408)

mag - ni con - si - li - i

32. Sic prima sacrosancti no(min)is iesus:[23] in ultimo respo(n)sorio prime d(omi)nice quadragesime. Ductus est iesus in desertu(m). duabus.

32. *In "Ductus est Jesus in desertum," the last responsory for Prime of Quadragesima Sunday, the first syllable of the holy name of Jesus is set to two notes [ex. 10]:*

EXAMPLE 10. Great responsory "Ductus est Jesus in desertum" (*Antiphonaire monastique . . . de Lucques,* in *Paléographie musicale* IX: 131)

Du – ctus est Ie – sus in de – ser – tum

33. In antiphona ad magnificat[24] quarte ferie pasche. Hoc iam tertio manifestavit se iesus. trib(us).[25]

33. *In "Hoc iam tertio manifestavit se Jesus," an antiphon to the Magnificat for the fourth feria [Wednesday] of Easter, it is set to three notes.*

34. In secunda antiphona matutinaru(m) in festo apostolor(um) petri e(t) pauli[26] Ait petrus. more biturico et parisio:[27] senonico vero in festo petri ad vincula[28] quinq(ue)[.]

34. *In "Ait Petrus," the second antiphon of Matins on the Feast of the Apostles Peter and Paul (according to the Biturgian and Parisian rites) and, moreover, on the Feast of Peter in Chains (according to the Senonic rite), it is set to five [ex. 11]:*

EXAMPLE 11. Antiphon "Ait Petrus" (Paris, Bibliothèque Nationale, MS lat. 1336 [from fifteenth century], fol. 63)

A – it Pe – trus prin – ci – pi – bus

sa – cer – do – tu(m) Ie – sum quem vos in –

35. In Alleluya. Surge(ns) ih(es)us.[29] dominice tertie post pascha more parisio. tredecim notis prote(n)ditur.[30]

35. *In the alleluia "Surgens Jesus [Dominus]" on the third Sunday after Easter (according to the Parisian rite), it is extended by thirteen notes.*

36. Que cum vera sint: miror[31] sup(er) errore cuiusdam ecclesie in galliis: que cum in quinto respo(n)-sorio dominice annu(n)ciationis[32] prima(m) eius vigintiquinq(ue) vel circiter notulis moduletur:[33] nichil-ominus in hymno. Ave maris stella. versu penultimo: ibi. ut videntes iesum. cantum suum di-mittens qui est la. re. super ii[34] iesum. conformiter ad versus pre-cede(n)[-] [o v^v] tes[35]

36. *In the light of these facts, I am sur-prised at the error of a certain church in the French domains. True, it sings the first syllable [of "Jesus"] in the fifth re-sponsory of Annunciation Sunday to twenty-five notes or thereabouts. Yet in the hymn "Ave maris stella," at "Ut vi-dentes Jesum" in the penultimate verse, dropping the interval A-D on the two syllables of "Jesum" in conformity to the previous verses [ex. 12],*

EXAMPLE 12. Hymn "Ave maris stella," line 3 of sixth stanza (*LU*, esp. 1260)

Ut   vi - den- tes   Je - sum_____

cantat re. re. tamq(ue) velociter pri-mu(m) re. preterit: ut novo quodam more atq(ue) inaudito: cum suo plano gravi et uniformi cantu. mi-nima(m) immo minimulam organi-cam[36] nigram videl(icet) atq(ue) retortam immiscere non vereatur.

it sings D-D, and so quickly escapes the first D as to adopt a certain new and un-precedented custom—it does not shy from interspersing a minim, nay even the ti-niest black flagged note of polyphony in its plain, serious, and uniform melody [ex. 13]:

EXAMPLE 13. Le Munerat seems to be describing the following alteration:

Ut   vi - den - tes   Je - sum_____

37. Quantum vero ad secundam propositi particulam: q(uod) super longas syllabas unica tantum nota pleru(m)q(ue) adiiciatur:[37] patet in prima de gaudeamus de omnes. de festum. super quarum quamlibet unica tantum nota apponitur.[38]

37. *As to the second part of our proposi-tion, that only one note is generally as-signed to long syllables, this is clear in the first syllable of "Gaudeamus," of "omnes," and of "festum," on each of which only one note is placed [ex. 14]:*

EXAMPLE 14. Introit "Gaudeamus omnes in Domino" (*LU*, 1368)

Gau-de - a - mus om - nes. in. Do - mi -

no,— di-em— fe - stum— ce - le - bran - tes—

38. Sed qui fuerunt isti asini (dicent prefati d(omi)ni maiores opinione(m) predictoru(m) philosophor(um)[39] et cetera que deduximus parvipendentes) qui nobis talia ministraveru(n)t?

39. Sane respo(n)detur. sancti hieronymus presbyter ecclesie romane et doctor ecclesie eximius. Damasus Celestinus. et Gelasius summi pontifices. Ambrosius ep(iscopu)s si-(mi)liter doctor ecclesie facundissimus. et Gregorius qui dictus est magnus papa scil(icet) sanctissimus: et doctor ecclesie pernecessarius.[40] qui ut in historiis legitur:[41] nedu(m) litterariu(m) divini officii contextum disposuerunt: sed ipsum etia(m) cantum institueru(n)t.

40. At quicquid sit de prioribus qualiter p(er) partes et successive illud ediderint. indubie de sancto gregorio q(ui) eor(um) postremus extitit. si historiis fide dignis credendu(m) est: cantu(m) ordinariu(m) instituit.[42]

41. Nam preter hoc q(uod) historie id clamant: ad perpetuam rei memo-

38. *But who were these nitwits who provided us with such practices? ask our elderly gentlemen, who think little of the aforesaid philosophers' opinion or of the arguments that we ourselves advanced.*

39. *The answer, to be sure, is Saint Jerome, a presbyter and distinguished doctor of the Roman church; the saints Damasus, Celestinus, and Gelasius, eminent popes; Saint Ambrose, bishop and likewise a most eloquent doctor of the church; and Saint Gregory, who is called the Great and most holy pope and a preeminent doctor of the church. As we read in the histories, they not only ordered the textual sequence of the Divine Office, but also established its melodies.*

40. *Yet whatever applies to the older ones, as to the way they gradually and successively produced the melodies, applies, with greater certainty, to Saint Gregory, who lived later than the others. If the histories may be considered reliable, he established the melodies for the services.*

41. *Beyond the fact that the histories declare as much, his accomplishment has*

ria(m) prima d(omi)nica adve(n)tus
ante introitu(m) misse in plerisq(ue)
ecclesiis: et signanter in ecclesia bituricensi in ipsius gradalis initio in-
scribitur tanq(uam) prohemiu(m)
libri: et cantatur q(uod) Gregorius
presul meritis e(t) no(m)i(n)e dignus:
renovavit monime(n)ta patrum. et
composuit hunc libellu(m) musice artis schole cantoru(m) anni
circulo[.]⁴³

42. Quod quide(m) intelligitur
de gradali romano: a quo nostra in
ecclesia latina derivata sunt: et in
modico differentia.

43. Fertur et in huius rei ampli-
ore(m) certitudine(m): q(uod) rome
(c)o(n)servatur locus seu schola cantus illius.⁴⁴

44. Insuper et codices cantus anti-
quissimi ab ipso confecti: i(n) quibus
pre vetustate vix aliquid po(tui)t
cognosci pro iocali precioso co(n)-
servantur et ostendu(n)tur.⁴⁵

45. Isti su(n)t illi boni asini: et i(n)ter
eos ultimus precipuus qui fecit
(c)o(n)summationem: qui nobis hoc
frumentu(m) saluberrimu(m) at-
tuleru(n)t et contriveru(n)t: quod
nostri dentes egroti masticare vel
fauces deglutire non possunt.

46. Sed quero ab ipsis dominis q(ui)
tam pias aures [o vi] ac teneras habent: ut nichil breve produci seu
prolongari: aut econtra audire valent:
nunquid secundu(m) regulas gram-

been memorialized on the first Sunday of
Advent before the introit of the Mass in
several churches, notably the Biturgian
church. At the beginning of its gradual,
a kind of prologue to the book has been
inscribed, where it is chanted that the
prelate Gregory, worthy in deeds and in
name, restored the monuments of the fathers and composed this book of music for
the Schola Cantorum according to the
yearly cycle.

42. We may understand this, actually, as
a reference to the Roman gradual, from
which the contents, only moderately different, of our own gradual in the Latin
church have been derived.

43. To throw greater light on the subject, it might be mentioned that Rome
still preserves the place or school of this
chant.

44. Above all, the oldest of the chant
codices to have been produced from it—
practically nothing can be deciphered
from them because of their antiquity—
are preserved and displayed as a precious
collection of relics.

45. These, then, are those good nitwits,
including, in particular, the last to complete the work; they purvey and pound
for us this most healthy grain which our
feeble teeth cannot chew and our throats
cannot swallow.

46. But I ask of these same gentlemen,
who have such pious and tender ears that
they are not at all capable of hearing a
short syllable prolonged or protracted (or
the contrary), whether it is necessary ac-

matice sue oportet prima(m) syllabam cuiuslibet dictio(n)is dis-
syllabe latine q(uan)tuncu(m)q(ue)
brevem in accentu longam fieri?[46]
47. Quod durius sonat vel[47] De torrente in via bibit. tertio vel septimo
tono modulatu(m):[48]

cording to the rules of their grammar for
the first syllable, however short, of any
word forming a Latin dissyllable to be
made long in conformity to its accent?
47. Or what sounds even harsher is "De
torrente in via bibet" sung in the third or
seventh tone [ex. 15]:

EXAMPLE 15

a) Psalm "Dixit Dominus" (verse 7): tone 3 (*LU*, 129)

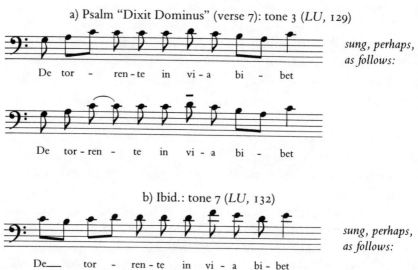

sung, perhaps,
as follows:

b) Ibid.: tone 7 (*LU*, 132)

sung, perhaps,
as follows:

vel Magnificat. secu(n)do vel oc-
tavo.[49]

or Magnificat in the second or eighth
tone [ex. 16]:

EXAMPLE 16

a) Magnificat: tone 2 (*LU*, 208)

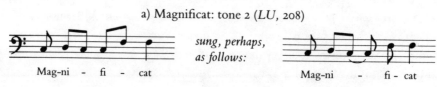

sung, perhaps,
as follows:

b) Ibid.: tone 8 (*LU*, 212)

sung, perhaps, as follows:

48. Vult unu(m) gra(m)matica. vult aliud et musica: que ut diximus in his est magistra.

49. Nam psalmodia q(uan)tum ad mediatione(m) et finitione(m) regitur grammatica: supposita⁵⁰ musica que prius dedit modulum suum sive cantum. qui in proposito dicitur tonus primus vel secundus. e(t)c.

50. Et bene (c)o(n)cordant in hoc passu gra(m)matica et musica. ita q(uod) supposito tono quem dedit musica: grammaticus adveniens optime reget psalmodia(m) cum dicto tono. ad quem etiam spectat: pone(n)do duas breves pro una longa: attendendo si est aliqua dictio monosyllaba que sit pars orationis de pri(n)cipalibus: aut dictio extranea sicut david israel e(t)c. quia secundum hoc variatur.

51. Nam in his requiru(n)tur pauciores syllabe. presertim in mediatione.

52. Non sic de principio psalmi: quia regitur totaliter cantu.

53. Quod patet. quia sive prima syllaba vel secu(n)da vel tertia sit brevis vel lo(n)ga: sit etiam dictio monossyllaba vel polissyllaba: latina vel barbara: nichilomin(us) uniformiter decantatur.

48. *Grammar calls for one approach, music for another, and in these matters music, as we said, is the mistress.*

49. *Psalmody is ruled by grammar for its [formulas of] mediation and termination. Added to grammar is music with its pre-established songs or melodies, designated respectively as first tone, second tone, etc.*

50. *Here grammar and music well agree in their paces, so that by adding the tone furnished by the music, the grammarian approaching his task will best rule the psalmody with the said tone. He looks to it, moreover, in setting two short syllables in the place of a long and in directing attention to any monosyllable among the main words of the text or to any foreign word, such as "David," "Israel," etc., where it must accordingly be varied.*

51. *In these places fewer syllables are required, especially for the mediation.*

52. *A different situation prevails at the beginning of the psalm, where it is totally directed by the melody.*

53. *Said otherwise, it matters little whether the first, second, or third syllable is short or long, whether the word is mono- or polysyllabic, Latin or foreign; it is nevertheless chanted in one and the same manner.*

54. Patet in Dixit d(omi)n(u)s et Beatus vir septimi toni e(t) aliorum tonorum.[51]

54. This is clear from "Dixit Dominus" and "Beatus vir" of the seventh and other tones [ex. 17]:

a) "Dixit Dominus" (Psalm 109): tone 7 (*LU*, 132)

b) "Beatus vir" (Psalm 111): tone 7 (*LU*, 146)

ubi no(n) obsta(n)te q(uod) prima de dixit sit lo(n)ga: e(t) de beatus brevis: nichilominus uniformiter decantantur.

55. In quibus manifeste patet differentia cantus et accentus.

56. Sunt et alia quedam in ecclesiastico officio cantu pariter et accentu moderata: ut prefatio. e(t) pater noster i(n) missa. lectiones puerorum tribus diebus ante pascha: passio-(n)es. Liber generationis. in matutinis natalis d(omi)ni.[52] e(t) similia. que q(uia) de verbo ad verbum sunt notata: nichil ibi dicitur: nisi q(uod) rite videntur composita.

57. Concluditur ergo inter cetera q(uod) hymnus Sanctorum meritis: de quo supra.[53] immo e(t) ceteri hymni: aut cantica uti notata sunt in

Though the first syllable of "Dixit" is long, and the first one of "Beatus" is short, the two are nevertheless chanted in one and the same manner.

55. In these matters, the difference between melody and accent is quite obvious.

56. Certain other items in the ecclesiastical office are shaped equally by melody and accent, such as the preface and the Pater noster in the Mass, the lessons of the boys on the three days before Easter, the Passions, the Book of the Generations at Matins of the Nativity of the Lord, and similar items. Since they have been notated from one word to another, nothing need be said except that they appear to be properly composed.

57. We may therefore conclude that, among other things, the hymn "Sanctorum meritis" (of which we spoke above) and indeed other hymns and canticles, in-

omnibus suis partibus nichil i[m]-mutando decantabuntur.

58. Magnificat etia(m) secu(n)di toni: octavi:[54] [o vi^v] et aliorum in suo tenore stabit. nec in aliquo corrigetur: s(ed) sicut antiqui sancti patres quos no(m)i(na)vimus ac p(rae)cipue (c)o(n)su(m)mator egregius sanctus gregorius: doctus[55] gra(m)matic(us): doctus musicus: et plenus spiritu sancto ea deca(n)tari instituit: inviolabiliter observabitur.

59. Similiter incipiendo introitu(m). antiphona(m). hymnu(m). et similia. ubi moris est p(ro)ducere seu modulare penultima(m) syllaba(m) non propter hoc si brevis occurrat: modulatio dimittetur.[56] sed equaliter[57] sup(er) longa(m) et breve(m) fiet. modulabiturq(ue) uniformiter penultima de Gaudeamus. de Statuit. de Ne timeas. et de Beata nobis gaudia.[58]

asmuch as they have been notated in all their phrases, should be chanted with no changes.

58. *Likewise, the Magnificat of the second, eighth, and other tones ought to remain as it is with nothing corrected. It should be inviolably observed just as the ancient holy fathers, whom we mentioned, ordered it to be sung—especially the one who completed the chants, the distinguished Saint Gregory, a learned grammarian and a learned musician, filled with the Holy Spirit.*

59. *As much may be said for beginning an introit, an antiphon, a hymn, and similar portions, where it is the custom to prolong the penultimate syllable or sing a melisma on it. If a short syllable occurs, that is no reason for the melisma to be removed. Rather the melisma may be placed equally on a long or a short syllable. The penultimate syllable of "Gaudeamus," of "Statuit," of "Ne timeas," and of "Beata nobis gaudia" ought to be uniformly sung* [ex. 18]:

EXAMPLE 18

a) Introit "Gaudeamus omnes in Domino" (*LU,* 1368)

b) Introit "Statuit ei Dominus" (*LU,* 1182)

c) Antiphon "Ne timeas Maria invenisti" (*LU,* 1417)

d) Hymn "Beata nobis gaudia anni" (*LU,* 876)

60. Similiter faciendu(m) est de penultima toti(us) cantici. introitus videl-
(icet). antiphone et hymni. q(uia)
merus ca(n)tus est.

61. Ubi aut(em) in lectionibus matu-
tinaru(m) aut misse co(m)parebu(n)t:
s(e)c(un)d(u)m leges gra(m)matice
debita q(uan)titate mensurabuntur.

62. Sic nec regulari habent p(rae)dic-
ta cantica pu(n)ctuali s(e)c(un)d(u)m
gra(m)matica(m) divisione: ita videl-
(icet) ut oporteat ab incipiente vel
i(n)cipie(n)tibus. vel etia(m) in
decursu a simul ca(n)ta(n)tib(us).
ad aliqua(m) etia(m) virgulare(m)
pausa(m) ut ibi q(ui)escatur de-
venire. s(ed) e(t) i(n)ter adiectivu(m)
e(t) s(u)b(stantivu)m. appositu(m)
e(t) suppositu(m). et alia q(uan)-
tu(m)cu(m)q(ue) suspe(n)siva. ubi
ca(n)tui seu canta(n)tib(us) cade(n)tia
seu pausa co(m)moda videbitur:
pausandu(m) est.

63. Hi(n)c rite i(n) eccl(es)ia p(ar)isi-
e(n)si q(ui) incipiu(n)t dicu(n)t t(an-
tu)m Regina. et chorus dicit. celi
letare e(t)c. q(uonia)m e(st) ibi
cade(n)tia s(e)c(un)d(u)m cantu(m)
q(ui)de(m): no(n) s(e)c(un)d(u)m
gra(m)matica(m) decentissi(m)a.[59]

60. *The same ought to be done on the*
penultimate of the whole piece, as, for
example, in an introit, an antiphon, or a
hymn, which are genuine melodies.

61. *But when the words appear in les-*
sons of Matins or of the Mass, they
ought to be measured in their due quan-
tity according to the laws of grammar.

62. *Thus the aforesaid pieces do not*
have to be regulated, at the divisions of
their punctuation, according to grammar,
in such a way, for example, as for the
opening singer or singers (or, in the con-
tinuation, for all the singers together) to
reach any division of a comma to make a
rest. Rather a pause should be made be-
tween a noun and the adjective apposed
or added to it, or between other parts of
speech, however incomplete, whenever a
cadence or a pause seems appropriate to
the melody or the singers.

63. *Hence they rightly begin in the Pari-*
sian church by merely saying "Regina,"
with the choir saying "caeli laetare," and
so on: because there is a cadence there
that, indeed, is most suitable according to
the melody, though not according to
grammar [ex. 19]:

EXAMPLE 19. Antiphon "Regina caeli laetare" (*LU*, 275)

Re - gi - na cae - li   lae - ta   re

articulated, for
musical reasons, as:

Re - gi - na cae - li   etc.

64. Qui v(er)o in l(e)c(ti)o(n)e i(n)ter Regina e(t) celi. aut si(mi)lia pausaret: ab o(mn)ib(us) pena i(n)famie strepitu videl(icet) plecte(n)d(us) e(ss)et.[60]

64. *He who, in reading, would pause between "Regina" and "caeli" or similar words ought, no doubt, to be loudly denounced by everyone under the pain of infamy.*

65. Sic i(n) p(ro)sa de s(an)c(t)o bartholomeo:[61] v(er)su q(ui) i(n)cipit Ruga care(n)s et:[62] ubi statim post et. quo nihil est magis suspe(n)sivu(m): (c)o(n)formiter ad v(er)su(m) p(rae)cedente(m) pausatur e(t) pausandu(m) e(st). ca(n)tu id exige(n)te.

65. *Thus in the sequence for Saint Bartholomew, in the verse that begins as "Ruga carens et," immediately after "et" where nothing could be more incomplete, a pause is and should be made in conformity to the preceding verse—the music requires it [ex. 20]:*

EXAMPLE 20

a) Sequence "Laudemus omnes inclita," stanza 12 (*Les proses d'Adam de Saint-Victor: texte et musique*, ed. L'Abbé E. Misset and Pierre Aubry, 301)

Mox pel-lem mu-tat In-di-a tin-cta bap-ti-smi gra-ti-a,

Ru-ga ca-rens et ma-cu-la ce-le-sti gau-det co-pu-la.

b) Ibid., the verse "Ruga carens et macula," as articulated from a musical standpoint

Ru-ga ca-rens et ma-cu-la

c) Ibid., the previous verse "Mox pellem mutat India," with its grammatical division between the verb "mutat" and the subject "India" and its corresponding musical division into two separate motives

Mox pel-lem mu-tat In-di-a

66. Precor aut(em) o(mn)es et singulos ut si q(ui)d (c)o(n)formiter ad ea q(uae) hic dicta vel scripta su(n)t: ad-

66. *I beg all persons and individuals who know or, in any way, can think of something to add to the substance of*

dere noveri(n)t: aut etia(m) aliter
senseri(n)t: michi Joha(n)ni le Munerat p(ar)isio scholastico. vel p(er)so-
naliter vel simili industria multiplica-
tu(m) notu(m) facia(n)t.
67. Nam desiderio inq(ui)re(n)de
veritatis: e(t) sedande discordie.
pauca hec a me descripta sunt.[63]
68. Explicit martirologiu(m): simul
et a(n)tiqua atq(ue) nova reg(u)la
canonica seu ecclesiastica:[64] cum
tractatu de (c)o(n)cordia gra(m)ma-
tice et musice in ecclesiastico officio.
Parisii per guidonem mercatoris:
p(ro)pe regia(m) scola(m) fra(n)cie
vulgata(m) navarre. ac domo
possessio(n)is eiusde(m) scole. arte
i(m)pressionis multiplicata. Anno
d(omi)ni millesimo. CCCC nonagesimo. Mensis iulii die ultimo.

*whatever has been said or written here
either to make it known to me (Jean Le
Munerat, Parisian scholastic) personally
or to invest similar efforts in having it
published.*
67. *I outlined these few things from the
desire to search for the truth and settle a
dispute.*
68. *Thus we have concluded the martyrology, along with the old and the new
canonical or ecclesiastical rule, with a
treatise on the concordance of grammar
and music in the ecclesiastical office. It
has been printed in Paris by Guy
Marchant, working near the royal
French school known as Navarre, in a
house belonging to the same school. The
date of publication is the last day of the
month of July in the year of our Lord
1490.*

Qui
precedenti tractatu
[1493]¹

1. [Fol. o vii] Qui precedenti tractatu nullam adesse rationem vel demo(n)-strativam vel ignorare: cur oporteat dicere gra(m)maticam subiectam musice asseruisse meminimus:² iam ministrante altissimo eam adinvenisse / vel putare / et hanc existere arbitramur.

2. Quia de omni iure / et secundu(m) o(mn)em intellectum / quandocu(m)q(ue) duo diversa seu disparata habent simul iungi / seu co(n)iugari vel co(m)binari: et unu(m) eoru(m) est regulare seu regulatu(m) / moderatu(m) seu mensuratu(m): Alteru(m) vero irregulare vel irregulatu(m) / et alias opposito modo se habens: Oportet co(m)binatione(m) vel coniu(n)ctionem / per regulatum fieri: non per reliquu(m): vel per tertiu(m) agens / sequens regulam regulati: no(n) irregularitatem irregulati.

1. *We recall having asserted in the previous treatise that there is no logical explanation, or that we do not know of one, for the statement that grammar is subject to music. Yet now, with the help of the Supreme Being, we believe that we have found one, or so we presume, and that it may be sustained.*

2. *By every right and understanding, whenever two different or disparate entities have to be joined, that is, connected or combined at the same time, and one of them is regular or regulated, meted or measured, while the other is irregular or unregulated, and otherwise contrary in its conduct, the combination or conjunction ought to be made through the regulated entity, not through an outside or third party. It follows the rules for a regulated entity, not the irregularity of an unregulated one.*

3. Constat autem q(uod) musica /
tam in suis principiis et discursu ad
conclusiones / sicut et quelibet alia
disciplina / q(uam) in suo actu vel
ef(f)ectu seu exercitio / qui dicitur
cantus: est tota regulata. precipue-
q(ue)[3] ipse eius actus / cantus scilicet
de quo loqui est animus: totus est
moderatus vel mensuratus: ut pro-
prie magis dici possit vel debeat numerus mensura vel modus: q(uam)
mensuratus vel moderatus: ut pote
qui ad minimu(m) usq(ue) vel indi-
visibile / si naturaliter dari posset:
modu(m) seu mensuram observat.
4. immo ipse cantus vel musica /
nichil aliud esse constat q(uam) arismetica voci a(n)i(m)alis / organi /
lire / timpani / aut alterius instru-
menti musici addita coniu(n)cta vel
associata. seu actus vel usus arisme-
tice / actui musice / scilicet cantui
causato ab ore animalis / seu in-
strumentis predictis additus / vel
associatus.

5. Gra(m)matica vero / etsi[4]
q(uan)tu(m) ad sua principia et dis-
cursu(m) ad conclusiones (si t(ame)n
principia habere dicatur: et non
magis ta(n)tum usus sit: ut tota eius
vis seu ratio vel fundamentum sit ab
autoritate: ut q(uod) hoc termino vel
modo loque(n)di usi sunt priscianus / cicero / quintilianus / valerius
maxim(us) / virgilius et ceteri pri-
ores gra(m)matici vel oratores.)[5] sit

3. *It so happens that music is completely
regulated not only in its principles and
by their elaboration toward their conclusions, as is the case with other disciplines, but also in its action, that is, by
its work or practice, which is known as
melody. It is particularly its action, that
is, melody, about which we intend to
speak: it is so completely meted or measured that it may or ought more properly
to be described as number, measure, or
meter than as meted or measured. The
reason is that whatever can be reproduced
so naturally up to its smallest indivisible
part observes meter or measure.*

4. *Indeed, that same melody or music
constitutes nothing else but an arithmetic
that has been added, joined, or connected
to the sounds of a living creature, an
organ, a lira, a drum, or other musical
instruments. Said otherwise: the action
or use of arithmetic has been added or
joined to the action of music, that is, the
melody produced by the mouth of a living creature or by the aforementioned
instruments.*

5. *Grammar, too, may be right or regulated with regard to its principles and by
their elaboration toward conclusions, for,
if we follow the opinion of sages and
savants, particularly the ones who established its foundations, it has a certain
rightness about it. (Yet one wonders
whether it can be said to have principles.
Perhaps it consists in no more than mere
usage. Hence all its strength and logic or
its foundations may derive from author-*

recta vel regulata (.nam sequi opiniones sapientu(m) vel eruditoru(m): eor(um) precipue qui fundame(n)ta stabilierunt rectu(m) quodda(m) est): 6. Ipsa tamen litera gra(m)maticalis qualis passim musice vel cantui decanta(n)da ministratur (siquide(m) litera modulatur non modulatio literatur: talia aute(m) sunt subiecta dicu(n)t dyaletici qualia permittuntur ab eor(um) predicatis)⁶ q(uan)tu(m) ad q(uan)titate(m) seu me(n)sura(m) suar(um) syllabar(um). tota est irregulata seu improporcionata nullu(m) in se modu(m) vel me(n)sura(m) observa(n)s.

7. Exe(m)pli gratia. in Gaudeamus o(mn)es in d(omi)no.⁷ q(uia) prima de gaudeamus est longa. secu(n)da brevis. tertia longa. quarta brevis. o(mn)es. co(n)stat ex duabus longis. in. breve est nisi propter positione(m) sicut in metro placeat lo(n)ga(m) dicere. d(omi)no. co(n)stat ex duabus p(ri)mis brevibus et ultima longa.

8. Sic in seque(n)tibus dictionibus nulla est proporcio q(uan)titatis: cu(m) qua possit cantus: qui ut dictu(m) est totus proporcionatus et me(n)su[-] [o viiᵛ] ratus est⁸ incedere vel a(m)bulare.

9. Sic in ceteris p(re)cibus officior(um) nulla est proportio debite. q(uan)titatis ut patet intue(n)ti. Quare oportet musica(m) seu ca(n)tum regere littera(m): et ut duce(m)

ity: Priscian, Cicero, Quintilian, Valerius Maximus, Vergil, and other early grammarians and orators have used this term or mode of discourse.)

6. Yet as often as this same grammatical speech is chanted to music or melody, it is controlled by the quantity or measure of its syllables. (We assume, of course, that speech is sung and song not spoken—the logicians maintain that such things are subjects as are allowed by their predicates.) Grammar is totally unregulated and unproportioned, for in itself it observes no meter or measure.

7. For example, in "Gaudeamus omnes in Domino," the first syllable of "Gaudeamus" is long, the second short, the third long, the fourth short ["Gāu-dĕ-ā-mŭs"]; "omnes" consists of two longs ["ōm-nēs"]; "in" is short unless by reason of its position it is rightly called long (as happens in metrical verse); "Domino" consists of two short first syllables and one long last one ["Dŏ-mĭ-nō"].

8. Thus in the sequence of these words there is no quantitative proportion with which melody might be able to proceed or advance (we already said that song is completely proportioned and measured).

9. Nor is there any proportion of due quantities in the remaining prayers of the Offices, as is evident to the observer. Hence it is necessary for music or melody to rule speech and, as leader or driver, to

vel auriga(m) curru(m)
silla(ba)ru(m) vel dictionu(m)
dirigere: et eas sue dicioni
subice(re)[.]⁹

10. Ac si musica vel ca(n)tus gra(m)-
matica(m) seu gra(m)maticale(m)
l(ite)ram talib(us) verbis alloque-
ret(ur). Soror mea gra(m)matica vel
gra(m)maticalis l(ite)ra / si simul nos
oportet seu actus n(ost)ros co(n)cur-
rere vel a(m)bulare: hoc est si vultis
nostris modulis deca(n)tari vel moderari: (Siquide(m) ut dixi l(ite)ra
modulat(ur) no(n) modulatio literatur. talia aut(em) su(n)t subiecta
qualia (e)tc.[)]¹⁰ cu(m) ita sit q(uod)
modu(m) seu me(n)sura(m) no(n)
observatis: nos aut(em) observare
constat: oportet vos sequi vias
n(ost)ras / seu leges vel regulas:
no(n) nos vestras.

11. Alias separati incedamus. et
nu(m)q(uam) contingat simul
ambulare.

12. Na(m) q(uan)tu(m) de nobis est
nulla l(ite)ra indigem(us). et equaliter
si placet sup(er) o(mn)em l(ite)ram /
latina(m) / greca(m) / hebraica(m) /
et q(uam)vis alia(m) nostros mo-
dulos formam(us) et ut dictum est
sine ipsis. Ut patet in supradictis in-
strume(n)tis corporalibus / organo /
lira / timpano / et ceteris.¹¹

13. inq(uam) ipso sono oris ho(mi-
n)is sine l(ite)ra iocamur et ludimus:
deu(m) angelos et ho(m)i(n)es
letificantes.

direct the chariot of syllables and words,
subjecting them to its own discourse.

10. *But if music or melody were to address grammar or grammatical speech in
the following words: "My sister grammar or grammatical speech: if it is necessary for us or for our action to meet or
advance at the same time, if you wish,
that is, to be chanted or shaped to our
measures" (provided, as I said, speech is
sung and song not spoken—'such things
are subjects as are . . .'), "as it is the
case that you do not observe meter or
measure, then it remains for you to observe us. It is necessary for you to follow
our ways or laws and our rules, and not
for us to follow yours."*

11. *"If not, then let us proceed separately, and may it never happen that we
advance together."*

12. *"As far as we are concerned, we
have no need of speech. We form our
songs equally well, if you please, on all
words, Latin, Greek, Hebrew, or any
other; or, as has been said, without
words, as is clear from the above-mentioned corporal instruments, the organ,
the lira, the drum, and others,"*

13. *then I myself would add: with the
very sound of man's voice, without
words, we jest and play, delighting God,
the angels, and men.*

14. Et hec ut credendum est causa
extitit: propter quam predicti phi-
losophi de quibus in tractatu precedenti archias et aristoxenus utrius-
q(ue) predicte artis preceptores /
moti sunt dicere grammaticam subiectam musice.[12] non quidem quia ei
subalternetur sicut geometria et
arismetica perspective: et quelibet
disciplina methaphisice: sed ob cau-
sam predictam: si oportet coniu(n)c-
tionem gra(m)matice (e)t musice
sive actuu(m) ipsarum fieri: oportet
ipsam litteram subici ca(n)tui:
fecitq(ue) necessitas ha(n)c legem ut
satis demonstratum puto oportere
litteram in q(uan)titate suarum sil-
labar(um) pati dist(o)r(t)i(o)ne(m):[13]
et indifferenter longas breves / et
breves longas fieri seu modulari.
Quod etia(m) usus manifeste
confirmat.

15. Vellem placidi(us) pro gra(m)-
matica que me a primordiis sicut ce-
teros fovit loqui et verbu(m) facere:
cuius etia(m) lacte / plusq(uam) musice paru(m) utriusq(ue) potatus /
lactatus su(m).[14]

16. Veru(m) quia a(m)bobus exi-
ste(n)tibus amicis vel non amicis /
iuxta catholica(m) doctrina(m) ubi
p(rae)cipue silentiu(m) sca(n)dalu(m)
generat (na(m) in plerisq(ue) ecclesiis
audivi controversia(m) dice(n)tibus
quibusda(m) sic: aliis sic debere
modulari vel decantari) nedu(m)

14. *We should recognize this as the reason why the aforesaid philosophers in the
previous treatise, Archytas and Aristoxenos, teachers of both arts under discussion, were moved to say that grammar is
subject to music. They said so not because grammar must submit to music in
the same way that geometry and arithmetic must submit to perspective or that
any other discipline must to metaphysics.
But rather because of the aforementioned
reason: if it is necessary to achieve a conjunction of grammar and music or of
their actions, then it is necessary for
speech to be subject to melody. Necessity
begets the law (as has, I think, been suf-
ficiently demonstrated), whereby speech
is required to suffer a distortion in the
quantity of its syllables: longs are indif-
ferently produced or sung as shorts and
shorts as longs. All this may be clearly
ascertained from practice.*

15. *I should like to speak and express
myself more amiably on behalf of grammar, which supported me as well as others from childhood. I was weaned on the
milk of grammar more than on that of
music, though both of them in some way
gave me drink.*

16. *Yet with the two of them acting now
as friends, now as enemies, it is, in line
with catholic doctrine, not just holy, but
necessary and well-advised, to indicate or
manifest the truth. Especially is this so
since by maintaining silence one precipi-
tates a scandal—in several churches I
witnessed a controversy between certain*

sanctu(m): veru(m) necessariu(m)
atq(ue) preceptu(m) est indicare seu
manifestare veritate(m):

17. idcirco pro modulo[15] hec di-
ce(m) vel scribe(m) / urgente co(n)-
scie(n)tia cogor et co(m)pellor
veritate(m) quide(m) dixerim vel
credita(m) seu putata(m): que si
no(n) est veritas. cuius. s(cilicet)
sicut ceteraru(m) tantu(m) apud
deu(m) clara est notitia: pro ipsa in-
vestiganda q(uan)tum nobis ipse dedit: sit hoc disceptationis iniciu(m):
satius[16] sentientiu(m) seu arbitra(n)-
tiu(m) su(m)mittens exercitio dispu-
tationi et iudicio.

persons who say that the chants should
be sung or chanted in one way and others
who say otherwise.

17. On behalf of the measure, I will, accordingly, speak or write these remarks:
I am driven and compelled by my press-
ing conscience. Thus I will speak the
truth, whether believed or supposed.
Granted, only God has a clear notion of
the truth in these and other matters.
Still, he gave it to us so that we might
investigate it as well as we can. If what
I say is not the truth, then let this mark
the beginning of a discussion, wherein
we submit rather to the experience, reasoning, and judgment of the listeners and
arbitrators.

FINIS

THE END

The Council of Basel: Its Regulations for Performing the Liturgy (1435)

Of the twelve articles contained in the Canonical Rule of the Council of Basel (*Ex sacro basiliensi concilio Canonica regula*), seven offer provisions for a dutiful celebration of Mass and the Divine Office. We reproduce the seven as recorded, with certain additions, by Jean Le Munerat on fols. n iv–o ii^v of the same volume containing his edition of Usuard's *Martirologium* (item no. 4 in chapter 2).

For the remaining five articles, treating collateral issues, see the listing in chapter 2 under item no. 9.

All numerals in the reading below, whether roman or arabic, are our own additions to the source.

I. Quomodo divinu(m) officium sit celebrandum

I. *How the Divine Office should be celebrated*

1. Si quis principem seculi rogaturus habitu honesto gestu decenti: prolatione no(n) precipiti sed distincta: attenta quoq(ue) mente: seipsu(m) ac verba audeat co(m)ponere: q(uan)to diligentius in sacro loco: o(mn)ipotentem oraturus deu(m): hec o(mn)ia facere curabit? Statuit igitur hec sancta sinodus: ut in cunctis cathedralib(us) ac collegiatis ecclesiis:

1. *Anyone about to petition the ruler of his generation undertakes to compose himself and his words in such a way as to exhibit an honest appearance, seemly gestures, an attentive mind, and a pronunciation not hasty, but distinct. Would he [not] take care to do all these things with even greater diligence in a holy place, when about to pray to almighty God? This holy synod ordains, there-*

horis debitis signis congrua pulsa-
tione premissis: laudes divine per
singulas horas: no(n) cursim ac fes-
tina(n)ter. sed tractim et cu(m) pausa
decenti: presertim i(n) medio
cuiuslibet versiculi psalmor(um): de-
bita(m) faciendo inter sole(n)ne et
feriale officiu(m) differentia(m): reverenter ab omnibus p(er)solvantur
horas canonicas dicturi[s]. cu(m)
tunica talari ac suppelliciis mundis
ultra medias tibias longis. vel cappis
iuxta tempor(um) regionu(m) di-
versitate(m) ecclesias ingrediantur.
no(n) capucia sed almucias vel bir-
reta tene(n)tes in capite.

*fore, that in all cathedrals and collegiate
churches, at the hours agreed upon in advance [and announced] by proper signals
and suitable ringing, the divine praises
for the separate hours be reverently performed by all those about to recite the
canonical hours. [They should do so] not
hastily or quickly, but slowly and with
seemly pauses, especially in the middle
of any psalm verse. [In reciting them,
moreover], they should make a proper
differentiation between a solemn and a
ferial office. They should enter the
churches with a cassock reaching to their
ankles; with a clean surplice extending
below the middle of their legs; with a
cope in accordance with the diversity of
the seasons [and] of the regions; not with
a cowl, but wearing an almuce and, on
their head, a biretta.*

2. Qui tum in choro fuerint: gravi-
tate(m) servent. quam et locus e(t)
officiu(m) exigu(n)t non insimul aut
cum aliis confabulantes vel collo-
quentes. aut litteras seu scripturas
alias legentes.[1] Nullus debet dicere
horas suas ad parte(m) [alicuius] in
libro vel breviario suo. Alias liceat
decano vel cantori libru(m) tollere a
manibus illu(m) tenentis. sed nec
litteras legere clausas vel apertas.[2]

*2. Those who are in the choir should
maintain the gravity required by the
place and the office. They should not
talk together or converse with others, nor
should they read letters or other writings.
Nobody ought to stand in for one of
them, reciting his hours in his book or
breviary. Should he do so, a deacon or
singer has permission to remove the book
from the hands of the one holding it,
though not to read any closed or open
letters.*

3. Et cum psallendi gratia ibidem
co(n)veniant: muta aut clausa labia
tenere non debent. Sed omnes p(re)-

*3. When they assemble there for the pur-
pose of chanting, they ought not to keep
their lips silent or closed. Rather all [of*

sertim qui maiori fungu(n)tur honore[3] in psalmis hymnis et canticis
deo alacriter modulentur. Cum dicitur Gloria patri et filio et sp(irit)ui
sancto: omnes consurgant. Cum
nominatur nomen gloriosum iesus:
in quo omne genuflectitur celestium
terrestrium et infernorum:[4] o(mn)es
caput inclinent.

4. Nemo ibidem dum hore in co(m)-
muni cantantur legat vel dicat pri-
vatim officiu(m). Nam no(n) so-
lu(m) obsequiu(m) quo obnoxius est
choro subtrahit: sed alios psallentes
perturbat. Sup(er) his debite obser-
vandis: aliisq(ue) ad divini officii
prosecutione(m) ac chori disci-
plina(m) spectantibus. decanus vel
cui onus incumbit diligenter invigilet
hinc inde ne quid i(n)ordinate fiat
circu(m)spicie(n)s[.] Horu(m) autem
transgressores illius hore in qua circa
predicta excesserint: vel alia maiori
prout transgressionis gravitas exegerit plectantur pena.[5]

II. Quo tempore quisq(ue) debeat
esse in choro

5. Qui in matutinis ante fine(m)
psalmi Venite exultemus:[6] in aliis
horis ante fine(m) primi psalmi. in

them], especially those who occupy a
higher post, ought eagerly to sing to God
in hymns, Psalms, and canticles. When
the [Lesser Doxology] "Gloria patri et
filio et spiritui sancto" [etc.] is recited,
all ought to rise. When the glorious
name of Jesus is mentioned, causing ev-
erything heavenly, earthly, and infernal
to kneel, all ought to bow their head.

4. When the hours are sung in common,
no one present should read or recite the
office separately. Not only does he under-
mine the ceremony in which he is responsible to the choir, but he also
disturbs others' chanting. Beyond these
matters to be duly observed as well as
others pertaining to the procedure of the
Divine Office and to [the maintenance
of] discipline in the choir, the deacon or
whoever discharges his duties ought hereafter to keep diligently on the alert lest
anything be done irregularly. Those
transgressors who infringe upon the
above-mentioned regulations and others
set for the [celebration of the] hour[s]
should be punished with a heavy penalty according to the gravity of their
transgression.

II. At what time each one should report
to choir

5. Anyone not present at Matins before
the end of the psalm "Venite exultemus," at other hours before the end

missa ante finem ultimi kirieleyson:
usq(ue) i(n) fine(m) divino officio
no(n) interfuerit: nisi forte necessi-
tate cogente ac petita et obtenta a
p(re)sidente chori lice(n)cia discedere
oporteat: pro illa hora absens ce(n)-
seatur. salvis ecclesiaru(m) (c)o(n)-
suetudinibus. si que forte circa hec
artiores existant[.] Ide(m) in his ob-
servetur qui a principio usq(ue) ad
fine(m) in processionibus non p(er)-
manserint. Pro cuius executio(n)e
deputetur aliquis onus habens notan-
di p(er)sonas singulas statuto tempore no(n) co(n)venie(n)tes: iura-
me(n)to astrictus agere fideliter et
nulli p(ar)cere . . .

*of the first psalm, and at Mass before the
end of the last Kyrie eleison, and not remaining until the end of the Divine Office, ought to be considered absent for
that hour. Exceptions occur when,
perchance, one is obliged to leave out of
necessity and permission is sought from
and granted by whoever is in charge of
the choir. [Further] exceptions should be
made for those churches whose customs
rule otherwise or, perchance, [already]
apply restrictions with regard to these
matters. The same [procedure] ought to
be observed in the case of those who do
not remain in processions from the beginning to the end. For its execution, someone will have to be delegated the
responsibility of marking [the names of]
those individual persons not assembling
at the appointed hour. He is bound by
oath to act faithfully and to spare no one.*

III. Qualiter hore canonice dicende
sunt extra choru(m)

*III. How the canonical hours should be
recited outside the choir*

6. Quoscu(m)q(ue) etia(m) alibi be-
neficiatos seu in sacris (c)o(n)stitutos
cu(m) ad horas canonicas tenea(n)-
tur: a(m)monet hec sancta sinodus:
ut si or(ati)ones suas deo acceptas
fore cupiu(n)t: non in gutture vel inter dentes: seu deglutie(n)do aut sin-
copa(n)do dictiones vel colloquia vel
risus intermisce(n)do: sed sive soli
sive associati diurnu(m) noctur-
nu(m)q(ue) officiu(m) reverenter

*6. This holy synod, moreover, advises
whichever persons otherwise hold bene-
fices or have been ordained in the holy
rites, inasmuch as they are bound to
[perform] the canonical hours, [to proceed as follows]. If they wish their
prayers to be accepted by God, they
ought to make sure, whether they are
alone or in a group, to perform the daily
and nightly offices reverently and with
clear[ly enunciated] words, not [produc-*

verbisq(ue) distinctis p(er)aga(n)t. ac tali in loco unde a devotione no(n) retrahantur. ad qua(m) se disponere e(t) preparare debent: iuxta illud quod scriptu(m) est. Ante orationem prepara animam tuam: ne sis quasi qui tentat deum.[7]

ing them] in their throat or between their teeth. The words should not be swallowed or syncopated and no talk or laughter should be interspersed. On such [earnest] occasions they should not withdraw from the devotion to which they ought to dispose and prepare themselves, according as is written: "Before prayer, prepare your soul, lest you be as one who tempts God."

IV. De his qui tempore divinoru(m) officioru(m) vagantur per ecclesiam

IV. *Regarding those who, at the time of the Divine Offices, wander about the church*

7. Quicunq(ue) in ecclesia beneficiatus p(re)sertim de maiorib(us). divinor(um) t(em)p(or)e p(er) ecclesia(m) vel foris circa ipsam deambulando aut cu(m) aliis colloquendo vagari visus fuerit: no(n) solu(m) illius hore sed totius p(re)sentia(m) diei ipso facto amittat. Qui si semel correctus non destiterit: p(er) me(n)sem distributio(n)ibus careat. vel graviori si p(er)tinacia exegerit pene subiaceat: ut tandem desistere cogatur. Prohibeatur etia(m) ne divina officia tumultuosi quoru(n)cu(m)que p(er) ecclesiam discursus impediant aut p(er)turbent. Regulares qui i(n) co(n)ventualibus ecclesiis circa predicta excesserint: gravi pena superiorum arbitrio castigentur.

7. *Any beneficed cleric, especially one of higher rank, who shall be seen, at the time of the Divine Offices, wandering about the church or walking around the premises outdoors or talking with others ought, for that reason, to lose his salary not only for that hour but for the whole day. If he does not desist [from doing so] once he has been set straight, he ought to forfeit his stipend for a month. If he perseveres, he ought to be subject to a [still] heavier penalty until, at last, he is forced to desist [from doing so]. The commotion of any [other] persons running to and fro within the church, whereby hindering or disturbing the Divine Offices, ought, moreover, to be prohibited. Regular clergy who shall have infringed upon these regulations in collegiate churches ought to be chastised with a heavy punishment by decision of their superiors.*

VI. De tabula pendente in choro

VI. *Regarding the tablet hanging in the choir*

8. Ut cuncta in domo dei ordinate p(ro)cedant: et quilibet sciat quid agendu(m) i(m)minet: statuatur tabula aliqua continue pendens in choro. i(n) qua per unu(m)que(m)q(ue) ex canonicis vel aliis beneficiatis in singulis horis p(er) ebdomada(m): aut maius te(m)pus cantandu(m) legendu(m)ve[8] sit describatur. Qui aute(m) secundu(m) quod ibi descriptum fuerit facere per se vel per alium neglexerit: pro qualibet hora distributiones unius diei amittat.

8. *In order for all things in the house of the Lord to proceed in an orderly fashion and for all persons to know what is scheduled for performance, one might establish some sort of tablet to hang permanently in the choir. Such a tablet would specify, on a weekly basis or over a larger period of time, whatever must be sung and read at the single office hours by each of the clerics and other beneficed ecclesiastics. Should anyone neglect, on his own or through another, to proceed according to what had been specified there, he ought to lose, for whatever hour he does so, the earnings of a full day.*

VII. De his qui in missa non co(m)plent Credo. vel cantant cantilenas. vel nimis basse missam legunt. aut sine ministro

VII. *Regarding those who, in Mass, do not complete the Credo, or who sing [profane] songs, or who read the Mass in too low a voice or without an episcopal officer [in attendance]*

9. Abusum aliquaru(m) ecclesiaru(m) in quibus credo in unu(m) deu(m). quod est simbolum et confessio fidei nostre no(n) complete usq(ue) in finem cantatur aut prefatio seu oratio dominica omittitur: vel in ecclesiis cantilene seculares voci ammiscentur: seu missa etiam privata sine ministro: aut preter secretas or(ati)ones: ita submissa voce dicitur: q(uod) a circu(m)stantibus

9. *We denounce the improper customs of those who, in some churches, do not sing the "Credo in unum deum," the symbol and confession of our faith, all the way through to the end; or who omit the preface or the Lord's Prayer [Pater noster]; or who, in the churches, admit secular songs to their voices; or who read the Mass in seclusion without an episcopal officer [in attendance]; or, beyond private prayers, who read the Mass in so*

audiri non potest abolentes. statuimus: ut qui in his transgressor
inventus fuerit: a superiore debite
castigetur.

*low a voice that it cannot be heard by the
bystanders. Hence we ordain that anyone
who has been found delinquent in these
matters should be duly punished by his
superior.*

IX. De spectaculis non faciendis

IX. *Regarding spectacles not to be held*

10. Turpe(m) etiam illu(m) abusum
i(n) quibusda(m) freque(n)tatu(m)
ecclesiis quo in certis anni celebri-
tatib(us). no(n)nulli cu(m) mitra
baculo ac vestibus pontificalibus
more ep(isc)o(po)r(um) benedi-
cu(n)t. Alii ut reges aut duces induti
su(n)t. quod festu(m) fatuor(um) vel
innocentiu(m) seu pueror(um) in
q(ui)busda(m) regionibus nu(n)cupa-
tur. Alii larvales ac theatrales iocos[.]
Alii coreas et tripudia mariu(m) ac
mulier(um) facie(n)tes ho(m)i(n)es
ad spectuacula et machinato(r)es
move(n)t. Alii co(m)messatio(n)es
e(t) co(n)vivia ibide(m) p(re)pa-
ra(n)t. Hec sa(n)cta sinodus detes-
ta(n)s statuit et iubet ta(m) ordinariis
q(uam) ecclesiaru(m) rectoribus: sub
pena suspe(n)sionis omniu(m) p(ro)-
ventuu(m) ecclesiasticor(um) triu(m)
mensiu(m) spacio: ne hec aut similia
ludibria. neq(ue) etia(m) mercantias
seu negociato(r)es nu(n)dinar(um)
i(n) ecclesia q(ui) domus or(ati)onis
esse d(ebet). et etia(m) in cimiterio
exerceri amplius p(er)mittant. trans-
gressoresq(ue) p(er) censura(m) ec-
clesiastica(m) aliaq(ue) iuris remedia

10. *This holy synod denounces, moreover, that shameful abuse, frequent in
various churches, whereby on certain annual celebrations some offer the benedic-
tion, in the manner of bishops, with a
miter, a staff, and pontifical garments,
while others are dressed as kings or
princes, which [abuse] is called in some
regions the Feast of Fools or [the Feast]
of Innocents or [the Feast] of Boys.
Some perform magic or theatrical stunts
while others perform round dances and
the capers of effeminate men and women:
[in so doing] they drive men and machi-
nists to [concoct] public displays. [Still]
others prepare banquets and feasts in the
same place. [This holy synod] enjoins
and orders both the overseers and the rectors of the churches no longer to permit
these or similar mockeries, nor [such others as] selling merchandise or trading
goods, to be practiced in the church,
which ought to be a house of prayer, or
in the cemetery. [Should they permit
them], they ought to be penalized by
suspending all ecclesiastical revenues for
the duration of three months. They
should not neglect to punish the transgressors by churchly reprimand and by*

punire no(n) negligant. Om(n)es
aute(m) (c)o(n)suetudines. statuta.
aut privilegia que his non (c)o(n)cor-
dant decretis: nisi forte maiores
adicerent penas: irrita esse hec sancta
sinodus decrevit.

*other legal remedies. This holy synod
further declares all customs, statutes, or
privileges which do not accord with these
decrees to be invalid, unless by chance
they apply [still] heavier penalties.*

Note on
the
Frontispiece

Entitled "typus musices," the woodcut belongs to the second edition (1504) of Gregor Reisch's *Margarita philosophica,* a comprehensive manual on liberal arts, philosophy, and theological studies, first printed in 1503, then reissued in at least thirteen subsequent editions until 1600. It differs from the woodcut for music in the first edition, as noted in the bibliography to this appendix. For present purposes, I shall limit my remarks to the 1504 edition, saving a detailed comparison of the woodcuts for music and the other *artes liberales* in the first, second, and remaining editions for a later study.

Lady *Musica* stands in the middle, dominating the assembly in size and stature. She holds a tablet with the pitches C D E F G A running up and down on two staves, the first in white, the second in black (here "hobnail") notation; the pitches comprise the six basic syllables (*ut re mi fa sol la*) that have been used, ever since Guido of Arezzo (d. after 1033), for the solmization of melodies (a seventh syllable, *si,* was added in the seventeenth century). The double notation suggests that "music" is of two kinds: plainchant (*musica plana*), written in black values; and part music, i.e., polyphony (*musica mensurata* or *figurata*), written, after 1440 or thereabouts, in white ones. Chant and polyphony form the two pillars of music education in Renaissance treatises (the early editions of Reisch's *Margarita philosophica* deal with *musica plana,* yet from 1512 on a section on *musica mensurata* was introduced).

To the left of *Musica* are various musicians playing their instruments (recorder, lute, harp, portative organ) and a *poeta,* who provides the texts to be sung, or, in the Boethian sense of *poeta* (to which Reisch refers in bk. 5, chap. 3), who composes melodies to verses. Together they belong to the realm of *musica activa,* or "practical music" (composition, performance) for instruments and voices. Though singers are absent from the depiction, vocal music may be inferred from the girl lutenist, who, from her facial expression, could be accompanying herself on her instrument; or, again, from the *poeta,* with a wreath on his head, and holding a *rotula,* to indicate his "literary" achievements; or from the harpist, perhaps an allusion to the harpist David, who, as we know, was both musician and poet (the latter as author of the Book of Psalms), both instrumentalist and vocalist ("And David and all Israel played before God with all their might, and with singing, and with harps": 1 Chronicles 13:8). The connection between Lady *Musica* and David had already been established in a miniature, for example, in a fourteenth-century copy of Boethius's *De musica* (Naples, Biblioteca Nazionale, Cod. V, A 14). There *Musica* sits on a richly ornamented throne, with a crown on her head, and playing an organ, while other musicians crowd alongside; King David's likeness appears in the upper part, in a medallion. (See Bachmann, in bibliography below, p. 49n.)

Musica, in the present woodcut, does not seem to be interested in the activities of the musicians to her left. As a *scientia,* she transcends *musica practica,* whether instrumental or vocal; as an autonomous *ars,* she bends poetry to her own designs. The *poeta* watches her from behind, as if deferring to her authority: "words" are clearly subservient to music. Perhaps the *poeta* is to be identified with one of the Hebrew prophets (*poetae*), in which case *Musica* looks away because he belongs to the old dispensation—his "book" is a scroll, referring to the Old Testament. *Musica* directs her attention to the right side of the picture, focusing on, and beyond, the young man with a rod, itself pointed upward to the right (a motif repeated in the ceiling supports and in the smith's hammer). Three figures may be discerned: Tubal (Jubal), or actually his half-brother Tubalcain, forging instruments of copper and iron on an anvil (Genesis 4:22); below him, Pythagoras (unnamed), carrying a balance, with hammers on the one scale and weights on the other; and, "conducting" the proceedings, the young man who holds a baton in his right hand and his hat in his left (as is clear from the parallel detail in the 1503 woodcut). This last figure is labeled a *pars viantis,* perhaps alluding musically to a "wandering part" (*pars vagans*). In polyphony such a part could be written in a higher or lower register as needed, hence it could be associated in its range with any of the voices from soprano to bass. It operates, then, as a kind of common denominator of the voices, which might explain its suitability to act as their leader.

The *pars viantis* appears to direct the viewer to another music, higher still: to *musica theoretica,* the property of a *musicus,* i.e., a musical judge, who contemplates music for its structure and significance; to *musica arithmetica*, or the numerical basis of music as determined by Pythagoras, who experimented with different hammers for producing sounds; to *musica mundana*, or music of the spheres, depending, as in real music, on the numerical proportions for consonance and dissonance; and last but not least, to *musica divina*, in particular the "new song" of the New Testament.

Musica divina seems to constitute the main subject of the woodcut, thus corresponding to the tendency throughout Reisch's treatise to proceed from liberal arts studies to the *studia divinitatis*, from the secular to the sacred, from the philosophical to the theological. As described in the treatise, the function of the "speculative intellect" is contemplation and its end knowledge; knowledge of the highest things is called *sapientia*, which in itself is "a recognition of divine matters" (bk. 12, chap. 9). There is music in paradise, we are informed, "though it is considerably different from ours" (bk. 5, chap. 1). The woodcut could be read to say that in order to perceive such music, one should follow the course marked by the *pars viantis*.

The very name *pars viantis*—I know of its occurrence in no other source—may have been coined after various passages in the New Testament, among them John 14:4 ("and whither I go you know and the way [*viam*] you know") and 14:6 ("I am the way [*via*], the truth, and the life"); Acts 16:17 ("which shew unto us the way [*viam*] of salvation"); and Hebrews 10:20 ("By a new and living way [*viam*], which he hath consecrated for us"). In the woodcut the *pars viantis* holds a "staff," which figures in its customary sense of journey, of pilgrimage. John the Baptist is often represented with a staff, for he prepared the way for Christ (Matthew 11:10: "Behold, I send my messenger [John] before thy face, which shall prepare the way [*viam*] before thee"). Like John the Baptist, who initiated believers into the faith, so the *pars viantis* would seem to lead on from lower to higher musical preoccupations.

Continuing in the same allegorical vein, one wonders whether the arched gate beyond the *pars viantis* was not deliberately set there to signify departure from earthly life (cf. Psalm 1:13: "thou that liftest me up from the gates of death") in order to ascend to paradise (of which one catches a glimpse in the upper right corner?). The scales carried by Pythagoras might allude to the Day of Judgment, when the souls of the dead will be weighed on a balance to adjudge their worthiness for entrance into paradise (Daniel 5:27; in depictions of the Last Judgment, they are usually carried by the archangel Michael).

In line with Jean Le Munerat's treatises, the woodcut may be construed, then, as a double parable. It recounts the numerical formation of music (different hammers, according to their weight, produce different pitches) and, similarly, of the cosmos. More generally, it recounts the power of music to guide the faithful, "via" a *pars viantis,* toward higher spheres. The same *pars* is a "conductor," in both a musical and an itinerary sense. As such, his task is to "coordinate" (*moderari*) the voices whereby creating "harmony" (*concordia*), whose true sound may be heard in the heavens. For Reisch, as for Le Munerat, music is a servant of theology. The same may be said of the other *artes,* for example grammar: in the woodcut for the "typus grammatices" in *Margarita philosophica,* the artist constructs a "tower of sciences," with the basic studies of grammar and poetry on the bottom stories; logic, rhetoric, and arithmetic on the third; astronomy, geometry, and music on the fourth; and at the very top of the edifice, "theologia sive metaphysica." Grammar enters the building through an arched front door, which, as in the woodcut for the "typus musices," introduces the *viator,* through gradual ascent, to higher knowledge. Though grammar and music "form two separate disciplines, they tend to submit and conform to the dictates of a third discipline, namely, the Divine Office" (*De moderatione et concordia,* 6).

Bibliography. The woodcut for *musica* has variously been reproduced (see, for example, the catalogue for an exhibition of *Early Music Printing in the Music Library of the University of California, Berkeley* [1977], [7]). Yet, as far as is known, it has never been discussed. For a similar, though emblematically much simpler, illustration of the "typus musices" from the first edition of Reisch's work (Freiburg, 1503), see *The Printed Note: Five Hundred Years of Music Printing and Engraving* (a catalogue for an exhibition held in the Toledo Museum of Art [Toledo, Ohio, 1957], [52]); it also appears on the cover of A. Hyatt King, *Four Hundred Years of Music Printing* (London, 1968).

For depictions of *musica* as a liberal art, see Werner Bachmann, "Bilddarstellungen der Musik im Rahmen der artes liberales," in *Bericht über den Internationalen Musikwissenschaftlichen Kongress Hamburg 1956* (Kassel, 1957), 46–55 (with bibliographical references in footnote 1, and a reproduction of the "typus grammatices" from the 1508 edition of Reisch's work as illustration 8); and for depictions of liberal arts in general, Paolo d'Ancona, "Le rappresentazioni allegoriche delle arti liberali nel trecento e nel rinascimento," *L'Arte* V (1902): 137–55, 211–28, 269–89, 370–85.

On Jubal, alias Tubal, versus Tubalcain, see Paul E. Beichner, *The Medieval Representative of Music, Jubal or Tubalcain?* (Notre Dame, 1954); also Judith Cohen, "Jubal in the Middle Ages," in vol. III of *Yuval: Studies of the Jewish*

Music Research Center, ed. Israel Adler and Bathja Bayer (Jerusalem, 1974), 83–99. On the controversy surrounding the priority of Jubal or Pythagoras as "inventors of music," see James W. McKinnon, "Jubal vel Pythagoras, quis sit inventor musicae?" *The Musical Quarterly* LXIV (1978): 1–28; also Howard Mayer Brown, ed., *A Florentine Chansonnier from the Time of Lorenzo the Magnificent* (Chicago, 1983, 2 vols.) I: 23–26 ("Tubalcain and the Coat of Arms").

For a number of illustrations of Lady *Musica,* Pythagoras, Tubal, and David, see Joseph Smits van Waesberghe, *Musikerziehung: Lehre und Theorie der Musik im Mittelalter* (Musikgeschichte in Bildern, vol. III, no. 3; Leipzig, 1969), 51–53, 57, 61 (Pythagoras with a staff), 63, 64 (Kind David with two hammers, striking bells; Pythagoras weighing hammers on scales), 65, 83 (*Musica,* with a banderole; Pythagoras), 93, etc.; and for Lady *Musica* in Italy, see Howard Mayer Brown, "St. Augustine, Lady Music, and the Gittern in Fourteenth-Century Italy," *Musica Disciplina* XXXVIII (1984): 25–66.

On iconographical symbols, see the practical manuals George Ferguson, *Signs and Symbols in Christian Art* (London, 1954), and Gertrude Sill, *A Handbook of Symbols in Christian Art* (New York, 1975); and on a larger scale, the following: LeRoy H. Appleton and Stephen Bridges, *Symbolism in Liturgical Art* (New York, 1959); Adolphe N. Didron, *Christian Iconography: The History of Christian Art in the Middle Ages* (New York, 1965, 2 vols.); André Grabar, *Christian Iconography: A Study of Its Origins* (Princeton, 1968); and Gertrud Schiller, *Iconography of Christian Art* (Greenwich, Conn., 1971, 2 vols.). For the music instruments and their allegorical representation, see Helmut Giesel, *Studien zur Symbolik der Musikinstrumente im Schrifttum der alten und mittelalterlichen Kirche* (Regensburg, 1978), and, more generally, Emanuel Winternitz, *Musical Instruments and Their Symbolism in Western Art* (London, 1967).

Notes

PREFACE

1. Page 25 (after Johann Forkel's *Allgemeine Geschichte der Musik* [1801], II: 323). For other references to Le Munerat and his treatise, see below, chap. 1, nn. 1–4.

2. See bibliography, and for other writings on humanism in relation to music, chap. 5, n. 16.

3. See bibliography for Gilbert Ouy's studies.

4. For details, see below, chap. 1, nn. 1, 4.

5. In the English translation of Le Munerat's treatises, many places follow substantive or syntactical emendations suggested by Professor Mathiesen, though others, for which I assume full responsibility, follow my own predilections (thus, for example, the reading of *numerus* not as "rhythm," but as "number," for reasons explained in note 17 to the first treatise; or the reading of *littera* not as "diction," but as "speech" or "words," for being more idiomatic; or varying translations of the knotty terms *modero, modulatio, modulo,* and *modus,* in preference to a fixed set of verbal equivalents, and this on contextual grounds).

6. A topic which, in the meantime, I have been able to develop further in a study on "The Concept of Battle in Music of the Renaissance" (see there for relevant literature).

7. The words are Le Munerat's; see chap. 2, end of item no. 6.

CHAPTER I

1. Mary Berry's entry on Le Munerat in *The New Grove Dictionary of Music and Musicians* X: 659.

2. Fétis, *Biographie universelle des musiciens* VI: 264; Eitner, *Biographisch-Bibliographisches Quellen-Lexikon* VI: 131 (Eitner's entry seems to be based on that of Fétis). For no tangible reason, Fétis described Le Munerat as a musician in the chapel of the College of France (the college was founded by Francis I around 1530, well after Le Munerat's time).

3. *Écrits imprimés concernant la musique* I: 495. The treatise was also listed some two centuries earlier in Johann Forkel's *Allgemeine Litteratur der Musik* (1792), 460.

4. With the exception of Mary Berry's dissertation on "The Performance of Plainsong in the Later Middle Ages and the Sixteenth Century," esp. pp. 134–43 (the treatise and a translation appear, unannotated, as appendix 1, on pp. 370–

93). More easily available is the same author's study, similarly entitled, in *Proceedings of the Royal Musical Association* (see bibliography); the discussion turns to Le Munerat's treatise on pp. 128ff.

5. Archival holdings in Bourges and in Sens are likely to yield additional data relative to Le Munerat's biography; they remain to be consulted.

6. Not to be confused with an earlier Jehan de Launay (or Lannoy), a musician in the French royal chapel in the 1450s–1460s: see Michel Brenet, *Musique et musiciens de la vieille France,* 30, 36, 38.

7. His freethinking in theological matters got him into trouble with the authorities, who excluded him from his teaching post at the Sorbonne in 1648. As an outspoken critic of hagiographical myths, he earned a reputation as a "dislodger (*dénicheur*) of saints."

8. Launoy, *Opera omnia, ad selectum ordinem revocata, ineditis opusculis aliquot, notis nonnullis dogmaticis, historicis et criticis,* etc., 1731–32 (see bibliography).

9. "M. Ioannes Launoyus . . . Doctor celeberrimus, Antiquitatis Ecclesiasticae et Academicae vir scientissimus, si quis unquam fuit": Boulay, *Historia universitatis parisiensis ipsius fundationem, nationes, facultates . . . complectens* IV: 97.

10. For details on both editions, see bibliography; our references here, and in later chapters, are to the earlier edition. Launoy and others used the terms *academia* and *gymnasium* as synonyms for *collegium.*

11. Part I contains a general history of the college from its origins until 1640; part II assembles various collegiate records; part IV reports on 163 teachers at the college.

12. "Ioannes Muneratus, qui se scholasticum Gymnasii Parisiensis Theologum nominat, duos illustres studiorum moderatores habuit, Joannem Raulinum, qui ex magno Navarrae Magistro Cluniacensis Monachus factus est; et Ludovicum Pinellam, qui ex eodem magno Magistro Parisiensis Cancellarius, atque ex Cancellario Meldensis Ecclesiae Antistes. Utrum plures Theologiae actus celebraverit, non constat; sed constat tantum eum nec magisterium, nec Licentiae gradum in Theologia consecutum esse. Id cum alia impedierunt, tum forte Concentoris (ut ipse loquitur) officium, quo in Navarrici Collegii Ecclesia fungebatur. Usuardi Martyrologium edidit anno MCCCCXC. et singulos pene natales dies, pluribus sanctorum Patrum sententiis illustravit. Illud tamen ad vetera exemplaria minime recognovit, ut quae post Usuardi tempus adjecta fuerant, notaret. Duos ad Martyrologii calcem tractatulos adjunxit. Unus est de divino Officio celebrando ex decretis Basilensis Concilii; alter de moderatione et concordia Grammaticae et Musicae in Officio Ecclesiastico. Tractatum de beatae Mariae Parisiensis Dedicatione juris publici fecit anno MCCCCXCIV. in 4°. recusus [recisus?] est anno MDXVI." The passage appears in bk. III of pt. III as chap. 4 ("De Joanne Munerato"); cf. Launoy, *Regii Navarrae gymnasii parisiensis historia* II: 610.

13. Lebeuf, *Histoire de la ville et de tout diocèse de Paris,* 1754 (for a later edition, see bibliography). Lebeuf has been included in recent works of musical lexicography (see Henry René Philippeau's entry for him in *Die Musik in Geschichte und Gegenwart,* VIII: cols. 411–12, and

Albert Cohen's entry for him in *The New Grove Dictionary* X: 578).

14. Lebeuf, *Traité historique et pratique sur le chant ecclésiastique,* 112–15.

15. See chap. 2, item no. 5.

16. The whole passage reads as follows: ". . . un témoin qui a été respecté en son tems; je veux dire, Jean le Munerat dans son Traité *De moderatione et concordia Grammaticae et Musicae,* imprimé à la fin de son édition du Martyrologe d'Usuard de l'an 1490. et celle de 1535. Il est bon de rapporter ici tout-au-long les termes de cet Ecrivain, qui étoit membre de l'Université de Paris, et qui eut en son tems la direction de la plûpart des ouvrages liturgiques de l'Eglise de Paris. (Il eut soin de la belle édition gothique du Breviaire de Paris *in-fol.* de l'an 1492. dont il y a un éxemplaire à la Bibliothèque de N. D. et un chez les Barnabites.)": Lebeuf, *Traité historique,* 112–13.

17. Boulay, *Historia* V: 924b; see below for further references to this inscription.

18. For biographical details, see *Gallia christiana, in provincias ecclesiasticas distributa* II: 90–91, 124. The dedication to Cadouet reappears as the only one in the second edition of 1536; it begins as follows: "Reverendissimo in xristo patri ac domino Domino petro. divina miseratione bituricensi archiepiscopo aquitanie primati Suus iohannes beate Marie de salis canonicus. ac gimnasii parisiensis scholasticus theologus," etc. (the remainder corresponding in its wording to the dedication to the bishop of Paris).

19. Cf. Alfred Baudrillart et al., *Dictionnaire d'histoire et de géographie ecclésiastiques* X: 182.

20. "Petrus Cadoüet ex canonico Bi-

turic[ensi] et priore B[eatae] Mariae de Salis 1462. archiep[iscopus] Bituric[ensis] circa an[no] 1485": *Gallia christiana* II: 124.

21. For his residence in Paris, see below, in connection with the College of Navarre.

22. "Biturgian" meaning "of Bourges." The commentary appears in an undated manuscript preserved in the Bibliothèque de l'Arsenal; for details, see chap. 2, item no. 6.

23. For the different liturgical traditions acknowledged by Le Munerat, see chap. 4.

24. Launoy, *Regii Navarrae* I: 213 (the full list covers pp. 207–20).

25. An inscription for 1497 has *baccalarius* appended to his name (see below).

26. On the requirements for the degrees of bachelor, licentiate, and master in the arts faculty at the University of Paris, see Hastings Rashdall, *The Universities of Europe in the Middle Ages* I: 439ff.

27. Cf. Charles Haskins, *The Rise of Universities,* 33–34; also Rashdall, *Universities* I: 323. For a Johannes Bonne (master of children at the Sainte-Chapelle), who became *magister artium* before embarking upon theological studies at the University of Paris, see Nan Carpenter, *Music in the Medieval and Renaissance Universities,* 53, reporting information contained in the *Chartularium universitatis parisiensis* IV: 82, no. 1796. On the different faculties at the University of Paris, see Charles Thurot, *De l'organisation de l'enseignement dans l'Université de Paris au Moyen-Âge,* esp. 35–108 (arts), 109–64 (theology).

28. Launoy, *Regii Navarrae* I: 214.

29. On Raulin, see ibid. I: 216–24; on

Pinelle, see ibid. II: 614–16 (also I: 217f., 220).

30. For the *moderatores* active at the college during the years 1480–1518, see Boulay, *Historia* IV: 97.

31. Boulay introduces his list of *moderatores* with the words "Interim Moderatorum, seu Magnorum, ut vocant, Magistrorum seriem qualemcunque contexere potui" (ibid.).

32. On the functions of the *grand maître* at the college, see under "Navarre (Collège de)" in *La grande encyclopédie* XXIV: 855.

33. Launoy, *Regii Navarrae* I: 219.

34. Once in the dedication to his edition of Usuard's Martyrology: "gi[m]nasii parisiensis scholasticus theologus," fol. a 1ᵛ (see chap. 2, item no. 4); and again in the dedication to his treatise on the consecration of Notre Dame: "et iam feliciter in xristo filio capelle regie schole francie vulgo navarre concentor modicus ac scholasticus theologus," fol. a i (see chap. 2, item no. 7).

35. Cf. Boulay, *Historia* V: 924b (see below).

36. For an English translation of these statutes, after *Chartularium universitatis parisiensis* I: 78–79, see Lynn Thorndike, *University Records and Life in the Middle Ages*, 27–30.

37. ". . . cappelle regie schole francie vulgo navarre parisii concentor." The same formula reappears in the dedication to the treatise on the consecration of Notre Dame, though now with "modest *concentor*" (see n. 34 above).

38. *Discantor* and *precentor* are general terms, the one referring to a singer of polyphony, the other to the main or leading singer in a choir. For *succentor* in medieval Paris, see Carpenter, *Medieval*

and Renaissance Universities, 52; for the same in Anglican music, see Watkins Shaw's entry on "Cathedral Music and Musicians, Anglican," *The New Grove Dictionary* IV: 9–11.

39. As may be supported by a passage in Isidore of Seville, *Etymologiarum sive originum libri XX,* where we read that "Concentor autem dicitur, quia consonat: qui autem consonat nec concinit, nec concentor erit" ("a *concentor* is so called, because he sounds together; yet he who sounds together, without singing together, is not to be considered a *concentor*"): VII. xii. 28. Isidore also refers to the terms *cantor, praecentor,* and *succentor* (ibid., 26–27). For the recurrence of Isidore's definitions of these and other terms in later writings, see Rhabanus Maurus, *De origine rerum* (early 9th cent.), quoted in Adrien de La Fage, ed., *Essais de diphthérographie musicale,* 363–72, esp. 371–72; also Joannes Presbyter, *De musica antiqua et moderna* (11th cent.), quoted in ibid., 392–408, esp. 405.

40. Boulay, *Historia* V: 919–24, esp. 924 (see above, notes 17, 35). Le Munerat's name is absent, however, from the persons connected with the University of Paris that Charles Jourdain listed in his *Index chronologicus chartarum pertinentium ad historiam universitatis parisiensis, ab ejus originibus ad finem decimi sexti saeculi.* For a Guillelmus Munerius, a *magister* active in the faculty of theology around 1350, see there, I: 145–46 (document no. DCXXXV).

41. See chap. 2, item no. 8.

CHAPTER 2

1. Launoy: nos. 4, 7, 9, 11; Lebeuf, nos. 4, 5, 11. For the two historians' reports

on Le Munerat, see chap. 1, esp. nn. 12, 16.

2. The four editions are nos. 1, 2, 3, and 5 (though the portion "Pray for Master Jean Le Munerat" was omitted from no. 2).

3. In the first book, the inscription reads: "Hunc librum dedit collegio theologorum de Navarra reverendus in Christo pater dominus Petrus de Allyaco, sacre theologie doctor et episcopus Cameracensis, quondam magister hujus collegij. Orate pro eo." In the second, it reads: "Bibliam istam legavit collegio Navarrae defunctus bone memorie magister Guillermus Ducis, quondam scolaris dicti collegij . . . anima cujus in pace requiescat. Amen." (Both examples are reported, after Launoy, in Alfred Franklin, *Histoire générale de Paris* I: 394f., 396.) The two books are now in Paris, Bibliothèque Mazarine, MSS 324 and 35 respectively, as are various others bequeathed to the college and similarly inscribed (MSS 329, 330, 418, 487, 905, etc.).

4. Printed in Dufay, *Opera omnia*, ed. Heinrich Besseler, V: 124–30. For Josquin's "Absolve, quaesumus, Domine," a funeral motet *a 6* for someone unspecified (space is left to fill in the name), see, in his *Werken*, the series *Motetten* XXIII: 109–13 (regarding its authenticity, cf. Myroslaw Antonowycz, "Zur Autorschaftsfrage der Motetten *Absolve, quaesumus, Domine* und *Inter natos mulierum*"). In another composer's setting of "Absolve," the deceased is identified as Josquin himself (cf. Martin Picker, "Josquiniana in Some Manuscripts at Piacenza," esp. 255–60).

5. Though *ordinarium* usually designates the Ordinary of the Mass, it seems also to have been employed in the general sense of a service book (J. F. Niermeyer, *Mediae latinitatis lexicon minus,* 744). In Charles Du Cange, *Glossarium mediae et infimae latinitatis,* it is defined, moreover, as a "liber continens ordinem divini officii" (VI: 58), which accords with its usage here; synonymous with *ordinarium* or *ordinarius* is *ordinale* or *ordinalis* ("liber in quo ordinatur modus dicendi et solemnizandi divinum officium": VI: 57).

6. Apparently in the same house occupied by Commin (rue Neuve-Notre-Dame à la Rose-Rouge).

7. For other printed breviaries from the time, see Hanns Bohatta, *Bibliographie der Breviere, 1501–1850;* for manuscript breviaries, see Victor Leroquais, *Les bréviaires manuscrits des bibliothèques publiques de France.*

8. On manuscript missals in French libraries, cf. Victor Leroquais, *Les sacramentaires et les missels manuscrits des bibliothèques publiques de France.*

9. In the copy bearing the shelf mark Rés. B 186 in the Bibliothèque Nationale, Paris, the word "ioannes" is followed by the handwritten annotation "le munerat."

10. For his biography, see Honoré Fisquet, *La France pontificale* I: 336–42. Among other episodes, Louis was excommunicated by his superior, the archbishop of Sens (Tristan de Salazar), for his refusal to participate in a council convoked by the archbishop in Sens on June 23, 1485 (the decree of excommunication was rescinded, however, on Dec. 13, 1485; on this and other ecclesiastical councils in the fifteenth century, see chap. 4). Fisquet misdated Le Munerat's edition of Usuard's Martyrology as 1492 (ibid. I: 340).

11. Here and elsewhere Le Munerat uses *multiplicare,* literally "to multiply," in the sense of "to reproduce"; he actually means "to print" (*imprimere*).

12. The martyrology is currently recited at Prime not after, but before, the words "Pretiosa," etc. (cf. *Liber usualis,* 233).

13. On early martyrologies, see Hans Achelis, *Die Martyrologien, ihre Geschichte und ihr Wert,* and Henri Quentin, *Les martyrologes historiques du Moyen-Âge.* As to the sources of Usuard's version, see Jacques Dubois's critical edition (*Le martyrologe d'Usuard*), esp. chaps. 2–3 (pp. 38–74); and, in the earlier reading in *Patrologia latina* (CXXIII: cols. 599–911, and CXXIV: cols. 9–860), the introduction, CXXIII: cols. 432–598, with reference to Le Munerat's edition, among the older prints consulted, in col. 546 (variants from the edition are cited throughout the footnote commentary in both volumes).

14. Cf. Quentin, *Les martyrologes,* where Usuard's Martyrology is discussed among "les dérivés du martyrologe d'Adon" (pp. 675–81). The College of Navarre had its own copy of Ado's Martyrology: MS 1695 of the Bibliothèque Mazarine carries, on its last page, the inscription "Hic liber fuit scriptus in collegio de Navarra Parisius, per dominum Philippum de Nivella, presbiterum, ibidem cappellanum, et finitus nonas novembris, anno quadrigentesimo quarto. Amen" (fol. 195ᵛ; cf. Auguste Molinier, *Catalogue des manuscrits de la Bibliothèque Mazarine* II: 172). For an English translation of the Roman Martyrology, i.e., the martyrology of the Roman Catholic church, first printed in its revised Latin version in 1584, see the

volume published under this name in Baltimore, 1907 (and for a Latin edition, the *Martyrologium romanum,* Turin, 1911).

15. For their listing, see Quentin, *Les martyrologes,* esp. 675–77 (Dubois's edition is based on the copy that bears the shelf mark MS lat. 13745).

16. Three copies are held in the Bibliothèque Nationale: Rés. G 212, 213, 591.

17. The Parisian print forms vol. II of *La mer des hystoires* (a translation of *Rudimentum novitiorum,* of which vol. I appeared in 1488); the copy in the Bibliothèque Nationale (Vélins 677) is described as originally belonging to Charles VIII.

18. Three copies are held in the Bibliothèque Nationale: Rés. H 223, 227, 228.

19. For the 1490s, at least two more copies of Usuard's Martyrology are known (Lyons, 1491; Paris, c. 1493). Until the reprint of Le Munerat's edition in 1536, various others appeared in the years 1506 (Lyons), 1507 (Rouen), 1515 (Cologne), 1517 (Venice), 1520 (Venice), 1521 (Paris). Another seven or more copies came out before the end of the sixteenth century. For information, see the various catalogues of Hain, Polain, the British Library, etc.

20. See chap. 1, n. 12.

21. For quotation, see chap. 1, n. 18. Of the five copies, H 277 and B 186 are the only ones to have red and blue inked letter rubrics added by hand.

22. Cf. Paul Marais, *Catalogue des incunables,* 302 (nos. 585 [588], 585 [588 A]). A third copy in the Bibliothèque Mazarine is listed as coming from "l'Église de Paris" (ibid., no. 584 [617]).

23. See item no. 8. Marchant's popular

"Danse macabre" (Paris, 1484) is available in a facsimile edition by Valentin Dufour (see also *La danse macabre,* ed. Pierre Champion after the 1486 printing); on its musical iconography, see Reinhold Hammerstein, *Tanz und Musik des Todes,* 70–71, 179–80.

24. A representative list of some fifteen titles may be found in vol. III of *Dictionary Catalogue of the History of Printing from . . . the Newberry Library.*

25. For the expression "historiis fide dignis," see the first treatise (*De moderatione,* sentence no. 40), and for *historiae* as "lives of the saints," n. 41 to same.

26. For a biography of Jean Simon (de Champigny), whose term as bishop lasted until 1502, see Fisquet, *La France pontificale* I: 344–47.

27. See chap. 1, n. 12.

28. Cf. Zechariah 9:9 ("exulta satis filia Sion iubila filia Hierusalem").

29. Cf. I Kings 6:9 ("et aedificavit domum et consummavit eam"), and 6:14 ("igitur aedificavit Salomon domum et consummavit eam").

30. Cf. Psalms 84:2–3 ("Quam dilecta tabernacula tua Domine virtutum, concupiscit et deficit anima mea in atria Domini"); became verse of introit to the Mass for the Dedication of a Church (*Liber usualis,* 1250).

31. For *stallum* as a "choir stall," see Niermeyer, *Mediae latinitatis lexicon minus,* 987 (3rd definition).

32. Louis IX, king of France from 1226 to 1270; see chap. 3.

CHAPTER 3

1. Jean de Launoy reviews the history of the college in pt. I of *Regii Navarrae gym-nasii parisiensis historia* (pt. I comprises three books, of which the first covers the period from 1304 to 1400, the second from 1400 to 1500, the third from 1500 to 1640). For a more fragmentary discussion, see César Boulay, *Historia universitatis parisiensis ipsius fundationem, nationes, facultates . . . complectens,* vols. IV for 1300–1400 (74–98), V for 1400–1500 (223, 673–74, 854–57), VI for 1500–1600 (140–47, 749). A useful entry for the college appears in *La grande encyclopédie: inventaire raisonné des sciences, des lettres et des arts* XXIV: 855.

2. North of Paris, in the département of Oise.

3. The college appears on a map of Paris around 1530 by Georges Braun and, in greater detail, on a map of Paris around 1552 by an unknown cartographer (copies in Paris, Bibliothèque Nationale, Salle de Cartes et Plans, vol. Ge CCI, nos. 3 and 8; also in *Reproductions d'anciens plans de Paris,* vol. I, for the years 1530–1675, assembled for internal use in the Salle de Travail of the library, vol. Gr. Fol. LK[7] 56877[(1)]). We reproduce part of the latter map as illustration 6. For a city plan (1575) by François de Belleforest, see the illustration in Alfred Franklin, *Histoire générale de Paris,* vol. I, *Les anciennes bibliothèques* [393]: the college figures as item no. 30.

4. Some of the other colleges in the vicinity were the College of Harcourt (founded in 1280), the College of Cardinal Lemoine (1302), of Montaigu (1314), of Plessis (1317), of Lisieux (1336), of La Marche (1362), and so on.

5. Quotation after entry in *La grande encyclopédie* XXIV: 855.

6. The library of the College of Navarre

is discussed by Franklin in his *Histoire générale de Paris* I: 393–404. Franklin drew his information from Aubert Miraeus, alias Le Mire (*Bibliotheca ecclesiastica sive de scriptoribus ecclesiasticis,* 1639 and 49), Louis Jacob (*Traicté des plus belles bibliothèques publiques et particulières . . . dans le monde,* 1644), not to speak of Launoy (*Regii Navarrae*) and others.

7. "Et s'il y a aucune chose de surcroist desdits deux mil livres de rente, ils seront reservez et gardez pour achepter livres de gramaire, de logique, de philosophie et de divinité, pour mettre au commun proufit des povres escholiers pour estudier" (Boulay, *Historia* IV: 74).

8. For a list of fifty-two donors, see Émile Châtelain, "Les manuscrits du Collège de Navarre en 1741," esp. appendix entitled "Bienfaiteurs de la Bibliothèque de Navarre," 400–411 (Châtelain set the sixteenth century as his upper limit). Further donors are mentioned in Henri Martin's report on the College of Navarre in his *Catalogue des manuscrits de la Bibliothèque de l'Arsenal* VIII: 510–18.

9. For Laginius, see Launoy, *Regii Navarrae* II: 896. For the copy of Usuard's Martyrology marked "De libris Cappelle collegii Navarre," see chap. 2, item no. 12.

10. After Châtelain, "Les manuscrits," 362.

11. Jean Raulin appears to have initiated the plan. Cf. Claude Héméré, *De academia parisiensi,* 140: "Anno 1506, bibliothecam Navarrae, in academia Parisiensi, quam Raulinus inchoarat, consummavit eleganti architectura, atque perfecit" (af-

ter Franklin, *Histoire générale de Paris* I: 399).

12. The words are those of François de Belleforest, writing in his edition of Sebastian Münster, *La cosmographie universelle de tout le monde* (1575; orig. *Cosmographia universalis lib. VI,* 1550) I: 194: "Ce que je voy en icelle maison de plus rare est la librairie, laquelle ne doibt guere grand chose a celle de Saint Victor, soit en nombre de livres ou en beauté et rareté de volumes des auteurs de toutes sciences et de toutes langues" (Franklin believed the report to be exaggerated; *Histoire générale de Paris* I: 401).

13. After Franklin, ibid., 401–2.

14. Milanges, *Catalogus generalis bibliothecae theologorum regiae Navarrae;* followed by a *Catalogus peculiaris librorum qui asservantur in armariis bibliothecae theologorum regiae Navarrae, vel quia duplices, vel quia commutandi.* The manuscript is held by the Bibliothèque Mazarine (shelf mark: MS 3139).

15. Davolé, *Catalogus bibliothecae regiae Navarrae, juxta ordinem materiarum digestus;* in the Bibliothèque Mazarine, MSS 3129–38.

16. Masson, *Catalogue des livres de la bibliothèque du Collège de Navarre;* in the Bibliothèque Nationale, MS fonds latin 9371. The list of manuscript items totals 1,272.

17. Châtelain, "Les manuscrits du Collège de Navarre en 1741." Of the various catalogues, we checked the ones by Masson and Châtelain. According to the latter, Masson's work reproduces, in abbreviated form, the earlier inventory by Davolé, with but two additional items; where Davolé goes into greater detail is

in providing the incipit, the size, the date of origin, the name of the donor, etc., for the various titles. In comparing the two, Châtelain proceeds only as far as fol. 32ᵛ of Masson's listing.

18. Masson, *Catalogue des livres*, fol. 204. Whether one of the copies was that deposited by Le Munerat in the chapel library cannot be determined.

19. Ibid., fol. 17.

20. Ibid., fols. 29ᵛ and 23 respectively. Châtelain identified the first of the two as, currently, MS 583 in the Bibliothèque Mazarine.

21. Ibid., fol. 31 (according to Châtelain now in the Bibliothèque de l'Arsenal, MS 257).

22. *Concilii basileensis acta multa;* cf. Masson, *Catalogue des livres*, fol. 9ᵛ.

23. See chap. 2, item no. 9; also appendix 1.

24. Masson, *Catalogue des livres*, fols. 17ᵛ, 32ᵛ.

25. Ibid., fols. 15ᵛ, 245ᵛ.

26. Ibid., fol. 223.

27. For the books now in the Bibliothèque Nationale, see Léopold Delisle, *Le cabinet des manuscrits de la Bibliothèque Nationale* II: 252–55; Châtelain, relevant indications in "Les manuscrits du Collège de Navarre en 1741"; also a list of 112 items once belonging to the college, in the Parisian library's *Catalogue général des manuscrits français, anciens petits fonds français* III: 410–11. For a general guide to the library's collections, see Werner Paravicini, *Die Nationalbibliothek: Ein Führer zu den Beständen aus dem Mittelalter und der Frühen Neuzeit* (with reference to the College of Navarre on p. 73).

28. See Martin, *Catalogue des manuscrits de la Bibliothèque de l'Arsenal,* esp. VIII: 510–18, also Châtelain, "Les manuscrits," 364. By consulting the notes left by D. Poirier (Arsenal, MS 6610), Martin was able to supplement the forty-nine with another fifty-three volumes.

29. Cf. Auguste Molinier, *Catalogue des manuscrits de la Bibliothèque Mazarine,* esp. vol. IV ("Table générale").

30. Referred to, in the writings of Launoy, Boulay, and others, variously as *capella, sacellum,* and *aedicula.*

31. "Statuimus nihilominus et praecipimus quod omnes Scholares festivitatibus solennibus et diebus Dominicis ad Capellam conveniant ordinatè ad pulsationem campanae, Matutinas, Missam et alias Canonicas horas dicturi" (reported in Boulay, *Historia* IV: 83).

32. See chap. 1, n. 12.

33. The first Sunday after Easter Day. Its name derives from the beginning of the introit to its Mass ("Quasi modo genite infantes": cf. *Liber usualis,* 809).

34. "Anno dom. *1309. Sabbato 12.* April. videlicet Sabbato post *Quasimodo* Reverendus Pater D. Simon Festu Dei gratia Meldensis Episcopus Executor excellentissimae D. Ioannae Franciae et Navarrae Regiae posuit et situavit primum lapidem in introitu Ecclesiae seu Capellae Congregationis Scholarium de Navarra" (after Boulay, *Historia* IV: 85).

35. "Et hoc anno interest Dedicationi Capellae Navarricae cum aliis plurimis Praelatis: ut habetur in tabella eiusdem Capellae, quae à dextra est ingredientibus per valvas ipsius: in qua haec verba leguntur. Anno Domino 1373. die Dom. quae fuit 16. mensis Octob. Indictione 11. fuit haec Capella dedicata per Reve-

rendum in Christo Patrem Dominum Petrum de Villaribus tunc Episcopum Nivernensem in honore sanctae Trinitatis, Victoriosissimae S. Crucis Christi, gloriosissimae Virginis Mariae, B. Ludovici Francorum Regis, B. Catharinae Virginis totiusque Curiae supernorum Civium" (after Boulay, *Historia* IV: 442).

36. "Insuper quinque Altaria per eundem consecrata sunt, pretiosis in eis SS. Reliquiis interclusis" (ibid.).

37. ". . . quemadmodùm et de caeteris Iocalibus, ornamentis Ecclesiasticis et alijs bonis . . . que desdits Ornemens, Ioyaux Reliquaires et autres biens estans en leurdite Chappelle" (ibid. V: 780).

38. Charles Du Cange, *Glossarium mediae et infimae latinitatis* IV: 421.

39. Le Munerat, *De moderatione et concordia,* 44.

40. "Charta qua magistri, provisores, capellanus et bursarii collegii Navarrae profitentur, organa quae in ejusdem collegii capella reponuntur, pertinere ad magistros Nationis Gallicanae, quorum expensis confecta fuerunt": Charles Jourdain, *Index chronologicus chartarum pertinentium ad historiam universitatis parisiensis,* 305 (also Nan Carpenter, *Music in the Medieval and Renaissance Universities,* 144n.).

41. Jourdain, *Index chronologicus,* 363: "Quittance par laquelle Josse Lebel, maître faiseur d'orgues et autres instruments de musique . . . confesse avoir reçu . . . de la Nation de France en l'Université de Paris la somme de deux cent trente livres tournois pour la façon des orgues par lui faites et livrées à l'église du collège de Navarre, pour ladite Nation de France"

(quoted by Carpenter, *Music in the Medieval and Renaissance Universities,* 144n.).

42. Michel Brenet, *Les musiciens de la Sainte-Chapelle du Palais,* 44 (after Henri Sauval, *Histoire et recherches des antiquités de la ville de Paris* I: 446): ". . . en 1499, au mois de janvier, les vieilles orgues de la Sainte-Chapelle furent vendues, à cause qu'elles n'étaient ni bonnes ni recevables pour telle église" (from a "compte des oeuvres royaux" for 1498–1500).

43. "Et an. 1309. die Sabbati 2. April. M. Simon Festu Episcopus Meldensis ex iis unus primum lapidem iecit in fundamenta Aediculae, quae S. Ludovico postea dedicata est" (Boulay, *Historia* IV: 85).

44. Cf. Launoy, *Regii Navarrae* I: 75 (also Boulay, *Historia* IV: 442).

45. Boulay, *Historia* IV: 96: ". . . verum hīc omittere non possum originem consuetudinis quae viget etiamnum hodie, concionem habendi publicam, seu sacrum sermonem die S. Ludovici, in cuius honorem Aedicula, seu Capella dedicata est." On *concio,* alias *contio,* as a dispute or controversy (*contentio*), see Du Cange, *Glossarium* II: 535 (the term otherwise refers to a meeting or an assembly [*congregatio, concilium, conventio*]: ibid. II: 480). One definition of *contentio* is "a conflict over the question of knowing which of two opinions is the more likely" (Félix Gaffiot, *Dictionnaire illustré latin-français,* 416).

46. "Legimus enim in Reg. Nationis Anglicanae, quae nunc Germanica dicitur, 'M. Simonem Doctorem Theologum anno 1364. die ultima Iulij supplicasse Universitati, ut liceret habere

quotannis concionem praedicta die S. Ludovici' . . . et concessa fuit supplicatio eius" (Boulay, *Historia* IV: 96). August 25 was, from then on, a day marked by "no lectures in any faculty and a sermon at the College of Navarre"; according to a "Fourteenth-Century Calendar of the University of Paris" (*Chartularium universitatis parisiensis,* ed. Henri Denifle and Émile Châtelain, II: 709–15; cf. Lynn Thorndike, *University Records and Life in the Middle Ages,* esp. 184).

47. The writer is Stephen Pascal (from his *Disquisitiones,* bk. V, chap. 23); after Thorndike, *University Records,* 342. André Pirro mentions the debate in his study "L'enseignement de la musique aux universités françaises," 32.

48. Item no. 12 among the publications listed in chap. 2. For original and translation, see pt. II.

49. Some of the grammarians active at the time are known to us from the college registers. Joannes Fromont is listed, in 1487, as "Regens in Grammaticis"; Andreas Perier, in 1489, as "Magister Grammaticorum, quorum nomina . . . desiderantur"; Petrus Cappel, in 1490, as "Regens in Grammaticis" (after Launoy, *Regii Navarrae* I: 218).

50. Le Munerat, *De moderatione et concordia,* 14–15.

51. On the word-music dichotomy, see chap. 5 (as it applies to Le Munerat's treatises) and the epilogue (as it applies to Renaissance music at large).

52. On Jean Gerson as a representative of incipient humanism in France, and on the College of Navarre as the "cradle of French humanism," see Gilbert Ouy,

"Le Collège de Navarre, berceau de l'humanisme français," passim, also idem, "Les premiers humanistes français et l'Europe," esp. 284–86. It might be mentioned that Gerson treated music, albeit allegorically, in three writings from the 1420s (*De canticorum originali ratione, De canticordo, De canticis*). See Joyce Irwin, "The Mystical Music of Jean Gerson," and from an organographical standpoint, Christopher Page, "Early Fifteenth-Century Instruments in Jean de Gerson's 'Tractatus de canticis.'" Music also figures in a didactic manual that Gerson composed for the choir school of Notre Dame (*Doctrina pro pueris ecclesie parisiensis,* 1411).

53. Gerson's various *tractatus de musica,* to which we just referred, date from a period following his tenure as chancellor of the University of Paris (1495–c. 1515), hence do not reflect any particular orientation in musical studies at the university.

54. Cf. Carpenter, *Music in the Medieval and Renaissance Universities,* 48. On various textbooks used in the thirteenth century, see Jeremy Yudkin, "The Influence of Aristotle on French University Music Texts" (consulted in typescript prior to publication, forthcoming, in the proceedings of the Notre Dame conference on music theory, 1987).

55. See Heinrich Hüschen, "Die Musik im Kreise der *artes liberales*"; Josef Koch, ed., '*Artes liberales': Von der antiken Bildung zur Wissenschaft des Mittelalters;* Edward A. Lippman, "The Place of Music in the System of Liberal Arts"; David Wagner, ed., *The Seven Liberal Arts in the Middle Ages.*

56. Extracted from his *Institutiones di-*

vinarum et humanarum litterarum, in *Patrologia latina* LXX: esp. cols. 1203–20.

57. Edited and translated into Latin by Giorgio Valla (*Écrits imprimés concernant la musique* I: 226); for Engl. tr., see Oliver Strunk, ed., *Source Readings in Music History,* 34–46.

58. In itself based on Nicomachos's lost *De musica* and, for bk. V, the beginning of Ptolemy's *Harmonics.*

59. Cf. William Harris Stahl and Richard Johnson, *Martianus Capella and the Seven Liberal Arts* (with Engl. tr. of Capella's treatise in vol. II).

60. Carpenter described it "as the musical text required of students in the arts faculty of many of the medieval (and even Renaissance) universities" (*Music in the Medieval and Renaissance Universities,* 65). For a modern reprint, see Martin Gerbert, ed., *Scriptores ecclesiastici de musica sacra potissimum* III: esp. 256–83.

61. Lefèvre's treatise was first printed in Paris in 1496; at least six later editions followed (until 1552), all of them Parisian (cf. *Écrits imprimés* I: 492–93).

62. Based largely on Boethius, Franco of Cologne, and Guido d'Arezzo (cf. Roger Bragard's edition of its seven books).

63. For details on editions, cf. *Écrits imprimés* II: 900. The *Enchiridion,* in its third edition (1512), is available in a facsimile reprint (see bibliography).

64. Paris: Nicolas Du Chemin, 1554; cf. François Lesure, "Bibliographie des éditions musicales publiées par Nicolas Du Chemin (1549–1576)," esp. I: 281, 309–10. On the treatise, see Isabelle Cazeaux, *French Music in the Fifteenth and Sixteenth Centuries,* 106.

65. Le Munerat, *De moderatione et concordia,* 19 (also 36).

66. For Jerome's *Tractatus* (after 1272), see the edition by Simon M. Cserba; for Anonymous IV's treatise "de mensuris et discantu" (between 1270 and 1280), see *Der Musiktraktat des Anonymus 4,* ed. Fritz Reckow; also Engl. tr. by Luther Dittmer; for Grocheo's *Ars musicae* (c. 1300), see *Der Musiktraktat des Johannes de Grocheo,* ed. Ernst Rohloff; also Engl. tr. by Albert Seay.

67. After Pirro, "L'enseignement de la musique aux universités françaises," 48f. On the *maîtrises* as preparatory schools for the university, see Cazeaux, *French Music,* 92ff., and at length, Otto Becker, "The 'Maîtrise' in Northern France and Burgundy during the Fifteenth Century." According to Guillaume de Van, it was the *maîtrise,* and not the university, where, in the fifteenth century, the fledgling composer received his basic training ("La pédagogie musicale à la fin du Moyen-Âge," esp. 78ff.). On the *maîtrise* of Notre Dame, see François-Léon Chartier, *L'ancien chapitre de Notre-Dame de Paris et sa maîtrise.*

68. On these productions, see Robert Bossuat, "Le théâtre scolaire au collège de Navarre (XIVme–XVIIme siècles)" (to which we owe our information here).

69. For music in the French theater, see Howard Mayer Brown, *Music in the French Secular Theater, 1400–1550.*

70. *Collège de Navarre rétabli d'aprés* [sic] *les bases de l'enseignement suivi dans l'Université de Paris; avec un pensionnat en pleine activité* (see bibliography).

71. After Psalms 147:18.

72. Nos. 5–21 (5th arrondissement); cf. Jacques Hillairet, *Dictionnaire historique des rues de Paris* I: 426–27.

73. Decree No. 77–839 (July 26, 1977),

printed in the explanatory brochure entitled *Institut Auguste Comte pour l'étude des sciences de l'action* (Paris, 1980), p. 2.

CHAPTER 4

1. See the examples provided in pt. II for the reading of the treatise.

2. Except for general surveys on the development of chant (the by now classic writings by Jean Lebeuf, *Traité historique et pratique sur le chant ecclésiastique* [1741], and Martin Gerbert, *De cantu et musica sacra a prima ecclesiae aetate usque ad praesens tempus* [1774, 2 vols.]), the subject has practically remained untouched. Amédée Gastoué followed the course of Parisian chant from its inception until the tenth century (*Histoire du chant liturgique à Paris des origines à la fin des temps carolingiens*). Mary Berry's study "The Performance of Plainsong in the Late Middle Ages and the Sixteenth Century" stands almost alone in dealing with chant practice in the period under discussion, though on a broader scale than the separate French traditions.

3. Le Munerat, *De moderatione et concordia,* 28.

4. Ibid., 34.

5. On the Parisian church, see Gérard Dubois, *Historia ecclesiae parisiensis* (2 vols.), also Jean Rupp, *Histoire de l'église de Paris.* French church history has an extensive literature; see, for example, René François W. Guettée, *Histoire de l'église de France* (12 vols.), and Charles Poulet, *Histoire de l'église de France* (3 vols.), not to mention *Gallia christiana, La France pontificale,* etc.

6. Lebeuf, *Traité historique et pratique,* 56.

7. These and other details relating to Le Munerat's connections with Bourges are recounted in chap. 1.

8. See chap. 2, under item no. 4.

9. For these and other references, see Ernest Émile Desjardins, *Géographie historique et administrative de la Gaule romaine* II: 381, 414–17, 426–27.

10. On the Biturgian church, see *Gallia christiana* II: 1–115 (and on religious life in fifteenth-century Bourges, Nicole Gotteri, "Le clergé et la vie religieuse dans le diocèse de Bourges au XVᵉ siècle d'après les suppliques en cour de Rome (1434–1484)"); on the council of 1438, see Noël Valois, *Histoire de la Pragmatique Sanction de Bourges sous Charles VII;* on the Cathedral of Bourges, see Auguste-Théodore de Girardot and Hyp. Durand, *La Cathédrale de Bourges, description historique et archéologique.* Paula Higgins has examined the surviving records of the Sainte-Chapelle of the Ducal Palace at Bourges, largely in connection with the shadowy figure Philippe Basiron: see "Antoine Busnois and Musical Culture in Late Fifteenth-Century France and Burgundy" (Ph.D. diss., Princeton Univ., 1987), esp. 255–57, and "Philippe Basiron, Philippon, Philippon de Bourges: An Enigma Resolved" (consulted in typescript prior to publication in *Acta Musicologica*); for a more general study, see Higgins, "Music and Musicians at the Sainte-Chapelle of the Bourges Palace, 1405–1515" (forthcoming in the congress proceedings of the International Musicological Society, Bologna, 1987).

11. Cf. Vincent Leroquais, *Les sacramentaires et les missels manuscrits des bibliothèques publiques de France* III: 185 (no. 757); shelf number in library, m. 39 (34).

12. Cf. W. H. Jacob Weale, *Bibliographia liturgica: catalogus missalium ritus latini ab anno M. CCCCLXXIV impressorum,* 33–34 (for the years 1493, 1500, 1512, 1522, 1526, 1527, 1547, 1651, 1741).

13. Cf. Auguste Molinier, *Catalogue des manuscrits de la Bibliothèque Mazarine* I: 141 (no. 386).

14. On the diocese of Sens and its role in church history, see, variously, *Gallia christiana* XII: 1–107; Honoré Fisquet, *France pontificale,* the volume entitled *Sens et Auxerre;* and Henri Bouvier, *Histoire de l'église de l'ancien archidiocèse de Sens* (3 vols.).

15. In the later fifteenth century. The details are related, after the ancient sources, in Lebeuf, *Histoire de la ville et de tout diocèse de Paris* I: 330.

16. Discussed, respectively, by Fisquet, in *Sens et Auxerre,* pp. 99–106.

17. After the entry on Sens, by Félix Raugel, in *Die Musik in Geschichte und Gegenwart* XII: cols. 519–20.

18. MS nouv. acq. lat. 1535; after Michel Huglo's entry on "Antiphoner" in *The New Grove Dictionary of Music and Musicians* I: esp. 484. Jacques Chailley refers, in his study "Motets inédits du XIVᵉ siècle à la Cathédrale de Sens," esp. 28, to a Senonic antiphonary from the end of the thirteenth century (Paris, Bibliothèque Nationale, MS lat. 1028). On French notation and its connection with the archbishopric of Sens, see Solange Corbin, "La notation musicale neumatique des quatre provinces lyonnaises: Lyon, Rouen, Tours et Sens"; for examples, see variously in the series *Paléographie musicale,* vols. III, VII, VIII, XVI.

19. Listed by Bruno Stäblein in his entry on "Graduale (Buch)" in *Die Musik in Geschichte und Gegenwart* V: esp. 632.

20. MS lat. 10502 (from first half of thirteenth century), MS lat. 864 (from first half of fifteenth century), MS lat. 880 (for the use of Melun, one of the five archdeaconates of the Senonic diocese; dated 1489). For a full description of these and other Senonic missals, see Leroquais, *Les sacramentaires et les missels manuscrits* II: 20 (no. 212), 81 (no. 262), 82 (no. 263), 172 (no. 356); III: 27 (no. 581), 155 (no. 720), 229 (no. 808).

21. For the five missals, along with two others from the eighteenth century, see Weale, *Bibliographia liturgica,* 242–43; for the antiphonary, see Ulysse Chevalier, *Répertoire des sources historiques du Moyen-Âge: Topo-bibliographie* II: col. 2926.

22. Source documents relating to the council are assembled in *Concilium basilense: Studien und Quellen zur Geschichte des Concils von Basel;* the proceedings are transcribed in the older compilations by Jean Hardouin and Gian Domenico Mansi (for details, see chap. 2, under item no. 9). For historical studies, see Carl Joseph Hefele, *Conziliengeschichte, nach den Quellen bearbeitet,* esp. vol. VII; and from the more recent literature, Antony Black, *Council and Commune: The Conciliar Movement and the Fifteenth-Century Heritage* (with particular reference to Juan de Segovia and the Council of Basel); Fredrich Kremple, "Cultural Aspects of the Councils of Constance and Basel"; Hermann Josef Sieben, *Traktate und Theorien zum Konzil: Von Beginn des grossen Schismas bis zum Vorabend der Reformation (1378–1521);* Joachim W.

Stieber, *Pope Eugenius IV, the Council of Basel and the Secular and Ecclesiastical Authorities in the Empire*. Johannes Helmrath reviews the literature, focusing on basic issues, in *Das Basler Konzil 1431–1449: Forschungsbestand und Probleme*. On various smaller councils headed by Senonic archbishops, see Honoré Fisquet, *La France pontificale,* esp. the volume on *Sens et Auxerre,* pp. 99ff.: a council convened by Jean II of Nanton in 1429 (it issued decrees calling for greater regularity and decency in the celebration of the canonical hours); a council convened by Louis I of Melun in 1460 (it reiterated the ordinances of the Council of Basel); a council convened by Tristan de Salazar in 1485 (it confirmed the decisions reached in 1460); and so forth. For source materials on French councils, see the early collection, in four volumes, by Jacques Sirmond, *Concilia antiqua Galliae.*

23. For the decisions of the council regarding the liturgy, in particular its call for greater discipline in delivering the sacred texts, see Ignaz von Wessenberg, *Die grossen Kirchenversammlungen des 15ten und 16ten Jahrhunderts* II: esp. 486–91.

24. Cf. chap. 2, items no. 4, 9.

25. See note 2 to appendix 1.

26. "Quod ad futuram utinam pro futuram rei memoriam" (as in previous note).

27. *Patrologia latina* LXVI: cols. 215–931 (or in Engl. tr., *Benedict of Nursia: The Rule of Saint Benedict*); for a recent critical reading, cf. John Chamberlin, ed., *The Rule of St. Benedict: The Abingdon Copy.* Two chapters are of particular rel-

evance to the celebration of the liturgy: nos. 19 ("De disciplina psallendi") and 20 ("De reverentia orationis"); cf. *Patrologia latina,* esp. cols. 475–84.

28. On these councils, cf. Théodore Gérold, *Les pères de l'Église et la musique,* 162f.

29. *Instituta patrum de modo psallendi sive cantandi,* in Martin Gerbert, ed., *Scriptores ecclesiastici de musica sacra potissimum* I: 5–8 (cf. S. A. van Dijk, "Saint Bernard and the *Instituta patrum* of Saint Gall"). Two kinds of instructions are included in the *Instituta:* those for singing (adapt the voice, in its size and expression, to the degree of liturgical solemnity; sing together; keep a steady voice); and those for delivering the text (use a moderate tempo in order for the words to be understood; sing happily or sadly according to the verbal content; articulate; attend to correct accentuation; etc.). For their discussion, see Don Harrán, *Word-Tone Relations in Musical Thought,* esp. 45–47.

30. Conrad von Zabern, *De modo bene cantandi choralem cantum in multitudine personarum* (1474), ed. Karl-Werner Gümpel; Rutgerus Sycamber de Venray, *De recta, congrua devotaque cantione dialogus* (c. 1500), ed. Fritz Soddemann; Biagio Rossetti, *Libellus de rudimentis musices* (1529).

31. "A psalm forms friendships, unites the divided, mediates between enemies . . . the singing of psalms brings love, the greatest of good things, contriving harmony like some bond of union and uniting the people in the symphony of a single choir": from the "Homily on the First Psalm," after

Oliver Strunk, ed., *Source Readings in Music History,* esp. 65.

32. Cf. Lynn Thorndike, *University Records and Life in the Middle Ages,* 343–49 (after *Chartularium universitatis parisiensis* IV: 652ff.).

33. Translation after Thorndike, *University Records,* esp. 344. On the Feast of Fools, see further E. K. Chambers, *The Medieval Stage* I: chaps. 13–14; Henri Villetard, "Office de Pierre de Corbeil (Office de la Circoncision), improprement appelé 'Office des Fous' "; Wulf Arlt, *Ein Festoffizium des Mittelalters aus Beauvais in seiner liturgischen und musikalischen Bedeutung* I: chap. 3; and more generally, Barbara Swain, *Fools and Folly during the Middle Ages and the Renaissance.*

34. Three editions as an independent tract (1499, c. 1505, 1509); six editions as a preface to the *Cantorinus* (from 1513 to 1566) and at least twenty-one as part of the *Rituale* (from 1523 to 1585). For details, see David Crawford, "The *Compendium musices:* Musical Continuity among the Sixteenth-Century Italian Clergy."

35. "Clericor(um) cantus non sit remissus: no(n) fractus: no(n) dissolutus sed honestus et gravis et uniformis et p(er) o(mn)ia humilis. Psalmodia plus redoleat suavitate(m) mentis: humilitate(m)q(ue) et devotione(m) q(uam) aliqua(m) ostentatione(m). Nam no(n) vacat a culpa animus qua(n)do cantantem plus delectat nota q(uam) res que canitur: omninoq(ue) abominabile est deo quando vocis elevatio plus fit propter audientes q(uam) propter deum": from *Compendium musices confectum ad faciliorem instructionem cantum choralem discentium* (Venice, 1513), fol. 16ʳ (after

copy of same in Sibley Music Library, Rochester, New York).

36. Cf. Gérold, *Les pères de l'Église,* for examples (Council of Glasgow [747], Bishop Chrodegang [d. 766], Bishop Abogard [d. 840], etc.), esp. pp. 162–69.

37. "Ipsum quoque cultum religionis incestat, quod ante conspectum Domini, in ipsis penetralibus sanctuarii, lascivientis vocis luxu, quadam ostentatione sui, muliebribus modis notularum articolorumque caesuris": *Polycraticus* (I. vi), in *Patrologia latina* CXCIX: esp. col. 402.

38. "Nunc vox stringitur, nunc frangitur, nunc impingitur, nunc diffusiori sonitu dilatatur. Aliquando, quod pudet dicere, in equinos hinnitus cogitur; aliquando virili vigore deposito, in femineae vocis gracilitates acuitur, nonnunquam artificiosa quadam circumvolutione torquetur et retorquetur. Videas aliquando hominem aperto ore quasi intercluso halitu exspirare, non cantare, ac ridiculosa quadam vocis interceptione quasi minitari silentium; nunc agones morientium, vel exstasim patientium imitari. Interim histrionicis quibusdam gestibus totum corpus agitatur, torquentur labia, rotant, ludunt humeri; et ad singulas quasque notas digitorum flexus respondet. Et haec ridiculosa dissolutio vocatur religio": *Speculum charitatis* (II. xxii), in *Patrologia latina* CXCV: esp. col. 571.

39. Le Munerat, *De moderatione et concordia,* 12, 62–65.

40. Ibid., esp. ex. 20b–c.

CHAPTER 5

1. Le Munerat, *De moderatione et concordia grammatice et musice* (1490), 15.

2. Ibid., 9 (cf. 47, 58).

3. Ibid., 10 (cf. 57).

4. Ibid., 2.

5. Ibid., 1 (cf. 68).

6. Ibid., 25.

7. Ibid., 24.

8. Ibid., 22–26, 66–67; *Qui precedenti tractatu* [1493], 1, 17.

9. *De moderatione*, 2, 9–10, 36, 46–67.

10. Ibid., 12–13, 62–64.

11. Ibid., 11.

12. Ibid., 2 (see also note 6 to same).

13. Ibid., 14–15, 38, 46.

14. Ibid., 7.

15. As we know from Gilbert Ouy's studies on "Les premiers humanistes français et l'Europe" and "Le Collège de Navarre, berceau de l'humanisme français."

16. On humanism as a growing tendency in Renaissance music, see Hans Albrecht, "Humanismus"; Willem Elders, "Humanism and Early Renaissance Music"; Don Harrán, *Word-Tone Relations in Musical Thought*, chap. 4 and passim; Harrán, *In Search of Harmony*, esp. pt. II; Warren Kirkendale, "Ciceronians versus Aristotelians on the Ricercar as Exordium, from Bembo to Bach"; Paul Kristeller, "Music and Learning in the Early Italian Renaissance"; Edward Lowinsky, "Humanism in the Music of the Renaissance"; Wendelin Müller-Blattau, "Der Humanismus in der Musikgeschichte Frankreichs und Deutschlands"; Helmuth Osthoff, "Der Durchbruch zum musikalischen Humanismus"; Claude Palisca, *Humanism in Italian Renaissance Musical Thought,* also "The Impact of the Revival of Ancient Learning on Music Theory"; Nino Pirrotta, "Music and Cultural Tendencies in

Fifteenth-Century Italy"; and most influential of all, perhaps, as the first of its kind, Daniel Pickering Walker, *Der musikalische Humanismus im 16. und 17. Jahrhundert.*

17. *De moderatione*, 9–10, 38–40.

18. Ibid., 45.

19. Ibid., 2, 9–13, 36, 46–47.

20. Ibid., 46.

21. Ibid., 46–47.

22. Ibid., 12.

23. *Qui precedenti,* 10–11.

24. Ibid., 3–5.

25. Ibid., 6–9.

26. Ibid., 15.

27. Ibid., 16–17.

28. *De moderatione*, 3, 6, 48, 62.

29. Ibid., 2, 14–15; *Qui precedenti,* 5.

30. *De moderatione*, 2, 28, 39–44, 58.

31. Ibid., 17–18, 28; *Qui precedenti,* 12.

32. *De moderatione*, 29–35, 37, 51, 59.

33. Ibid., 17, 19, 49–52, 59, 62–65; *Qui precedenti,* 12.

34. *De moderatione*, 2, also 28, 57–58.

35. Ibid., 14–15.

36. Ibid., 3–5, 24, 56.

37. Ibid., 5, 61.

38. Ibid., 6. In sentence 2, Le Munerat spoke of "plain speech" versus "speech sung to notes or neumes."

39. Ibid., 4.

40. Cf. *Qui precedenti,* 9–10, 14.

41. Ibid., 14.

42. *De moderatione*, 6. In *Qui precedenti,* Le Munerat refers both to vocal music (with or without text) and to instrumental music: "the sounds of a living creature, an organ, a lira," etc. (4); or more clearly, "we form our songs equally well, if you please, on all words . . . or . . . [we form them] without words, as is clear from the above-mentioned

corporal instruments [viz., voices], the organ, the lira," etc. (12).

43. *De moderatione, 49–55*. On the different considerations pertaining to the initial and terminal formulae of psalm tones, see *The New Grove Dictionary of Music and Musicians* XV: 328–29.

44. *De moderatione*, 17.

45. Cf. ibid., 23.

46. Ibid., 16 (also 21, 26, and in *Qui precedenti*, 14).

47. *De moderatione*, 18.

48. Ibid., 19.

49. Ibid., 17 (cf. *Qui precedenti*, 9).

50. *De moderatione*, 62–65.

51. Ibid., 20.

52. Ibid., 21 (cf. *Qui precedenti*, 2, 6, 9–10).

53. See note 46 above.

54. *De moderatione*, 27.

55. Ibid., 28–35 (also 39, 42–44, 57–58).

56. Ibid., 2, 18, 28–35, 53–54 (cf. *Qui precedenti*, end of 14).

57. *De moderatione*, 29–30.

58. Ibid., 39–44, also 57–58.

59. Ibid., 39.

60. Ibid., 40. Cf. chap. 2, n. 5.

61. See, for example, Helmut Hucke, "Toward a New Historical View of Gregorian Chant."

62. *De moderatione*, 44.

63. Ibid., 8, 48–50, 56.

64. On confusion in its celebration, see ibid., 8, 11.

65. On disputes over the mode of performance, see ibid., 2, 24, 67 (also *Qui precedenti*, 16).

66. *De moderatione*, 6.

67. Ibid., 49–54.

68. Ibid., 50.

69. Ibid., 56.

70. Ibid., 57–59.

71. Beyond sentences 57–59, cf. end of 2, 9–11, 28–35, 37.

72. Ibid., end of 59, 60.

73. Ibid., 53.

74. The differentiation into these three varieties of penultimate syllables may be assumed from his examples, where he refers to one word ("Gaudeamus," or "Statuit"), two words ("Ne timeas"), three words ("Beata nobis gaudia"), and "the penultimate of the whole piece" (by which he means larger groupings of words into sentences or periods).

75. *De moderatione*, 62–65.

76. For "macula," see *De moderatione*, ex. 20a–b.

77. Cf. ibid., 61.

78. Ibid., 22.

79. Ibid., 24, 16 (also 26).

80. Ibid., 23.

81. As may be concluded from the handwritten annotation on the back flyleaf of Le Munerat's own copy of Usuard's Martyrology (see under item no. 12 in chap. 2).

82. *Qui precedenti*, 2.

83. Ibid., 3, 5, end of 6, 7–8.

84. Ibid., 6, 9, end of 10.

85. Ibid., 14 (where Le Munerat refers to the first treatise on this point).

86. In *Qui precedenti*, musical tradition is described periphrastically as the "principles" of music, "their elaboration toward their conclusions," and the "action" or procedures of music (3).

87. *Qui precedenti*, 2.

88. Ibid., 6 (see there, note 6, for double meaning of *subiecta* as "subjects" and "subjected," as well as for source references).

89. Ibid., 10 (parenthetical statement).

90. Cf. *De moderatione*, 5, 61.

91. *Qui precedenti,* 12.

92. Ibid., 3–4 (for music) versus 7–8 (for speech).

93. Ibid., 9.

94. Ibid., 10 (middle).

95. Ibid., 5.

96. *De moderatione,* 26. Le Munerat refers to the musical customs inaugurated and sanctioned by the church fathers (38–44). The chants should be performed "according to the way the ancient Holy Fathers . . . ordered [them] to be sung" (58).

97. Note his evasive wording in *Qui precedenti,* 5–6: "Grammar, too, *may* be right or regulated . . . *if* we follow the opinion of sages and savants . . . (*yet* one *wonders whether* . . . ; *perhaps* it consists . . . hence all its strength and logic . . . *may* derive from authority . . .). *Yet* as often . . . ," etc.

98. Ibid., 6 (end)–9.

99. Ibid., 8.

100. Ibid., 3.

101. Ibid., 3 (end)–4.

102. As announced in the initial thesis (ibid., 2) and its subsequent reinforcement (6, 9–10).

103. Euclid, *Elementa,* vol. III of *Opera omnia,* ed. I. L. Heiberg and H. Menge; and for the infiltration of these ideas into Renaissance theory, Franchinus Gaffurius, *Practica musicae* (1496), bk. IV, chap. 1.

104. *Qui precedenti,* 4.

105. *De moderatione,* 17–19.

106. *Qui precedenti,* 15.

EPILOGUE

1. Jean Le Munerat, *De moderatione et concordia,* 48.

2. Ibid., 7–8.

3. Cf. Priscian, "Accentus namque est certa lex et regula ad elevandam et deprimendam syllabam uniuscuiusque particulae orationis," etc., from his *De accentibus liber,* in *Grammatici latini,* ed. Heinrich Keil, III: 519f.

4. ". . . accentus, quas Graeci προσ-ῳδίας vocant": cf. Quintilian, *Institutio oratoria* I. v. 22 (also XII. x. 33). For *accentus* as *adcantus,* cf. Servius Honoratus's commentary to Donatus's *Ars grammatica:* "Accentus autem est quasi adcantus dictus, quod ad cantilenam vocis nos facit agnoscere syllabas" (*Grammatici latini* IV: 451).

5. For examples of deviation from metrical and tonic orderings, see Thomas J. Mathiesen's studies on "New Fragments of Ancient Greek Music" and "Rhythm and Meter in Ancient Greek Music."

6. "And the melody and rhythm will depend upon the words": *The Republic* III. 398d. 8–9 (after translation by Benjamin Jowett, *The Dialogues of Plato* III: 84).

7. Many of his works are conflations of others' writings, as in the case of the three to which we refer in the paragraphs below, viz., his *Prosodia in usum iuventutis northusianae* (1535), *Quaestiones musicae in usum scholae northusianae* (1536), *Trivii erotemata, hoc est grammaticae, dialecticae, rhetoricae, quaestiones* (1544); for details, see bibliography.

8. "Est ars, docens quo accentu quaeque dictionis syllaba proferenda sit": Spangenberg, *Prosodia,* fol. A 2.

9. A practice that began in the early sixteenth century: recall Conrad Celtes's use of musical examples by Tritonius for his lectures, at the University of Ingolstadt, on Horatian meters (*Melopoiae*

sive harmoniae tetracenticae, Augsburg, 1507).

10. "Quid est accentus? Est lex levandae vel deprimendae syllabae": Spangenberg, *Trivii erotemata,* fol. 58 (cf. Priscian, n. 3 above).

11. "Quotuplex est Accentus? Duplex, productus et correptus. Productus est, quando syllaba naturaliter elevatur, ut fortuna, natura. Correptus est, quando syllaba naturaliter deprimitur, ut dominus, tabula": Spangenberg, *Trivii erotemata,* fol. 58.

12. "Quid est Accentus? Est lex levandae vel deprimendae syllabae, cuiusque particulae orationis. Quotuplex est Accentus? Triplex. Acutus, gravis, circumflexus. Acutus, est quo syllaba vocis acuitur et elevatur, ut sum, es, est. Gravis, est quo syllaba deprimitur et deorsum praecipitatur. Circumflexus, est quo syllaba in gyrum flectitur, in medioque subsistit": ibid., fol. 72–72ᵛ.

13. On these and other treatises, in this connection, see chap. 5 of Don Harrán, *Word-Tone Relations in Musical Thought.*

14. "Est melodia quae dictionum syllabas iuxta accentus sui naturalis exigentiam, regulate pronunciat": Spangenberg, *Quaestiones musicae,* fol. D 2 (from the chapter "De accentu musico," fols. D 2–4ᵛ).

15. "Dictiones monosyllabae, item barbarae, Graecae, Hebraicae, Latinam inflexionem non habentes, acuuntur, ut me, te, se, nos, vos, sum, est. Ascaroth, Senaherib, Babylon, Abraham. Hinc excipiuntur encleticae coniunctiones, que, ne, ve, quae habent accentem gravem" (ibid., fol. D 3).

16. "Quomodo cognoscitur ille accentus [*referred to previously as* accentus Eccle-

siasticus]? per punctum, in textu positum . . . si in una oratione, inter plures dictiones distinctio repereatur, eas in unisono esse proferendas demonstrat. Si autem comma, hoc est, duo puncti: tunc ultima syllaba ad tertiam deprimitur, excepta dictione monosyllaba, et hebraica, quae in proximam secundam levantur. Quando vero Colon, hoc est punctus ante literam capitalem, invenitur, indicat ultimam syllabam, debere gravari ad quintam, dictione hebraica et monosyllaba dempta, quae ad locum sui descensus vult elevari, iuxta quantitatem syllabarum": Lampadius, *Compendium musices* (1537), from 1554 ed., fols. G viᵛ–vii.

17. Nicolaus Wollick, for example, writes as follows: "Positura . . . est figura ad distinguendos sensus per cola et commata et periodos que cum suo ordine examussim apponitur lectionis sensum nobis aperit" (*Enchiridion musices* [1509], from 1512 ed., fol. g ii).

18. Le Munerat, *De moderatione,* 46.

19. "Dictio dissyllaba, accentum recipit in prima, sive ea syllaba sit longa sive brevis": Spangenberg, *Quaestiones musicae,* fol. D 3.

20. Andreas Guarna, *Bellum grammaticale Nominis et Verbi regum, de principalitate orationis inter se contendentium* (see bibliography).

21. For details of later readings, see *Andrea Guarnas "Bellum grammaticale" und seine Nachahmungen,* ed. Johannes Bolte. At least twenty-eight editions were issued in Paris, beginning with the second one from 1512–13. For an English translation from 1569, see John Somers, ed., *A Collection of Scarce and Valuable Tracts* I: 533–54 ("A Discourse of Great War

and Dissention between 2 Worthy
Princes the Noun and the Verb,
Contending for the Chefe Place or
Dignitie in Oration"; under Guarna in
bibliography).

22. For its redaction by Robert
Schneider, see under Guarna in
bibliography.

23. "In principio erat Verbum et Verbum
erat apud Deum et Deus erat Verbum"
(*The Gospel according to John* 1:1). The
basic division of language into nouns
and verbs may be traced back to Plato's
Sophist; see *The Dialogues of Plato,* tr.
Benjamin Jowett, IV: 339–407, esp.
396–401.

24. Brandolino (c. 1465–1517), Inghirami (1470–1516), Marso (c. 1442–
1512).

25. Claudio Sebastiani, *Bellum musicale,
inter plani et mensuralis cantus reges, de
principatu in musicae provincia obtinendo,
contendentes* (1563).

26. "Qui quidem cum saltem nominum
et verborum in grammatica bellum de-
scripserit, ego tamen praeter id Deorum,
Musarum, hominum, ferarum, avium,
instrumentorum Musicalium et eorum
qui istorum inventores extiterunt, om-
niumque rerum sonarum quarum memi-
nisse potui, controversias inservi":
Sebastiani, *Bellum musicale,* fol. A 2. On
Sebastiani's debt to Guarna, see *Andrea
Guarnas "Bellum grammaticale,"* ed.
Bolte, pp. *86–88.

27. Chap. 37 of Sebastiani's *Bellum musicale* is headed thus: "Sequuntur decem
praecepta, omni canenti necessaria ex su-
pradicto Andrea Ornitoparcho excerpta"
(fol. X 2).

28. ". . . singularis eruditionis virum"
(fol. R 4ᵛ).

29. For his music treatise, see above,
chap. 3, n. 61; for his place in intellec-
tual history, see Eugene F. Rice, Jr.,
"Humanist Aristotelianism in France:
Jacques Lefèvre d'Étaples and his Circle," in A. H. T. Levi, ed., *Humanism in
France at the End of the Middle Ages and in
the Early Renaissance,* 132–49.

30. A shadowy figure, identified as the
progenitor of the Thracian Bistones and,
variously, as the son of Ares, of Paion,
of Kikon, and of Terpsichore (see *Paulys
Realencyclopädie der classischen Altertumswissenschaft* V: col. 504).

31. Erasmus Sartorius, *Belligerasmus, id
est Historia belli exorti in regno musico*
(Hamburg, 1622, 3rd ed. prepared by
Peter Lauremberg, 1639, under the title
Musomachia, id est Bellum musicale); information after entry on Sartorius (d.
1637), by Martin Ruhnke, in *Die Musik
in Geschichte und Gegenwart* XI: col.
1420. Another treatise in the same line
of descent is Johann Bähr's *Bellum musi-
cum oder musikalischer Krieg* (n.p., 1701).

32. Bolte commented that "this charm-
ingly executed idea, which seems in particular to have conferred on the book its
far-reaching renown, stands, to all appearances, as Guarna's own property":
Andrea Guarnas "Bellum grammaticale,"
*13.

33. Andreas Ornithoparcus, *Musice active
micrologus* (1517), tr. John Dowland as
*Micrologus, or Introduction: Containing the
Art of Singing* (1609), 68f.

34. ". . . exceptis responsoriis, gradu-
alibus, et introitibus, in quibus sunt
ligaturae, neumae, et species coniunc-
tionum in his nequimus ordinem diu ob-
servatum permutare quia debemus
implere omnes colores musicae, et hic

grammatica ancilla est musicae sicut affirmaverunt vates sapientissimi architas namque et Aristoxenus subiectam musicae grammaticen dixerunt": Biagio Rossetti, *Libellus de rudimentis musices* (1529), fol. c ii^v.

35. ". . . sed in hymnis et prosis vel sequentiis et in psalmis et antiphonis possumus de ancilla grammatica facere dominam": ibid.

36. Cf. Le Munerat, *De moderatione,* 6 (viz., the notion of the Divine Office as a "third discipline," to which grammar and music are subservient); also Rossetti, *Libellus de rudimentis musices,* where, as early as the title, the author speaks of his intention to write about a fitting celebration of the holy rites ("de modo debite solvendi divinum pensum").

37. See Gilbert Ouy's studies on the humanist ferment at the college; and for a broader treatment of French humanism, Werner L. Gundersheimer, ed., *French Humanism, 1470–1600,* also A. H. T. Levi, ed., *Humanism in France.*

38. See Harrán, *Word-Tone Relations,* app., nos. 49ff. and 89ff.

39. ". . . dovemo osservare, di accommodare in tal maniera le parole della Oratione alle figure cantabili, con tali Numeri, che non si oda alcun Barbarismo; si come quando si fà proferire nel canto una sillaba longa, che si doverebbe far proferir breve: o per il contrario una breve, che si doverebbe far proferir longa": Gioseffo Zarlino, *Le institutioni harmoniche* (1558), 340.

40. "Et si debbe per ogni modo osservar quello, che gia molti de gli Antichi hanno osservato; cioè di non porre tali Pause, se non nel fine delle Clausule, o

punti della Oratione, sopra la quale è composta la cantilena, et simigliantemente nel fine di ogni Periodo. Il che fa dibisogno, che li Compositori etiandio avertiscano; accioche li Membri della oratione siano divisi, et la sentenza delle parole si oda, et intenda interamente": ibid., 212.

41. On the gradual "verbalization of polyphonic music," see Helmuth Osthoff, "Der Durchbruch zum musikalischen Humanismus," 31.

42. By Aristotle, for one, in his *Politics,* 1342*b* (cf. Oliver Strunk, ed., *Source Readings in Music History,* 23).

43. ". . . oltre che non sono mancati et non mancano tra piu famosi, di quelli che hanno prima composte le note secondo i loro capricci, et adattattovi poi quelle parole che è paruto loro; senza haver fatto alcuna stima, che tra le parole et le note, sia la medesima ò maggiore disformità di quella che si è detta essere tra il Dithirambo et l'harmonia Doria": Vincenzo Galilei, *Dialogo della musica antica, et della moderna* (1581), 87. (The dithyramb properly belonged to the Phrygian mode, which, in its emotional character, stood in contrast to the calm Dorian.)

44. On the humanist movement in music of the Renaissance, see the writings mentioned in chap. 5, n. 16.

45. For the tug of war between liberal and reactionary theologians at the University of Paris, see James K. Farge, *Orthodoxy and Reform in Early Reformation France: The Faculty of Theology of Paris, 1500–1543.*

46. Le Munerat, *De moderatione,* 2.

47. Ibid.

48. Rossetti's revisions are discussed by

Raphael Molitor in *Die Nach-Tridentinische Choral-Reform zu Rom* I: 121ff.; see also Harrán, *Word-Tone Relations,* 116–18.

49. Maurus P. Pfaff, for one, wrote about the edition "that the arrangers arbitrarily shortened or displaced melismas; that the rhythmic system in back of the notation remains unelucidated; that such groupings of neumes are introduced as have no place in the tradition; that the principles employed by the editors, said to be Anerio and Suriano, can neither be explained nor demonstrated—contemporary chant theory has nothing to say about them" ("Die liturgische Einstimmigkeit in ihren Editionen nach 1600," 52f.).

50. On music as having its own language, see, for *musica antiqua,* Mathias Bielitz, *Musik und Grammatik: Studien zur mittelalterlichen Musiktheorie.* In considering pitches, rhythms, etc., in relation to language, it is useful to bear in mind the distinction between music as *sprachähnlich,* i.e., patterned after linguistic procedures, and music as *sprachlich,* i.e., forming its own closed system of communication: the dividing line between the two would seem to fall in the seventeenth century (see Fritz Reckow on "Tonsprache" in *Handwörterbuch der musikalischen Terminologie,* ed. Hans Heinrich Eggebrecht [Wiesbaden: Franz Steiner, 1972 on], installment for 1979, pp. 1–6). For some recent studies on music as a language of sound, and the problems of defining its content, see, for example, Eggebrecht, "Musik als Tonsprache," *Archiv für Musikwissenschaft* XVIII (1961): 73–100; Nelson Goodman, *Languages of Art: An Approach to a Theory of Symbols*

(Indianapolis: Bobbs-Merrill, 1968), esp. 3–43 (a structuralist consideration of imitation, representation, etc.); Peter Faltin, "Musikalische Syntax. Ein Beitrag zum Problem des musikalischen Sinngehaltes," *Archiv für Musikwissenschaft* XXXIV (1977): 1–19; Ivo Supičić, "Expression and Meaning in Music," *International Review of the Aesthetics and Sociology of Music* II (1971): 193–212; Tibor Kneif, "Bedeutung, Struktur, Gegenfigur. Zur Theorie des musikalischen 'Meinens,'" ibid., 213–39; various items in *Beiträge zur musikalischen Hermeneutik,* ed. Carl Dahlhaus (Regensburg: Gustav Bosse, 1975), and so on (all of them employing post-Renaissance methods of analysis); to these add the literature on Schenkerian analysis and, growing strong, on musical semiotics and the phenomenology of music.

DE MODERATIONE

1. The treatise is presented here after its original redaction (1490), both in its spellings and in its punctuation. I numbered its sentences for purposes of reference and for ease of comparison with the suggested translation. (In the source, sentences 38, 57, 66, and 68 were indented as new paragraphs.) Periods lacking in the original have been supplied in brackets. As customary, parentheses are used in my reading of the Latin for words printed in abbreviation. Except for some additional periods and a few orthographical variants (duly recorded here in footnote), the 1536 edition reproduces the original to the letter. Though Le Munerat named specific musical examples, he did not include them:

all such examples, therefore, are editorial additions. Where the chants to which the author referred were readily available in the *Liber usualis,* they have been quoted, for convenience' sake, from that source (designated here by the siglum *LU*). Their values have been reduced at the rate of 16 to 1, whereby a breve [*punctum*] of the original equals an eighth note of the transcription.

2. A misprint for fol. o iii (all subsequent folio listings here should be lowered by one digit).

3. On *moderatio* as "measurement," see under note 7 below. The terms *moderatio, modulatio, concordia,* and others used here have multiple meanings that modern English cannot duplicate, but can only approximate; they have been rendered, for the most part, according to their function in context (cf. note 5 to preface).

4. 1536 ed.: "syllabaru(m)."

5. Ibid.: "syllaba."

6. "Prosodi[a]ce" (an adjective) seems to be set in attribution to *prosodie,* hence "grammatice prosodie vel prosodi[a]ce [prosodie]" ("grammatical accentuation or metrical [accentuation]"). By "grammatical accentuation" the author would be referring to the long-short properties of syllables as determined by their vowels; by "metrical accentuation," to the long-short properties of syllables as determined by their location in metrical schemes. Yet by "grammatical accentuation" he is also referring to the acute-grave properties of syllables as determined by their verbal inflection (after the notion of *prosodia* as accent: for a quotation from Quintilian, see epilogue,

n. 4). For Johann Spangenberg's comments on *prosodia,* particularly as they bear on qualitative accentuation, see epilogue, nn. 10–12. Gioseffo Zarlino maintained that "grammarians . . . observe the accents [of words] not according to the measure of durations, but according solely to the usages of inflection" ("i Grammatici, i quali osservano i loro Accenti, non secondo la misura de i Tempi; ma secondo l'uso solamente del loro Declinare"): *Sopplimenti musicali* (1588), 322.

7. The verb *modulari* in its participial form "modulata" appears to be used here in the sense "to sing." Cf. Jean Lebeuf, *Traité historique et pratique sur le chant ecclésiastique* (1741), 19n., where, speaking of the responsory "Congregati sunt," the author writes that it "appears to have been invented [*fabriqué*] in France and to have been sung [*modulé*] in Paris, or in Sens, or even in Chartres." On *modulari* and *moderari* as synonyms, see below, specifically, "moderatur vel modulatur" (fol. o iv–iv^v), "mensuratus vel moderatus" (o vii), "decantari vel modulari" (o vii^v). The notion of song as number (or singing, *modulari,* as measuring, *moderari* or *mensurare*) derives from the Pythagorean definition of music as the science of numbers (cf. "moderatum seu mensuratum," fol. o vii).

8. 1536 ed.: "lungas."

9. Period after 1536 ed., as is the case with the periods that follow sentences 7, 14, 15, 21 and that follow the word "quadragesime" in sentence 32, the word "Alleluya" in sentence 35, and the words "hymno" and "stella" in sentence 36.

10. Here the author refers to the deriva-

tion of *accentus* from *ad-cantus* ("melody adjoined to it"), after the Greek *prosodia*, i.e., πρός (*ad*) plus ὠδή (*cantus*). For quotation from Servius Honoratus, see epilogue, n. 4.

11. The hymn, that is, is employed on feasts of three or nine lessons in the Parisian rite. 1536 ed.: "lectionu(m)."

12. Le Munerat's meaning is not completely clear: in the above example, the singers could well have found a "suitable way out" by resetting "for" of "fortia" to C-D (with "tia" on C-C) and "op" of "optimum" to C-D-C (with "timum" on B-A). Perhaps the author was referring to a more melismatic version of the chant melody (mode 2) than the readings in modern editions (beyond the one quoted from *LU,* which follows that of the *Antiphonale romanum,* [36], see another in the *Antiphonale monasticum,* 646, and those in Bruno Stäblein, ed., *Die mittelalterlichen Hymnenmelodien des Abendlandes,* 61, 198). An examination of "Parisian" sources may turn up examples with more ornate figures on the penultimate syllables of "fortia" and "optimum," whose resetting would, as Le Munerat predicted, have been detrimental to the overall design of the melody.

13. These pauses on short syllables mark the verse endings.

14. For other readings beyond the one quoted in ex. 5, see Stäblein, *Die mittelalterlichen Hymnenmelodien,* 46 (mode 8), 304 (mode 1); *LU,* 952, also *Graduale romanum,* 139★ (mode 1); *Antiphonale romanum,* 106★, also *Graduale romanum,* 138★, and *LU,* 920 (mode 4).

15. 1536 ed.: "presertim."

16. Cf. Quintilian, *Institutio oratoria,* I. x. 17: "Transeamus igitur id quoque, quod grammatice quondam ac musice iunctae fuerunt: si quidem Archytas atque Euenus etiam subiectam grammaticen musicae putaverunt." The reference is to Archytas and Euenus (the first a philosopher and Pythagorean mathematician resident in Tarentum [southern Italy] and active in the years 400–350 B.C., the second a poet and sophist contemporary with Plato). Aristoxenos's name turns up a few lines later (I. x. 22), yet in a somewhat different connection (viz., "Vocis rationem Aristoxenus dividit in ῥυθμὸν et μέλος, quorum alterum modulatione, alterum canore ac sonis constat").

17. Though *numerus* is often used in music theory as a synonym for rhythm, it appears to be understood by Le Munerat in its literal sense as number. Cf. *Qui precedenti tractatu,* 4, where music is defined as "arithmetic."

18. It is not clear what Le Munerat means by *duplex nota.* In a previous reference to the same on the "fi" of "Magnificat," he specified a two-note neume (see ex. 1). Now, however, by counterpoising *duplex nota* with *minima,* the author might have had any one of three possibilities in mind: (1) a minim preceded by a note of double value, i.e., a semibreve (♩ ♩); (2) a two-note su - per- neume followed by a single note (♩ ♩ ♩); or, more figuratively, (3) a su - per- melisma of three or more notes (on "su") followed by a smaller number of notes (on "per"). In ex. 6, quotations are

drawn to illustrate each of the three.

19. Usually spelled as "problemate."

20. 1536 ed.: "initio."

21. Feast day for Saints Gervase and Protase: June 19.

22. 1536 ed.: "consilii."

23. The name "Iesus" was originally tri-syllabic ("Ĭ-ē-sus," after Greek Ἰ-η-σοῦς), and only later dissyllabic ("Iē-sus"). In Latin, the stress accent falls on the first syllable "Ie"; yet in Greek, French, and, presumably, frenchified Latin, it falls on the second syllable "sus" (hence "sus" would ordinarily have received the melisma, not "Ie" as in the examples below).

24. 1536 ed.: the "m" of "magnificat" is capitalized.

25. Such a three-note melisma could not be traced. The reading of "Hoc iam tertio manifestavit se Iesus" contained in the *Antiphonaire monastique . . . de Lucques* (*Paléographie musicale* IX: 220) has two notes for the first syllable "Ie" of "Iesus" while the one in the *Antiphonaire monastique . . . de Worcester* (*Paléographie musicale* XII: 135) has only a single note for the same. Le Munerat might have misread three notes in the former by combining the second note on "se" with the two notes on "Ie," thus:

Hoc— iam— ter-ti - - o ma-ni-fe-sta-vit se— Ie - sus

altered to

se Ie - sus

26. The Feast of the Apostles Peter and Paul is celebrated on June 29.

27. Text included in the *Breviarium sanctae . . . bituricensis ecclesie* (1522), fol.

lxxx^v, and in Le Munerat's edition of the *Breviarium parisiense* (1488), fol. DD i.

28. The Feast of Peter in Chains is celebrated on August 1.

29. 1536 ed.: "ies(us)."

30. Chant not identified. The reading contained in the *Graduel de Saint-Yrieix* (*Paléographie musicale* XIII: 163) has the first syllable of "Ihesus" set to a melisma of eight notes, thus:

Sur-gens_____ Ihe - sus

31. The portion from "miror" to "vereatur" (the last word before ex. 13) is quoted by Lebeuf in his *Traité historique,* p. 113 (with "vocem" inserted between "eius" and "vigintiquinque").

32. Annunciation Sunday: March 25.

33. Chant not identified. The author seems to be referring to the responsory "Ecce virgo concipiet et pariet filium et vocabitur nomen eius ihesus," etc. (whose text is included in the *Breviarium sanctae,* fol. lvii).

34. Both editions (1490, 1536) have "li" (as does Lebeuf in his quotation; see note 31).

35. Of the numerous versions of the Vesper hymn "Ave maris stella," the author appears to be referring to the one given in ex. 12 (after *LU,* 1259f., as well as *Antiphonale romanum,* [117], *Antiphonale monasticum,* 704, etc.). The figure on "Jesum" falls, in previous stanzas, on "Virgo" (stanza 1), "pace" (2), "pelle" (3), "natus" (4), and "(so)lutos" (5).

36. On *organicus* (adjectival form of *organum*) as a synonym for (*musica*) *mensurata,* see *The New Grove Dictionary of Music and Musicians* XIII: 797–98 (under

etymology of *organum*), also 809–10 (for studies relative to terminology). Though I had originally construed Le Munerat's words to refer to the succession A-D-D, with "Je" on the first two notes and "sum" on the third, Thomas Mathiesen suggested an even better reading, which I gratefully reproduce in ex. 13.

37. Le Munerat refers, for this provision, to the last portion of sentence 2 above.

38. In the version of the chant "Gaudeamus omnes in Domino" quoted in ex. 14 (common to the various feasts for the Proper of the Saints), it will be noted that "om" of "omnes" is set not to one note, but to a liquescent neume.

39. Referring to Archytas and Aristoxenos, mentioned above.

40. Jerome: c. 340–420. Damasus I: pope 366–84. Celestinus I: pope 422–32. Gelasius I: pope 492–96. Ambrose: bishop 374–97. Gregory I: pope 590–604.

41. Le Munerat is referring to such biographical reports as are included in the standard "lives of the saints" and, for that matter, in his own edition of Usuard's Martyrology. The library of the College of Navarre is known to have owned copies of a *Summa de vitis sanctorum* and a volume *De vitis sanctorum* (listed under the *codices manuscripti* in Gabriel Masson, comp., *Catalogue des livres de la bibliothèque du Collège de Navarre,* fol. 17 [nos. 400–401]).

42. Sources ascribing to Gregory the final ordering of the chant may be traced back to the eighth and ninth centuries; particularly influential was the testimony of John the Deacon, who, in his biogra-phy of Gregory (872–82), spoke of the latter's having "compiled" the antiphonary as a patchwork of materials ("Antiphonarium centonem . . . compilavit," *Sancti Gregorii Magni Vita,* II. vi. 17; in *Patrologia latina* LXXV: 90). Cf. Walther Lipphardt, "Gregor der Grosse und sein Anteil am römischen Antiphonar." On Gregory's role in disseminating the chants, see Helmut Hucke, "Die Entste-hung der Überlieferung von einer mu-sikalischen Tätigkeit Gregors des Grossen"; Joseph Schmit, "Die gottes-dienstlichen Gesänge in Rom und ihre Ordnung unter Benedikt und Gregor"; and Leo Treitler, "Homer and Gregory: The Transmission of Epic Poetry and Plainchant." On *ordinarium,* see chap. 2, n. 5.

43. The prologue appears in a number of chant books, containing items both for the Mass and for the Divine Office; its text is ascribed, in an eleventh-century manuscript from the monastery of St. Martial, Limoges, to Pope Hadrian I (772–95). Of its ten versions, at least two were sung prior to the first introit of Advent ("Ad te levavi," *LU,* 318). (The copy of the later *Graduale bituricense* [Bourges, 1741, 2 vols.] checked by this writer in Paris, Bibliothèque Nationale, lacks vol. I, which might have contained the prologue; vol. II begins with the first Sunday after Easter.) Le Munerat quotes directly from the prologue, as is clear from the portion printed in Helmut Hucke's entry on "Gregory the Great" in *The New Grove Dictionary* VII: 699. For a separate study, see Bruno Stäblein, "Gregorius Praesul: der Prolog zum römischen Antiphonale" (with musical

examples of the prologue, from various traditions, on pp. 557–58). On the Schola Cantorum, i.e., the papal choir, see below.

44. On the Schola Cantorum, see S. J. P. van Dijk, "Gregory the Great, Founder of the Urban 'Schola Cantorum' "; and, more extensively, Franz Xaver Haberl, "Die römische 'schola cantorum' und die päpstlichen Kapellsänger bis zur Mitte des 16. Jahrhunderts" (as well as Elaine Debenedictis, "The 'Schola Cantorum' in Rome during the High Middle Ages [Italy]"). For the connection between the early chant books, particularly Gregory's (supposed) antiphonary, and later manuscripts of Frankish provenance, see Karl Gustav Fellerer, "Die römische Schola cantorum und die Verbreitung des liturgischen Gesangs," also Helmut Hucke, "Toward a New Historical View of Gregorian Chant," esp. 446ff., 464–66.

45. For the word "iocale" in connection with the treasures belonging to the chapel of the College of Navarre, see chap. 3, nn. 37–38.

46. The author appears to be referring to the practice of lengthening short syllables of dissyllabic words to correspond to their stress accent. Hence ♪ ♪ and

♪ ♪ for example, might be per-
bī - bet

formed as ♪♪ and ♪♪ (see ex. 15).
       ví - a   bí - bet

47. In the 1536 ed., "vel" appears in red type, as does the next "vel" (preceding "Magnificat"), the "e(t)c." at the end of sentence 49, the "e(t)c." following "israel" in sentence 50, the "et" following "dominus" in sentence 54, the fourfold "de" in sentence 59, the phrase "et

chorus dicit" in sentence 63, the word "e(t)c." (following "letare") in the same, and "e(t)" following "Regina" in sentence 64.

48. "De torrente in via bibet" (misspelled in source as "bibit") forms the first hemistich of the seventh and last verse of the psalm beginning "Dixit Dominus Domino meo" (Psalm 109). The author seems to be referring to the first unaccented syllable of "torrente," with its two-note neume.

49. Both "ni" and "fi" of "Magnificat" are short syllables. Le Munerat already mentioned the practice of altering "Magnificat" in performance (see the sentence preceding ex. 1).

50. On the word "supposita" as "added" or "subjoined," see sentence 62, specifically the portion reading "inter adiectivum et substantivum appositum et suppositum."

51. By "other tones," the author is referring to tones 2, 5, and 8 for both "Dixit Dominus" and "Beatus vir." In tones 1, 3, 4, and 6, the two syllables of "Dixit" are set to a *punctum* plus *podatus*

(•), and the three of "Beatus" to a
Di - xit

punctum plus *podatus* and *punctum*

Be - a - tus

52. For the preface, beginning "Vere dignum et justum est," see *LU*, 4, 8–10 (it introduces the Sanctus); for Pater noster, see *LU*, 6. As for the lessons chanted by boys (so we are told) on the three days preceding Easter, they appear to be the various portions of the Lamentations of Jeremiah recited during the First Nocturn of Matins, on Maundy Thursday, Good Friday, and Holy Saturday, as part

of the Tenebrae service (cf. *LU,* 626–32, 669–75, 715–22). The Passions, i.e., the Gospel narratives of the sufferings of Jesus from the night of the Last Supper to his death, are read at Mass on Palm Sunday (*LU,* 596–99, according to Matthew), on Tuesday of Holy Week (*LU,* 607–10, according to Mark), on Wednesday of Holy Week (*LU,* 606–19, according to Luke), and on Good Friday (*LU,* 700–702, according to John). The Book of the Generations ("Liber generationis Jesu Christi, filii David, filii Abraham," etc.) belonged to Matins of Christmas Day until its removal from the liturgy with the adoption of the Tridentine breviary (cf. Peter Wagner, *Einführung in die gregorianischen Melodien* III: 251–57, including references, on p. 252n., to early studies by Emil Bohn, Dom Joseph Pothier, and others in the *Revue du Chant Grégorien* [1897], *Kirchenmusik* [1908] and the *Gregoriusblatt* [1908, 1915, 1916]).

53. See ex. 2.

54. See exx. 1 and 16.

55. 1536 ed.: "doctor."

56. Ibid.: "dimittitur" (i.e., present instead of the future tense "dimittetur" in 1490).

57. Both editions have the misprint "sede qualiter."

58. For earlier references to "Gaudeamus [omnes in Domino]" and "Statuit [ei Dominus]," see exx. 8a–b, 14. In the case of "Statuit," "timeas," and "gaudia," the author would seem to be referring, not to the penultimate, but to the antepenultimate syllable. For other versions of "Ne timeas" (limiting ourselves to antiphons and introits), see *Antiphonaire monastique . . . de Worcester,*

in *Paléographie musicale* XII: 320 ("Ne timeas a facie," antiphon, with "timeas" set as), *Graduale romanum,* 504 ("Ne timeas Zacharia . . . oratio," introit, with "timeas" as), etc. For other readings of the hymn "Beata nobis," see Bruno Stäblein, ed., *Die mittelalterlichen Hymnenmelodien,* 339, 421 (mode 1); 146 (mode 3); 232, 354, 449 (mode 4); etc.

59. For another verson of this antiphon, with "Regina caeli" set as , see *Antiphonale romanum,* [131]; and for a still simpler version, with "Regina caeli" set as , see *LU,* 278. In all readings, the portion "Regina caeli," as edited, is intoned by the soloist, with the chorus following on "laetare," etc.

60. The rhetoric implies, though without stating it: "But this is not the case in music."

61. Feast day for Saint Bartholomew: August 24.

62. The verse "Ruga carens et" may be traced to the sequence "Laudemus omnes inclita Bartholomei merita." For the text, tentatively ascribed to Adam of St. Victor (d. 1177 or 1192), see *Analecta hymnica medii aevi,* ed. Guido Dreves and Clemens Blume, vol. 55 (*Thesauri hymnologici prosarium. Die Sequenzen des Thesaurus Hymnologicus H. A. Daniels und anderer Sequenzenausgaben* [pt. II, vol. II]), pp. 104–06. It appears there, under "Sequentiae rhythmicae et rigmatae," as a series of twelve couplets, two octaves,

one quatrain, and five final couplets
("Ruga carens" introducing a couplet
numbered 17). As arranged in *Les proses
d'Adam de Saint-Victor,* the sequence consists of fifteen quatrains, of which "Ruga
carens" opens the third line of the
twelfth (see under ex. 20a); the text is
printed there on pp. 211–12, its musical
setting on pp. 300–302 (the latter based
on Paris, Bibliothèque Nationale, MS
fonds latin 14452, a gradual from the
Abbey of St. Victor prior to 1239). For a
listing of the sequence under "the first
extant Victorine sequence repertory,"
see Margot E. Fassler, "Who was Adam
of St. Victor? The Evidence of the Sequence Manuscripts," esp. 246.

63. In the 1536 ed., the concluding para-
graph (explicit plus colophon) is replaced by a new colophon: "Imprimebat
desiderius Maheu bibliopole parisij i(m)-
pensis honesti viri Ambrosij Girault.
anno a nato christo. M. D. xxxvj.
Mense Januarij."

64. By the "old . . . rule," Le Munerat
refers to part of the prefatory material to
the martyrology, namely, the section entitled "Prologus primus pro lectionibus
moralibus ecclesiastice discipline regulam continentibus" (fols. a ii–iii). By
the "new . . . rule," he refers to the regulations of the Council of Basel for performing the liturgy (printed, after the
martyrology, on fols. n iv–o ii^v; see appendix 1).

QUI PRECEDENTI TRACTATU

1. All editorial additions are indicated by
brackets. Parentheses are used for the
completion of words printed in abbreviation. In the source, sentences 3,

5, 14, and 15 were indented as new
paragraphs.

2. Le Munerat refers here to his remarks
under sentences 22–25 of the previous
treatise.

3. In the print, "precipue" and "q(ue)"
are separated.

4. Printed as "et si."

5. Priscian (early 6th cent.), author of
the *Institutiones grammaticae,* exceeding all
works of the Latin grammarians in detail
and breadth of coverage (it occupies
vols. II–III of the *Grammatici latini,* ed.
Heinrich Keil). Cicero (106–44 B.C.),
who, in addition to his philosophical
works and his letters, composed more
than a hundred orations (of which some
forty-eight are lost) and several works
on rhetoric (*De inventione, De oratore,
Brutus, Orator, De optimo genere oratorum,
Partitiones oratoriae, Topica*). Quintilian
(A.D. 1st cent.), author of the *Institutio
oratoria* in twelve books, covering the
education of an orator from childhood
to full maturity ("vir bonus dicendi pe-
ritus": XII. i. 1) Valerius Maximus, author of a book of historical anecdotes for
the use of rhetoricians (*Factorum et dictorum memorabilium libri IX,* dated A.D.
c. 31); in book VIII, chap. 10, he relates
the story of Gaius Graccus's basing his
oration on musical accents. Vergil (70–
19 B.C.), author of no known grammatical or rhetorical works, though he
studied the *artes sermonicales,* as was
customary, in his youth; as the greatest
poet of Roman antiquity, he epitomized
a literary approach to composition.

6. Here Le Munerat seems to be using
"subiectum" in the double sense of
"subject" and "subjected" (i.e., subordinate), the latter after the first treatise,

sentences 15, 21, and the present one, sentences 1, 9, 14. He sets up the categorical proposition "speech is sung," in which "speech" functions as subject and "is sung" as predicate. Since the predicate "allows" the singing of speech, it follows that speech is subordinate to song. Said otherwise, speech forms a species or subgenus of the larger category formed by song. On predicates and predication in formal logic, see Aristotle, *Categories,* 1ᵇ10–24, 2ᵃ11–4ᵇ19, 10ᵇ17–23, 11ᵇ38–12ᵃ17, 12ᵃ40, ᵇ29; *De interpretatione,* 17ᵃ40, ᵇ12–16, 19ᵇ19, 20ᵇ31–21ᵃ32; *Metaphysics,* book VI (or *Zeta*); *Prior Analytics,* 24ᵇ17, ᵇ26, 25ᵇ22, 41ᵃ15, 43ᵃ25, 48ᵃ41, 49ᵃ16.

7. See *De moderatione et concordia,* exx. 8b, 14, 18a.

8. Refers to sentence 3 on the measurability of song.

9. For similar statements in writings of Aristides Quintilianos, Dionysios of Halicarnassus, Aristoxenos, and others, see Thomas Mathiesen, "Rhythm and Meter in Ancient Greek Music," esp. 160–65.

10. Here Le Munerat refers to that portion of sentence 6 reading "talia autem sunt subiecta dicunt dyaletici qualia permittuntur ab eorum predicatis."

11. See sentence 4, where Le Munerat names the same instruments, though using "vox animalis" for the present "instrumenta corporalia." By "animal" or "corporal" means of sound production, the theorist refers to human voices, which, as we know from sentence 13, can dispense with words yet still create melodies.

12. See *De moderatione,* sentence 16.

13. The original reads "distrīen"

(the "en" seemingly a typographical inversion).

14. The Latin of the portion from "cuius" to end of sentence is corrupt.

15. The "measure," that is, of melody and speech.

16. Original reads "satvis."

APPENDIX I

1. Here Le Munerat interjects his own comment (in parentheses): "Nota q(uod) tanta erat nostris diebus in ecclesia parisiensi huius constitutionis observantia: ut etia(m) cu(m) decreto suo p(ar)ticulari irritante quod sequit(ur) districte observaret(ur)." Or in translation: "Note that, in our day, the observance of this regulation was so widespread in the Parisian church as [for the regulation] to be strictly observed along with its particular decree instigating the following [action to be taken in case of its violation]." The text continues as above ("Nullus debet," etc.).

2. To which Le Munerat adds parenthetically: "Quod ad futura(m) utina(m) pro futura(m) rei me(m)oria(m) ut cetere ecclesie tam seculares q(uam) regulares si que fortassis no(n) observant: ad observa(n)tia(m) co(n)simile(m) excitentur appositu(m) est." Or in translation: "As has been designated for the future recollection of this matter—let us hope it is advantageous—so that other churches both secular and regular, if any possibly do not observe [the instructions], may be aroused to a similar observance [of them]." The text continues as above ("Et cum psallendi," etc.).

3. The reference may be to solo singers

or, more likely, to those of superior rank in the clerical hierarchy.

4. After Philippians 2:10; the Vulgate has "ut in nomine Iesu omni genu flectat caelestium et terrestrium et infernorum" (cf. *Biblia sacra iuxta vulgatam versionem* II: 1817).

5. Here Le Munerat interjects his own comment: "Salvis tamen laudabilibus consuetudinibus statutis ac observantiis specialibus ecclesiarum singularu(m) regni et delphinatus." Or in translation: "Exceptions occur, however, when praiseworthy customs, statutes, and spe-cial observances of individual churches within the kingdom or the Dauphiné rule otherwise." The text continues with regulation II above ("Quo tempore," etc.).

6. Psalm 94 (the Invitatory Psalm), sung at the beginning of Matins (cf. *Liber usualis,* 368, 765, 863, etc.).

7. After Ecclesiasticus 18:23; the Vulgate has "et noli esse quasi homo qui temptat Deum" for the second hemistich (cf. *Biblia sacra* II: 1051).

8. "Legendu(m)" and "ve" are separated in print.

Bibliography

Only those items to which reference is made in the body of the text or in the footnote material are entered. Titles having an initial article or preposition are filed according to their first noun or adjective: thus *La danse,* etc., occurs under the letter D, or *Ex sacro,* etc., under the letter S. Most edited works are listed by title.

Primary Sources. They include editions of music (listed by their composer or their title) and anthologies of theoretical writings. Among the more important works consulted, though not recorded below, are the *Auctarium chartularii universitatis parisiensis,* ed. H. Denifle, É. Châtelain et al. (Paris, 1894–1942, 5 vols.), and a number of music manuscripts in Paris, Bibliothèque Nationale (MSS lat. 864[1], 880[1], 1140, 1331, 1336, etc.).

Secondary Literature. Library inventories are indexed by name of library, then city (e.g., Newberry Library, Chicago), but for the library of the College of Navarre, see under Navarre. Other works consulted as a matter of course include *The Catholic Encyclopedia* (New York, 1907–14, 16 vols.), the British Library General Catalogue, the *Catalogue général des livres imprimés de la Biblio-* *thèque Nationale (auteurs),* John Bryden and David Hughes's *Index of Gregorian Chant* (Cambridge, Mass., 1969, 2 vols.), Carl Marbach's *Carmina scripturarum* (Strasbourg, 1907), and Andrew Hughes's *Medieval Manuscripts for Mass and Office* (Toronto, 1982), to name a few.

PRIMARY SOURCES

Adam of St. Victor (d. 1177 or 1192). *Les proses d'Adam de Saint-Victor: texte et musique,* ed. L'Abbé E. Misset and Pierre Aubry. Paris: H. Welter, 1900. Repr. New York: Broude, 1969.

Agricola, Alexander (c. 1446–1506). *Opera omnia,* ed. Edward Lerner. Rome: American Institute of Musicology, 1961–70, 5 vols.

Ailred (or Aelred [Aelredus abbas rievallensis]; d. 1167). *Speculum charitatis.* In vol. CXCV of *Patrologia latina,* cols. 501–658.

Analecta hymnica medii aevi, ed. Guido Dreves and Clemens Blume. Leipzig: O. R. Reisland, 1886–1922, 55 vols. See also *Register,* ed. Max Lutolf (Bern: Francke, 1978, 3 vols.).

Anonymous IV. *De mensuris et discantu* (between 1270 and 1280). See *Der Musiktraktat des Anonymus 4,* ed. Fritz

Reckow (Wiesbaden: Franz Steiner, 1967, 2 vols.), also *Anonymus IV,* ed. and tr. Luther Dittmer (Brooklyn: Institute of Medieval Music, 1959).

Antiphonaire monastique . . . de Lucques (Lucca, Biblioteca Capitolare, MS 601; 12th cent.). See vol. IX of *Paléographie musicale* (1906).

Antiphonaire monastique . . . de Worcester (Worcester, Cathedral Library, MS F. 160; 13th cent.). See vol. XII of *Paléographie musicale* (1922).

Antiphonale monasticum pro diurnis horis. Paris: Desclée, 1934.

Antiphonale romanum (Antiphonale sacrosanctae romanae ecclesiae pro diurnis horis). Paris: Desclée, 1924.

Aristotle (384–22 B.C.). *Categories* and *De interpretatione,* tr. with notes by J. L. Ackrill. Oxford: Clarendon, 1963.

———. *Metaphysics (Metaphysica),* ed. and tr. W. D. Ross. Oxford: Clarendon, 1908. 2nd ed. 1928 (vol. VIII in *The Works of Aristotle,* ed. W. D. Ross, Oxford, 1928–52, 12 vols.).

———. *Prior Analytics,* ed. and tr. Hugh Tredennick. London: Heinemann, 1938.

Basil. "Homily on Psalm 1" (later 4th cent.). For Engl. tr., see Oliver Strunk, ed., *Source Readings in Music History,* 64–66.

Benedict (Benedictus de Nursia). Rule (*Regula monachorum;* c. 540). In vol. LXVI of *Patrologia latina,* cols. 215–931. See also *The Rule of St. Benedict: The Abingdon Copy,* ed. John Chamberlin (Leiden: Brill, 1982), and for Latin-English version, *Benedict of Nursia: The Rule of Saint Benedict,* ed.

D. O. Hunter Blair (Fort Augustus, Scotland: The Abbey Press, 1934).

Biblia sacra iuxta vulgatam versionem. 2nd rev. ed. Stuttgart: Württembergische Bibelanstalt, 1975, 2 vols.

Boethius, Anicius Manlius Torquatus Severinus (c. 480–c. 524). *De institutione musica libri quinque,* ed. Gottfried Friedlein. Leipzig: Teubner, 1867.

Breviarium magnum ad usum parisiensem, ed. Jean Le Munerat. Paris: Jean Dupré, 1492. (See above, chap. 2, no. 5.)

Breviarium parisiense, ed. Jean Le Munerat. Paris: printed by Pierre Le Rouge for Vincent Commin, 1488. (See above, chap. 2, no. 1.)

Breviarium sanctae, patriarcalis, ac metropolitane bituricensis ecclesie. Opus profecto emendatissimum. In quo singula officia festivitatum totius anni cum regulis amplissimis continentur. Limoges: Paul Berton, 1522.

Brumel, Antoine (c. 1460–c. 1515). *Opera omnia,* ed. Barton Hudson. Rome: American Institute of Musicology, 1969–72, 6 vols.

Capella, Martianus (early 5th cent.). *De nuptiis Philologiae et Mercurii.* See Stahl, William Harris and Richard Johnson, *Martianus Capella,* etc. (under Secondary Literature).

Cassiodorus, Marcus Aurelius (c. 485–c. 580). *De quatuor mathematicis disciplinis,* extracted from his *Institutiones divinarum et humanarum litterarum.* In vol. LXX of *Patrologia latina,* esp. cols. 1203–20.

Chartularium universitatis parisiensis, ed. Henri Denifle and Émile Châtelain. Paris: Delalain, 1889–97, 4 vols. (covering period from 1200 to 1452).

Claudin de Sermisy (c. 1490–1562). *Opera omnia,* ed. Gaston Allaire and Isabelle Cazeaux. Rome: American Institute of Musicology, 1970 on (5 vols. to 1977).

Clemens non Papa (c. 1515–1555 or 1556). *Opera omnia,* ed. K. Ph. Bernet Kempers. Rome: American Institute of Musicology, 1953 on (20 vols. to 1973).

Cleonides (A.D. 2nd cent.). *Introduction to Harmonics.* For Engl. tr., see Oliver Strunk, ed., *Source Readings in Music History,* 34–46.

Compendium musices confectum ad faciliorem instructionem cantum choralem discentium. Venice: Lucantonio Giunta, 1513.

Concilium basilense: Studien und Quellen zur Geschichte des Concils von Basel, ed. Johann Haller, G. Beckmann, R. Wackernagel and G. Coggiola. Basel: R. Reich, 1896–1904, 5 vols.

Conrad von Zabern. *De modo bene cantandi choralem cantum in multitudine personarum.* Mainz: Peter Schöffer, 1474. For a modern edition, see Karl-Werner Gümpel, "Die Musiktraktate Conrads von Zabern," *Akademie der Wissenschaften und der Literatur: Abhandlungen der Geistes- und sozialwissenschaftlichen Klasse* nos. 1–7 (1956): 260–80.

La danse macabre. Paris: Guy Marchant, 1486. Facs. repr. (with notes by Pierre Champion) Paris: Éditions des Quatre Chemins, 1925 (and another one, with notes by Valentin Dufour, after the *editio princeps* [1484]; Paris: L. Willem, 1875).

Denis le Chartreux. *Speculum aureum animae peccatricis.* Paris: Guy Marchant, 1499. (Copy in Paris, Bibliothèque Nationale, D 13121⁵, entitled *Opusculum aureum,* etc.)

Donatus, Aelius (A.D. 4th cent.). *Ars grammatica* (two books, *minor* and *maior*). In vol. IV of *Grammatici latini,* ed. Heinrich Keil, 355–402.

Dufay, Guillaume (c. 1400–1474). *Opera omnia,* ed. Heinrich Besseler and Guillaume de Van. Rome: American Institute of Musicology, 1947–64, 6 vols.

Euclid (fl. c. 300 B.C.). *Opera omnia,* ed. I. L. Heiberg and H. Menge. Leipzig: Teubner, 1883–1916, 8 vols. plus supp.

Gaffurius, Franchinus. *Practica musicae.* Milan: Guillaume Le Signerre, 1496. Facs. ed. Farnborough: Gregg, 1967.

Galilei, Vincenzo. *Dialogo della musica antica, et della moderna.* Florence: Giorgio Marescotti, 1581. Facs. ed. New York: Broude, 1967.

Gallia christiana. See under Secondary Literature.

Genet (Carpentras), Elzéar (c. 1470–1548). *Opera omnia,* ed. Albert Seay. Rome: American Institute of Musicology, 1972–73, 5 vols. in 7.

Gerbert, Martin, ed. *Scriptores ecclesiastici de musica sacra potissimum.* St. Blaise: Typis San-Blasianis, 1784, 3 vols. Repr. Hildesheim: Georg Olms, 1963.

Graduale bituricense. Bourges: J. Boyer & J.-B. Christ, 1741, 2 vols.

Graduale romanum (Graduale sacrosanctae romanae ecclesiae de tempore et de sanctis). Paris: Desclée, 1924.

Graduel de Saint-Yrieix (Paris, Bibliothèque Nationale, MS 903; 11th cent.). See vol. XIII of *Paléographie musicale* (1925).

Grammatici latini, ed. Heinrich Keil. Leipzig: Teubner, 1855–70, 8 vols.

Guarna, Andreas (c. 1470–1517). *Bellum grammaticale Nominis et Verbi regum, de principalitate orationis inter se contendentium* (Cremona, 1511, and many later editions). Paris: ex officina Roberti Stephani, 1539. Johann Spangenberg (d. 1550) reworked it in 1534; see Robert Schneider, ed. and tr., *Grammatischer Krieg* (2nd ed. Berlin: Friedberg & Mode, 1895). For an Engl. tr. from 1569 (*Guarna's "Bellum grammaticale": A Discourse of Great War and Dissention between 2 Worthy Princes the Noun and the Verb, Contending for the Chefe Place or Dignitie in Oration*), see John Somers, ed., *A Collection of Scarce and Valuable Tracts* (2nd ed. London: T. Cadell and W. Davies, 1809–15, 13 vols.) I: 533–54. Johannes Bolte edited the original and commented on its various reworkings in his *Andrea Guarnas "Bellum grammaticale" und seine Nachahmungen* (Berlin: A. Hofmann, 1908).

Guerson, Guillaume. *Utilissime musicales regule necessarie plani cantus simplicis contrapuncti* (c. 1495). 8th ed. Paris: F. Regnault, 1518.

Guilliaud, Maximilian. *Rudiments de musique practique*. Paris: Nicolas Du Chemin, 1554.

Hardouin, Jean, ed. *Conciliorum collectio regia maxima*. Paris: ex typographia regia, 1714–15, 12 vols.

Instituta patrum de modo psallendi sive cantandi (early 13th cent.). In Martin Gerbert, ed., *Scriptores ecclesiastici* I: 5–8.

Isidore of Seville. *Etymologiarum sive originum libri XX* (622–33), ed. W. M. Lindsay. Oxford: Clarendon, 1911.

Jacob, Louis. *Traicté des plus belles bibliothèques,* etc. See under Secondary Literature.

Jacques [Jacobus] de Liège. *Speculum musicae* (1330–40), ed. Roger Bragard. Rome: American Institute of Musicology, 1955–73, 7 vols.

Jean de Muris. *Musica speculativa* (1323). In Martin Gerbert, ed., *Scriptores ecclesiastici* III: 249–83.

Jerome of Moravia. *Tractatus de musica* (after 1272), ed. Simon M. Cserba. Regensburg: Friedrich Pustet, 1935.

Johannes de Grocheo. *Ars musicae* (or *De musica;* c. 1300). See *Der Musiktraktat des Johannes de Grocheo,* ed. Ernst Rohloff (Leipzig: Reinecke, 1943), also *Concerning Music,* tr. Albert Seay (Colorado Springs: Colorado College, 1967).

John the Deacon (Johannes diaconus romanus). *Sancti Gregorii Magni Vita* (872–82). In vol. LXXV of *Patrologia latina,* cols. 59–242.

John of Salisbury (Johannes parvus saresberiensis). *Polycraticus, sive de nugis curialium et vestigiis philosophorum* (1159). In vol. CXCIX of *Patrologia latina,* cols. 379–822.

Josquin des Prez (c. 1440–1521). *Werken,* ed. Albert Smijers et al. Leipzig, Amsterdam: C. F. W. Siegel, F. Kistner, G. Alsbach, 1921–69, 55 fascicles.

La Fage, Adrien de, ed. *Essais de diphthérographie musicale*. Paris:

O. Legouix, 1864. Repr. Amsterdam: Knuf, 1964.

Lampadius. *Compendium musices, tam figurati quàm plani cantus ad formam dialoghi* (1537). 5th ed. Bern: Samuel Apiarius, 1554.

Launoy, Jean de. *Opera omnia, etc.* See under Secondary Literature.

Lebeuf, Jean. *Traité historique et pratique sur le chant ecclésiastique.* Paris: C. J. B. Hérissant, 1741. Repr. Geneva: Minkoff, 1972.

Lefèvre, Jacques, d'Étaples (Jacobus Faber stapulensis). *Musica libris demonstrata quatuor.* Paris: Johann Higman & Wolfgang Hopyl, 1496.

Le Munerat, Jean. Commentary on a sequence (*prosa*) belonging to the liturgy for Bourges. Paris, Bibliothèque de l'Arsenal, MS 848, fols. 56ᵛ–58ᵛ. (See chap. 2, item no. 6.)

———. *Compendium divinorum officiorum sive Tabula sine quo esse nolo.* Paris: Jean Dupré, 1496. (See chap. 2, item no. 10.)

———. *De dedicatione ecclesie parisiensis.* Paris: Guy Marchant, 1496. Later ed. Paris: Pierre Targa, 1633. (See chap. 2, item no. 7.)

———. *De moderatione et concordia grammatice et musice,* in volume containing Le Munerat's edition of Usuard's Martyrology (Paris: Guy Marchant, 1490), fols. o iv–viᵛ (*recte* o iii–vᵛ). (See chap. 2, item no. 11, and for full transcription, pt. II, first treatise.)

———. *Qui precedenti tractatu nullam adesse rationem vel demonstrativum.* [Paris: Guy Marchant, 1493.] Added, as extra folio, to Le Munerat's personal copy of his edition of Usuard's

Martyrology, which he later presented to the chapel library of the College of Navarre. (See chap. 2, item no. 12, and for full transcription, pt. II, second treatise.)

———. *Sancta et salubris cogitatio,* at end of Denis le Chartreux, *Speculum* (or *Opusculum) aureum anime peccatricis* (Paris: Guy Marchant, 1499), fol. c iv (= 36ʳ). (See chap. 2, item no. 8.)

For Jean Le Munerat's editions, see separate works by title.

Liber usualis. 1st ed. 1896. Tournai: Desclée, 1952. Abbreviated *LU.*

Mansi, Gian Domenico, ed. *Sacrorum conciliorum nova, et amplissima collectio.* Florence: A. Zatta, 1759–98, 31 vols.

Martirologium (by Usuard), ed. Jean Le Munerat. Paris: Guy Marchant, 1490. 2nd ed. Paris: Ambroise Girault, 1536. (See chap. 2, item no. 4, also entry below for Usuard.)

Martyrologium romanum. Turin: P. Marietti, 1911. For Engl. tr., see *The Roman Martyrology* (Baltimore: John Murphy, 1907).

Missale ad usum ecclesie cathalaunensis, ed. Jean Le Munerat. Paris: Jean Dupré, 1489. (See chap. 2, item no. 3.)

Missale parisiense, ed. Jean Le Munerat. Paris: Guillaume Le Caron, Jean Belin & Jean Dupré, 1489. (See chap. 2, item no. 2.)

Münster, Sebastian (1489–1552). *La cosmographie universelle de tout le monde,* ed. François de Belleforest. Paris: M. Sonnius, 1575, 2 vols. in 3. (Originally *Cosmographiae universalis lib. VI;* Basel: Heinrich Petri, 1550.)

Ornithoparcus, Andreas. *Musice active micrologus.* Leipzig: Valentin Schumann, 1517. Tr. by John Dowland as *Micrologus, or Introduction: Containing the Art of Singing* (London: Thomas Adams, 1609; facs. ed. New York: Da Capo, 1969).

Paléographie musicale. Solesmes: Abbaye Saint-Pierre (and other imprints for later volumes in series), 1889–1958, 17 vols. Repr. Bern: H. Lang, 1969 on.

Patrologia latina (Patrologia cursus completus . . . series latina), ed. Jacques P. Migne. Paris: Garnier, 1841–1905, 221 vols.

Plato (d. 347 B.C.). *The Dialogues of Plato,* tr. Benjamin Jowett (1871). 3rd ed. London: Oxford University, 1892, 5 vols.

Priscian (Priscianus; early 6th cent.). *Institutiones grammaticae,* also *De accentibus liber,* in *Grammatici latini,* ed. Heinrich Keil, vols. II–III.

Processionale monasticum ad usum congregationis gallicae ordinis sancti Benedicti. Solesmes: Abbaye Saint-Pierre, 1893.

Quintilian (Marcus Fabius Quintilianus; A.D. 1st cent.). *Institutio oratoria (Institutionis oratoriae libri XII),* ed. M. Winterbottom. Oxford: Clarendon, 1970, 2 vols.

Raulin, Jean. *Collatio de perfecta religionis plantatione, incremento, et instauratione.* Paris: Guy Marchant, 1499.

Rossetti, Biagio. *Libellus de rudimentis musices.* Verona: Stefano e fratelli de Nicolinis de Sabio, 1529. Facs. ed. New York: Broude, 1968.

Rutgerus Sycamber de Venray. *Dialogus de musica (or De recta, congrua devotaque cantione dialogus; c. 1500),* ed. Fritz Soddemann. Cologne: Arno Volk, 1963.

Ex sacro basiliensi concilio Canonica regula, ed. Jean Le Munerat, in volume containing his edition of Usuard's Martyrology (Paris: Guy Marchant, 1490), fols. n iv–o ii^v. (See chap. 2, item no. 9, and for a transcription of part of the *Canonica regula,* see appendix 1.)

Sebastiani, Claudio. *Bellum musicale, inter plani et mensuralis cantus reges, de principatu in musicae provincia obtinendo, contendentes.* Strasbourg: Paulus Machaeropoeus, 1563.

Sirmond, Jacques, ed. *Concilia antiqua Galliae cum epistolis pontificum, principum constitutionibus et aliis gallicanae rei ecclesiasticae monumentis.* Paris: Sébastien Cramoisy, 1629, 3 vols., plus supp. by P. Delalande, 1666. Repr. Aalen: Scientia, 1970–72.

Spangenberg, Johann. *Bellum grammaticale.* See under Guarna, Andreas.

———. *Prosodia in usum iuventutis northusianae, congesta per Ioan. Spang.* Wittenberg: Georg Rhau, 1535.

———. *Quaestiones musicae in usum scholae northusianae, per Ioann. Spang. Herdess. collectae.* Nuremberg: Johann Petreius, 1536.

———. *Trivii erotemata, hoc est grammaticae, dialecticae, rhetoricae, quaestiones, ex doctissimorum nostri seculi virorum libris, in puerorum usum congestae, per Ioannem Spangenberg.* N.p., 1544. (In later eds. [1545, 1549], title begins *Erotemata trivii;* no listing in *Écrits imprimés.*)

Stäblein, Bruno, ed. *Die mittelalterlichen Hymnenmelodien des Abendlandes.* Kassel: Bärenreiter, 1956.

Strunk, Oliver, ed. *Source Readings in*

Music History. New York: Norton, 1950.

Usuard (Usuardus; d. c. 875). *Le martyrologe d'Usuard,* ed. Jacques Dubois (after Paris, Bibliothèque Nationale, MS lat. 13745). Brussels: Société des Bollandistes, 1965.

———. *Martyrologium.* In *Patrologia latina* CXXIII: cols. 599–911, and CXXIV: cols. 9–860. (The introduction, in vol. CXXIII: cols. 432–598, contains an extensive review of manuscript and printed sources.)

Valerius Maximus. *Factorum et dictorum memorabilium libri IX* (A.D. c. 31), ed. Carl Kempf. Leipzig: Teubner, 1888.

Vulgate. See *Biblia sacra iuxta vulgatam versionem.*

Wollick (Volcyr), Nicolaus. *Enchiridion musices* (1509). 3rd ed. Paris: Jehan Petit & François Regnault, 1512. Facs. ed. Geneva: Minkoff, 1972.

Zarlino, Gioseffo. *Le istitutioni harmoniche.* Venice, 1558. Facs. ed. New York: Broude, 1965.

———. *Sopplimenti musicali.* Venice: Francesco de' Franceschi Senese, 1588 (vol. III in the series *De tutte l'opere del R. M. Gioseffo Zarlino da Chioggia,* 1588–89, 4 vols.). Facs. ed. Ridgewood, New Jersey: Gregg, 1967.

SECONDARY LITERATURE

Achelis, Hans. *Die Martyrologien, ihre Geschichte und ihr Wert.* Berlin: Weidmann, 1900.

Albrecht, Hans. "Humanismus." In vol. VI of *Die Musik in Geschichte und Gegenwart,* cols. 895–918 (preceded there by August Buck, "Der Humanismus als geistige Bewegung," cols. 877–95).

Antonowcyz, Myroslaw. "Zur Autorschaftsfrage der Motetten *Absolve, quaesumus, Domine* und *Inter natos mulierum.*" *Tijdschrift van de Vereniging voor Nederlandse Muziekgeschiedenis* XX (1966): 154–69.

Arlt, Wulf. *Ein Festoffizium des Mittelalters aus Beauvais in seiner liturgischen und musikalischen Bedeutung.* Cologne: Volk, 1970, 2 vols.

Baudrillart, Alfred, et al. *Dictionnaire d'histoire et de géographie ecclésiastiques.* Paris: Letouzay & Ané, 1912–38, 10 vols.

Becker, Otto Frederick. "The 'Maîtrise' in Northern France and Burgundy during the Fifteenth Century." Ph.D. diss., George Peabody College for Teachers (Nashville, Tenn.), 1967.

Berry, Mary (Sister Thomas More). "The Performance of Plainsong in the Later Middle Ages and the Sixteenth Century." Ph.D. diss., Cambridge University, 1968.

———. "The Performance of Plainsong in the Later Middle Ages and the Sixteenth Century." *Proceedings of the Royal Musical Association* XCII (1965–66): 121–34.

Bibliothèque de l'Arsenal (Paris). Martin, Henri. *Catalogue des manuscrits de la Bibliothèque de l'Arsenal.* Paris: Plon, 1885–99, 8 vols.

Bibliothèque Mazarine (Paris). Marais, Paul. *Catalogue des incunables de la Bibliothèque Mazarine.* Paris: Welter, 1893.

———. Molinier, Auguste. *Catalogue des manuscrits de la Bibliothèque Mazarine.* Paris: Plon, 1885–92, 4 vols.

Bibliothèque Nationale (Paris). *Catalogue général des manuscrits français, anciens petits fonds français*. Paris: Bibliothèque Nationale, 1897–1902, 3 vols.

———. Delisle, Léopold. *Le cabinet des manuscrits de la Bibliothèque Nationale*. Paris: Imprimerie Nationale, 1868–81, 4 vols.

Bielitz, Mathias. *Musik und Grammatik: Studien zur mittelalterlichen Musiktheorie*. Munich: Katzbichler, 1977.

Black, Antony. *Council and Commune: The Conciliar Movement and the Fifteenth-Century Heritage*. Shepherdtown, W. Va.: Patmos, 1979.

Bohatta, Hanns. *Bibliographie der Breviere, 1501–1850*. Leipzig: K. W. Hiersemann, 1937.

Bossuat, Robert. "Le théâtre scolaire au collège de Navarre (XIVme–XVIIme siècles)." In *Mélanges d'histoire du théâtre du Moyen-Âge et de la Renaissance offerts à Gustave Cohen* (Paris: Nizet, 1950), 165–76.

Boulay, César Égasse de. *Historia universitatis parisiensis ipsius fundationem, nationes, facultates . . . à Carolo M[agno] ad nostra tempora ordine chronologico complectens*. Paris: François Noël, 1665–73, 6 vols. Repr. Frankfurt: Minerva, 1966.

Bouvier, Henri. *Histoire de l'église de l'ancien archidiocèse de Sens*. Paris: Alphonse Picard, 1906–11, 3 vols.

Brenet, Michel [Marie Bobillier]. *Les musiciens de la Sainte-Chapelle du Palais*. Paris: Alphonse Picard, 1910. Repr. Geneva: Minkoff, 1973.

———. *Musique et musiciens de la vieille France*. Paris: Félix Alcan, 1911.

British Library (London). *Catalogue of Books Printed in the Fifteenth Century Now in the British Museum* [= British Library]. London: British Museum, 1908 on, in 9 pts.

Brown, Howard Mayer. *Music in the French Secular Theater, 1400–1550*. Cambridge, Mass.: Harvard University, 1963.

Carpenter, Nan. *Music in the Medieval and Renaissance Universities*. Norman, Okla.: University of Oklahoma, 1958. Repr. New York: Da Capo, 1972.

Cazeaux, Isabelle. *French Music in the Fifteenth and Sixteenth Centuries*. Oxford: Basil Blackwood, 1975.

Chailley, Jacques. "Motets inédits du XIVe siècle à la Cathédrale de Sens." *Revue de Musicologie* XXIX (1950): 27–34.

Chambers, Edmund K. *The Medieval Stage*. Oxford: Clarendon, 1903, 2 vols.

Chartier, François-Léon. *L'ancien chapitre de Notre-Dame de Paris et sa maîtrise d'après les documents capitulaires (1326–1790)*. Paris: Perrin, 1897. Repr. Geneva: Minkoff, 1971.

Chevalier, Ulysse. *Répertoire des sources historiques du Moyen-Âge: Topo-bibliographie*. Montbeliard: Société Anonyme de l'Imprimerie Montbéliardaise, 1894 and 1903, 2 vols.

Christian, Arthur. *Débuts de l'imprimerie en France*. Paris: Imprimerie Nationale, 1904.

Claudin, Anatole. *Histoire de l'imprimerie en France au XVe et au XVIe siècle*. Paris: Imprimerie Nationale, 1900–1915, 5 vols.

Collège de Navarre rétabli d'après [sic] les bases de l'enseignement suivi dans l'Université de Paris; avec un pensionnat en pleine activité. Paris: Sétier, 1800.

Copinger, W. A. *Supplement to Hain's*

"Repertorium bibliographicum" or Collections toward a New Edition of that Work. London: Henry Sotheran, 1895–1902, 3 vols.

Corbin, Solange. "La notation musicale neumatique des quatre provinces lyonnaises: Lyon, Rouen, Tours et Sens." Diss., University of Paris, 1957.

Crawford, David. "The *Compendium musices:* Musical Continuity among the Sixteenth-Century Italian Clergy." In *Report of the Thirteenth Congress of the International Musicological Society, Strasbourg 1982,* ed. Marc Honegger, Christian Meyer, and Paul Prévost (Strasbourg: Association des Publications près les Universités de Strasbourg, 1986, 2 vols.) II: 195–216.

Debenedictis, Elaine. "The 'Schola Cantorum' in Rome during the High Middle Ages (Italy)." Ph.D. diss., Bryn Mawr College, 1983.

Desjardins, Ernest Émile. *Géographie historique et administrative de la Gaule romaine.* Paris: Hachette, 1876–93, 4 vols.

Dijk, S. A. van. "Saint Bernard and the *Instituta patrum* of Saint Gall." *Musica Disciplina* IV (1950): 99–109.

——— (now as Dijk, S. J. P. van). "Gregory the Great, Founder of the Urban 'Schola Cantorum.'" *Ephemerides Liturgicae* LXXVII (1963): 345–56.

Dubois, Gérard. *Historia ecclesiae parisiensis.* Paris: F. Muguet, 1690 and 1710, 2 vols.

Du Cange, Charles du Fresne. *Glossarium mediae et infimae latinitatis.* Rev. ed. Niort: L. Favre, 1883–87, 10 vols.

Écrits imprimés concernant la musique, ed.

François Lesure. Munich-Duisburg: G. Henle, 1971, 2 vols.

Eitner, Robert. *Biographisch-Bibliographisches Quellen-Lexikon der Musiker und Musikgelehrten der christlichen Zeitrechnung bis zur Mitte des 19. Jahrhunderts.* Leipzig: Breitkopf & Härtel, 1898–1904, 10 vols.

Elders, Willem. "Humanism and Early Renaissance Music: A Study of the Ceremonial Music by Ciconia and Dufay." *Tijdschrift van de Vereniging voor Nederlandse Muziekgeschiedenis* XXVII (1977): 65–101.

Fabricius, Johann Albert. *Bibliotheca latina mediae et infimae aetatis cum supplemento Christiani Schoettnegii* (1734–46), ed. Gian Domenico Mansi. Padua: Joannes Manfrè, 1754, 6 vols. in 3. Repr. Florence: T. Baracchi, 1858–59.

Farge, James K. *Orthodoxy and Reform in Early Reformation France. The Faculty of Theology of Paris, 1500–1543.* Leiden: Brill, 1985.

Fassler, Margot E. "Who was Adam of St. Victor? The Evidence of the Sequence Manuscripts." *Journal of the American Musicological Society* XXXVII (1984): 233–69.

Fellerer, Karl Gustav. "Die römische Schola cantorum und die Verbreitung des liturgischen Gesangs." In *Geschichte der katholischen Kirchenmusik,* ed. Karl Gustav Fellerer (Kassel: Bärenreiter, 1972 and 76, 2 vols.) I: 182–84.

Fétis, François J. *Biographie universelle des musiciens et bibliographie générale de la musique.* 2nd ed. Paris: Firmin Didot, 1866–70, 8 vols.

Fisquet, Honoré. *La France pontificale (Gallia christiana). Histoire chronologique et biographique des archevêques et* évêques de tous les diocèses de France depuis l'établissement du christianisme jusqu'à nos jours, divisée en 17 provinces ecclésiastiques. Paris: E. Repos, 1864–73, 21 vols.

Forkel, Johann N. *Allgemeine Geschichte der Musik.* Leipzig: Schwickert, 1788 and 1801, 2 vols. Repr. Graz: Akademische Druck- u. Verlagsanstalt, 1967.

———. *Allgemeine Litteratur der Musik.* Leipzig: Schwickert, 1792. Repr. Hildesheim: Georg Olms, 1962.

Franklin, Alfred. *Histoire générale de Paris. Les anciennes bibliothèques de Paris. Églises, monastères, collèges, etc.* Paris: Imprimerie Impériale, 1867–73, 3 vols.

Gaffiot, Félix. *Dictionnaire illustré latin-français.* Paris: Hachette, 1934.

Gallia christiana, in provincias ecclesiasticas distributa; qua series et historia archiepiscoporum, episcoporum, et abbatum Franciae vicinarumque ditionum ab origine ecclesiarum ad nostra tempora deducitur. Paris: Jean-Baptiste Coignard, 1715–1865, 16 vols. Repr. Farnborough, Hampshire: Gregg International, 1970.

Gastoué, Amédée. *Histoire du chant liturgique à Paris des origines à la fin des temps carolingiens.* Paris: Poussielgue, 1904.

Gerbert, Martin. *De cantu et musica sacra a prima ecclesiae aetate usque ad praesens tempus.* St. Blaise: Typis San-Blasianiis, 1774, 2 vols. Repr. Graz: Akademische Druck- u. Verlagsanstalt, 1968.

Gérold, Théodore. *Les pères de l'Église et la musique.* Strasbourg: Imprimerie Alsacienne, 1931. Repr. Geneva: Minkoff, 1973.

Girardot, Auguste-Théodore de and Hyp. Durand. *La Cathédrale de Bourges, description historique et archéologique.* Moulins: P.-A. Desrosiers, 1849.

Gotteri, Nicole. "Le clergé et la vie religieuse dans le diocèse de Bourges au XVᵉ siècle d'après les suppliques en cour de Rome (1434–1484)." Diss., University of Paris, 1974.

La grande encyclopédie: inventaire raisonné des sciences, des lettres et des arts. Paris: Lamirault, [1886–1902], 31 vols.

Guettée, René François Wladimir. *Histoire de l'église de France, composée sur les documents originaux et authentiques.* Lyons and Paris: Guyot, 1847–56, 12 vols.

Gundersheimer, Werner L., ed. *French Humanism, 1470–1600.* London: Macmillan, 1969.

Haberl, Franz Xaver. "Die römische 'schola cantorum' und die päpstlichen Kapellsänger bis zur Mitte des 16. Jahrhunderts." *Vierteljahrsschrift für Musikwissenschaft* III (1887): 189–296.

Hain, Ludwig. *Repertorium bibliographicum, in quo libri omnes ab arte typographica inventa, usque ad annum MD.* Stuttgart and Paris: J. G. Cottae and Jul. Renouard, 1826–38, 4 vols.

Hammerstein, Reinhold. *Tanz und Musik des Todes: Die mittelalterlichen Totentänze und ihr Nachleben.* Bern: Francke, 1980.

Harrán, Don. "The Concept of Battle in Music of the Renaissance." *The Journal of Medieval and Renaissance Studies* XVII (1987): 175–94.

———. *In Search of Harmony: Hebrew and Humanist Elements in Sixteenth-Century Musical Thought.* Neuhausen-Stuttgart: Hänssler-Verlag for the

American Institute of Musicology, 1988.

———. *Word-Tone Relations in Musical Thought. From Antiquity to the Seventeenth Century.* Neuhausen-Stuttgart: Hänssler-Verlag for the American Institute of Musicology, 1986.

Haskins, Charles Homer. *The Rise of Universities.* 1st ed. 1923. Ithaca, New York: Great Seal Books, 1957.

Hefele, Carl Joseph. *Conziliengeschichte, nach den Quellen bearbeitet.* Freiburg im Breisgau: Herder, 1855–90, 9 vols.

Helmrath, Johannes. *Das Basler Konzil 1431–1449: Forschungsbestand und Probleme.* Vienna: Böhlau, 1987.

Héméré, Claude. *De academia parisiensi, qualis primo fuit in insula et episcoporum scholis liber.* Paris: Sébastien Cramoisy, 1637.

Hillairet, Jacques. *Dictionnaire historique des rues de Paris.* Paris: Éditions de Minuit, 1963, 2 vols.

Hucke, Helmut. "Die Entstehung der Überlieferung von einer musikalischen Tätigkeit Gregors des Grossen." *Musikforschung* VIII (1955): 259–64.

———. "Toward a New Historical View of Gregorian Chant." *Journal of the American Musicological Society* XXXIII (1980): 437–67.

Hüschen, Heinrich. "Die Musik im Kreise der *artes liberales.*" In *Gesellschaft für Musikforschung, Kongress-Bericht, Hamburg 1956* (Kassel: Bärenreiter, 1957), 117–23.

Irwin, Joyce. "The Mystical Music of Jean Gerson." In *Early Music History: Studies in Medieval and Early Modern Music,* ed. Iain Fenlon (Cambridge: Cambridge University, 1981 on) I: 187–201.

Jacob, Louis. *Traicté des plus belles bibliothèques publiques et particulières, qui ont esté, et qui sont à présent dans le monde.* Paris: R. le Duc, 1644.

Jourdain, Charles Marie. *Index chronologicus chartarum pertinentium ad historiam universitatis parisiensis, ab ejus originibus ad finem decimi sexti saeculi.* Paris: L. Hachette, 1862.

Kirkendale, Warren. "Ciceronians versus Aristotelians on the Ricercar as Exordium, from Bembo to Bach." *Journal of the American Musicological Society* XXXII (1979): 1–44.

Koch, Josef, ed. *'Artes liberales': Von der antiken Bildung zur Wissenschaft des Mittelalters.* Leiden: Brill, 1959. See esp. Karl Gustav Fellerer, "Die Musica in den *Artes liberales,*" 33–49.

Kremple, Fredrich Awalde. "Cultural Aspects of the Councils of Constance and Basel." Ph.D. diss., University of Minnesota, 1954.

Kristeller, Paul. "Music and Learning in the Early Italian Renaissance." *Journal of Renaissance and Baroque Music* I (1947): 255–74.

Launoy, Jean de. *Opera omnia, ad selectum ordinem revocata, ineditis opusculis aliquot, notis nonnullis dogmaticis, historicis et criticis, auctoris vita . . . aucta et illustrata.* Allobrogian Colony [now Savoy]: Fabre & Barrillot, 1731–32, 5 pts. in 10 vols.

———. *Regii Navarrae gymnasii parisiensis historia.* Paris: widow of Edmond Martin, 1677, 2 vols. 2nd ed. entitled *Academia parisiensis illustrata, quatuor partibus divisa* (Paris: widow of E. Martin and J. Baudot, 1682, 2 vols.).

Lebeuf, Jean. *Histoire de la ville et de tout diocèse de Paris* (1754). New ed. Paris: A. Durand, 1863–70, 4 vols.

Le Brun, Pierre. *Explication literale, historique et dogmatique des prieres et des ceremonies de la messe, suivant les anciens auteurs, et les monumens* [sic] *de la plupart des eglises: avec des dissertations et des notes sur les endroits difficiles, et sur l'origine des rits* [sic]. Paris: F. Delauine, 1716–26, 4 vols.

Leroquais, Victor. *Les bréviaires manuscrits des bibliothèques publiques de France*. Paris: Mâcon & Protat, 1934, 6 vols.

———. *Les sacramentaires et les missels manuscrits des bibliothèques publiques de France*. Paris: Mâcon & Protat, 1924, 4 vols.

Lesure, François. "Bibliographie des éditions musicales publiées par Nicolas Du Chemin (1549–1576)." *Annales Musicologiques* I (1953): 269–373, plus supplements: IV (1956): 251–53; VI (1958–63): 403–06.

Levi, A. H. T., ed. *Humanism in France at the End of the Middle Ages and in the Early Renaissance*. New York: Barnes and Noble, 1970.

Lipphardt, Walther. "Gregor der Grosse und sein Anteil am römischen Antiphonar." In *Atti del Congresso di Musica Sacra, Roma 1950* (Tournai: Desclée, 1952), 248–54.

Lippman, Edward A. "The Place of Music in the System of Liberal Arts." In *Aspects of Medieval and Renaissance Music: A Birthday Offering to Gustave Reese*, ed. Jan LaRue et al. (New York: Norton, 1966), 545–59.

Lowinsky, Edward E. "Humanism in the Music of the Renaissance." In *Medieval and Renaissance Studies,* ed. Frank Tirro (Durham, North Carolina: Duke University, 1982), 87–200.

Mathiesen, Thomas J. "New Fragments of Ancient Greek Music." *Acta Musicologica* LIII (1981): 14–32.

———. "Rhythm and Meter in Ancient Greek Music." *Music Theory Spectrum* VII (1985): 159–80.

Miraeus (or Le Mire), Aubert. *Bibliotheca ecclesiastica sive de scriptoribus ecclesiasticis qui ab anno Christo . . . ad usque tempora nostra floruerunt*. Antwerp: J. Mesius, 1636 and 49, 2 vols.

Molitor, Raphael. *Die Nach-Tridentinische Choral-Reform zu Rom*. Leipzig: F. E. C. Leuckart, 1901 and 1902, 2 vols.

Müller-Blattau, Wendelin. "Der Humanismus in der Musikgeschichte Frankreichs und Deutschlands." In *Festschrift für Walter Wiora zum 30. Dezember 1966,* ed. Ludwig Finscher and Christoph-Hellmut Mahling (Kassel: Bärenreiter, 1967), 296–303.

Die Musik in Geschichte und Gegenwart, ed. Friedrich Blume. Kassel: Bärenreiter, 1949–68, 14 vols., plus supp., 1973 and 1979, 2 vols.

Navarre, College of (Paris): Library. Châtelain, Émile. "Les manuscrits du Collège de Navarre en 1741." *Revue des Bibliothèques* XI (1901): 362–411.

———. Davolé (or Duvollé), Pierre. *Catalogus bibliothecae regiae Navarrae, juxta ordinem materiarum digestus.* 10 vols. in manuscript, 1721 (now in Paris, Bibliothèque Mazarine, MSS 3129–38).

———. Masson, Gabriel. *Catalogue des livres de la bibliothèque du Collège de*

Navarre. In manuscript, 1741 (now in Paris, Bibliothèque Nationale, MS fonds latin 9371).

———. Milanges, Étienne. *Catalogus generalis bibliothecae theologorum regiae Navarrae . . . tum primum confectus, et in ordinem digestus . . .* (followed by *Catalogus peculiaris librorum qui asservantur in armariis cancellatis bibliothecae theologorum regiae Navarre, vel quia duplices, vel quia commutandi*). In manuscript, 1708 (now in Paris, Bibliothèque Mazarine, MS 3139).

Newberry Library (Chicago). *Dictionary Catalogue of the History of Printing from the John M. Wing Foundation in the Newberry Library.* Boston: G. K. Hall, 1961, 6 vols., plus supp., 1970, 3 vols.

The New Grove Dictionary of Music and Musicians, ed. Stanley Sadie. London: Macmillan, 1970, 20 vols.

Niermeyer, J. F. *Mediae latinitatis lexicon minus.* Leiden: Brill, 1984.

Osthoff, Helmuth. "Der Durchbruch zum musikalischen Humanismus." In *Report of the Eighth International Congress [of the International Musicological Society], New York 1961,* ed. Jan LaRue (Kassel: Bärenreiter, 1961, 2 vols.) II: 31–39.

Ouy, Gilbert. "Le Collège de Navarre, berceau de l'humanisme français." In *Actes du 95ᵉ Congrès National des Sociétés Savantes, Reims 1970* (Paris: Bibliothèque Nationale, 1975, 2 vols.) I: 276–99.

———. "Les premiers humanistes français et l'Europe." In *La conscience européenne au XVᵉᵐᵉ et au XVIᵉᵐᵉ siècle* (Paris: École Normale Supérieure de Jeunes Filles, 1982), 280–95.

Page, Christopher. "Early Fifteenth-Century Instruments in Jean de Gerson's 'Tractatus de canticis.'" *Early Music* VI (1978): 339–49.

Palisca, Claude. *Humanism in Italian Renaissance Musical Thought.* New Haven: Yale University, 1985.

———. "The Impact of the Revival of Ancient Learning on Music Theory." In *Report of the Twelfth Congress [of the International Musicological Society], Berkeley 1977,* ed. Daniel Heartz and Bonnie Wade (Kassel: Bärenreiter, 1981), 870–78.

Paravicini, Werner. *Die Nationalbibliothek: Ein Führer zu den Beständen aus dem Mittelalter und der Frühen Neuzeit.* Munich: K. G. Saur, 1981.

Paulys Realencyclopädie der classischen Altertumswissenschaft. Stuttgart: Metzler, 1897–1976, 85 vols.

Pellechet, Marie. *Catalogue général des incunables des bibliothèques publiques de France.* Paris: Alphonse Picard, 1897–1909, 3 vols. (of which vols. II–III were edited by Louis Polain; reprinted and completed after MS Nendeln, Liechtenstein: Kraus-Thomas, 1970, 26 vols.).

Pfaff, Maurus P. "Die liturgische Einstimmigkeit in ihren Editionen nach 1600." In *Musikalische Edition im Wandel des historischen Bewusstseins,* ed. Thrasybulos Georgiades (Kassel: Bärenreiter, 1971), 50–61.

Picker, Martin. "Josquiniana in Some Manuscripts at Piacenza." In *Josquin des Prez,* ed. Edward E. Lowinsky in collaboration with Bonnie J. Blackburn (London: Oxford University, 1976), 247–60.

Pirro, André. "L'enseignement de la

musique aux universités françaises."
*Mitteilungen der Internationalen
Gesellschaft für Musikwissenschaft* II
(1930): 26–32, 45–56.

Pirrotta, Nino. "Music and Cultural
Tendencies in Fifteenth-Century
Italy." *Journal of the American Musi-
cological Society* XIX (1966): 127–61.

Polain, Louis. *Catalogue des livres imprimés au quinzième siècle des bibliothèques de Belgique.* Brussels: Société
des Bibliophiles et Iconophiles de
Belgique, 1932, 4 vols., plus supp.,
1978.

Pothier, Dom Joseph. "Chant de la Gé-
néalogie à la Nuit de Noël." *Revue du
Chant Grégorien* VI (1897): 65–71.

Poulet, Charles. *Histoire de l'église de
France.* Paris: Beauchesne, 1944, 3
vols.

Quentin, Henri. *Les martyrologes historiques du Moyen-Âge. Étude sur la formation du Martyrologe romain.* Paris:
J. Gabalda, 1908.

Rashdall, Hastings. *The Universities of
Europe in the Middle Ages* (1895), ed.
F. M. Powicke and A. B. Emden.
Oxford: Oxford University, 1936, 2
vols. in 3.

Renouard, Philippe. *Répertoire des imprimeurs parisiens (libraires, fondeurs de
caractères et correcteurs d'imprimerie)
depuis l'introduction de l'imprimerie à
Paris (1470) jusqu'à la fin du seizième
siècle.* Paris: Lettres Modernes, 1965.

Rupp, Jean. *Histoire de l'église de Paris.*
Paris: R. Laffont, 1948.

Sauval, Henri. *Histoire et recherches des
antiquités de la ville de Paris.* Paris:
C. Moette, 1724, 3 vols.

Schmit, Joseph. "Die gottesdienstlichen
Gesänge in Rom und ihre Ordnung

unter Benedikt und Gregor." In
*Geschichte der katholischen Kirchen-
musik,* ed. Karl Gustav Fellerer (Kassel: Bärenreiter, 1972 and 76, 2 vols.)
I: 178–81.

Sieben, Hermann Josef. *Traktate und
Theorien zum Konzil. Von Beginn des
grossen Schismas bis zum Vorabend der
Reformation (1378–1521).* Frankfurt:
Knecht, 1984.

Stäblein, Bruno. "Gregorius Praesul: der
Prolog zum römischen Antiphonale."
In *Musik und Verlag: Karl Vötterle zum
65. Geburtstag* (Kassel: Bärenreiter,
1968), 537–61.

Stahl, William Harris and Richard
Johnson. *Martianus Capella and the
Seven Liberal Arts.* New York: Columbia University, 1971 and 77, 2
vols. (with Engl. tr. of Capella's
treatise *De nuptiis* in vol. II).

Stieber, Joachim W. *Pope Eugenius IV, the
Council of Basel and the Secular and Ecclesiastical Authorities in the Empire:
The Conflict over Supreme Authority
and Power in the Church.* Leiden: Brill,
1978.

Swain, Barbara. *Fools and Folly during the
Middle Ages and the Renaissance.* New
York: Columbia University, 1932.

Thorndike, Lynn. *University Records and
Life in the Middle Ages.* New York:
Columbia University, 1944.

Thurot, Charles. *De l'organisation de l'en-
seignement dans l'Université de Paris au
Moyen-Âge.* Paris: Dezobry & E.
Magdeleine, 1850.

Treitler, Leo. "Homer and Gregory: The
Transmission of Epic Poetry and
Plainchant." *The Musical Quarterly*
LX (1974): 333–72.

Unger, Hans-Heinrich. *Die Beziehungen*

Bibliography

zwischen Musik und Rhetorik im 16.–
18. Jahrhundert. Würzburg: Triltsch,
1941. Repr. Hildesheim: Georg
Olms, 1969.

Valois, Noël. *Histoire de la Pragmatique
Sanction de Bourges sous Charles VII.*
Paris: Alphonse Picard, 1906.

Van, Guillaume de. "La pédagogie musicale à la fin du Moyen-Âge." *Musica
Disciplina* II (1948): 75–94.

Villetard, Henri. "Office de Pierre de
Corbeil (Office de Circoncision), im-
proprement appelé 'Office des
Fous.'" *Bibliothèque musicologique* IV
(Paris, 1907): 65–73.

Wagner, David, ed. *The Seven Liberal
Arts in the Middle Ages.* Bloomington,
Indiana: Indiana University, 1983.

Wagner, Peter. *Einführung in die gre-*
gorianischen Melodien (1911–21). 2nd
ed. Leipzig: Breitkopf & Härtel,
1921. Repr. Hildesheim: Georg
Olms, 1962, 3 vols.

Walker, Daniel Pickering. *Der musikalische Humanismus im 16. und 17. Jahrhundert.* Kassel: Bärenreiter, 1949.

Weale, W. H. Iacob. *Bibliographia liturgica: catalogus missalium ritus latini ab
anno M. CCCCLXXIV impressorum,* ed.
Hanns Bohatta. London: Bernard
Quaritch, 1928.

Wessenberg, Ignaz Heinrich Karl von.
*Die grossen Kirchenversammlungen des
15ten und 16ten Jahrhunderts in Bezie-
hung auf Kirchenverbesserung
geschichtlich und kritisch dargestellt.*
Constance: C. Glüther, 1840, 4 vols.

Index

Index

Index

Villars, Pierre de (bishop), 33, 130
Villetard, Henri, 136

Waesberghe, Joseph Smits van, 119
Wagner, Peter, 149
Walker, Daniel Pickering, 137
War: humanists ("grammarians") versus musicians, xi–xii, 22, 24, 37, 51–59, 64, 67–77, 81–82, 100, 105–6, 131 (*see also* Accentuation, conflict between grammatical and musical approaches to); nouns against verbs, 71–72, 140–41 (*see also* Guarna, Andreas); plainchant against polyphony, 72, 141
Wessenberg, Ignaz Heinrich Karl von, 135
Willaert, Adrian, 75
Winternitz, Emanuel, 119

Wollick (Volcyr), Nicolaus, 39, 69, 132, 140
Words, adapting music to, 37, 51–52, 55, 67–68, 70–71. *See also* Accentuation, adapting music to; Syntax: adapting music to

Yudkin, Jeremy, 131

Zarlino, Gioseffo, 74–75, 142, 144
Zoilo, Annibale, 76